AFRICAN HISTORICAL DICTIONARIES
Edited by Jon Woronoff

1. *Cameroon,* by Victor T. LeVine and Roger P. Nye. 1974
2. *The Congo (Brazzaville),* by Virginia Thompson and Richard Adloff. 1974
3. *Swaziland,* by John J. Grotpeter. 1975
4. *The Gambia,* by Harry A. Gailey. 1975
5. *Botswana,* by Richard P. Stevens. 1975
6. *Somalia,* by Margaret F. Castagno. 1975
7. *Dahomey,* by Samuel Decalo. 1975
8. *Burundi,* by Warren Weinstein. 1976
9. *Togo,* by Samuel Decalo. 1976
10. *Lesotho,* by Gordon Haliburton. 1977
11. *Mali,* by Pascal James Imperato. 1977
12. *Sierra Leone,* by Cyril Patrick Foray. 1977
13. *Chad,* by Samuel Decalo. 1977
14. *Upper Volta,* by Daniel Miles McFarland. 1978
15. *Tanzania,* by Laura S. Kurtz. 1978
16. *Guinea,* by Thomas O'Toole. 1978
17. *Sudan,* by John Voll. 1978
18. *Rhodesia/Zimbabwe,* by R. Kent Rasmussen. 1979
19. *Zambia,* by John J. Grotpeter. 1979
20. *Niger,* by Samuel Decalo. 1979
21. *Equatorial Guinea,* by Max Liniger-Goumaz. 1979
22. *Guinea-Bissau,* by Richard Lobban. 1979
23. *Senegal,* by Lucie G. Colvin. 1981
24. *Morocco,* by William Spencer. 1980
25. *Malaŵi,* by Cynthia A. Crosby. 1980
26. *Angola,* by Phyllis Martin. 1980
27. *The Central African Republic,* by Pierre Kalck. 1980
28. *Algeria,* by Alf Andrew Heggoy. 1981
29. *Kenya,* by Bethwell A. Ogot. 1981
30. *Gabon,* by David E. Gardinier. 1981
31. *Mauritania,* by Alfred G. Gerteiny. 1981
32. *Ethiopia,* by Chris Prouty and Eugene Rosenfeld. 1981
33. *Libya,* by Lorna Hahn. 1981

Historical Dictionary of GABON

by

DAVID E. GARDINIER

African Historical Dictionaries, No. 30

The Scarecrow Press, Inc.
Metuchen, N.J., & London
1981

Library of Congress Cataloging in Publication Data

Gardinier, David E.
Historical dictionary of Gabon.

(African historical dictionaries ; no. 30)
Bibliography: p.
1. Gabon--History--Dictionaries. I. Title. II. Series.
DT546.15.G37 967'.21'00321 81-5290
ISBN 0-8108-1435-8 AACR2

Manufactured in the United States of America

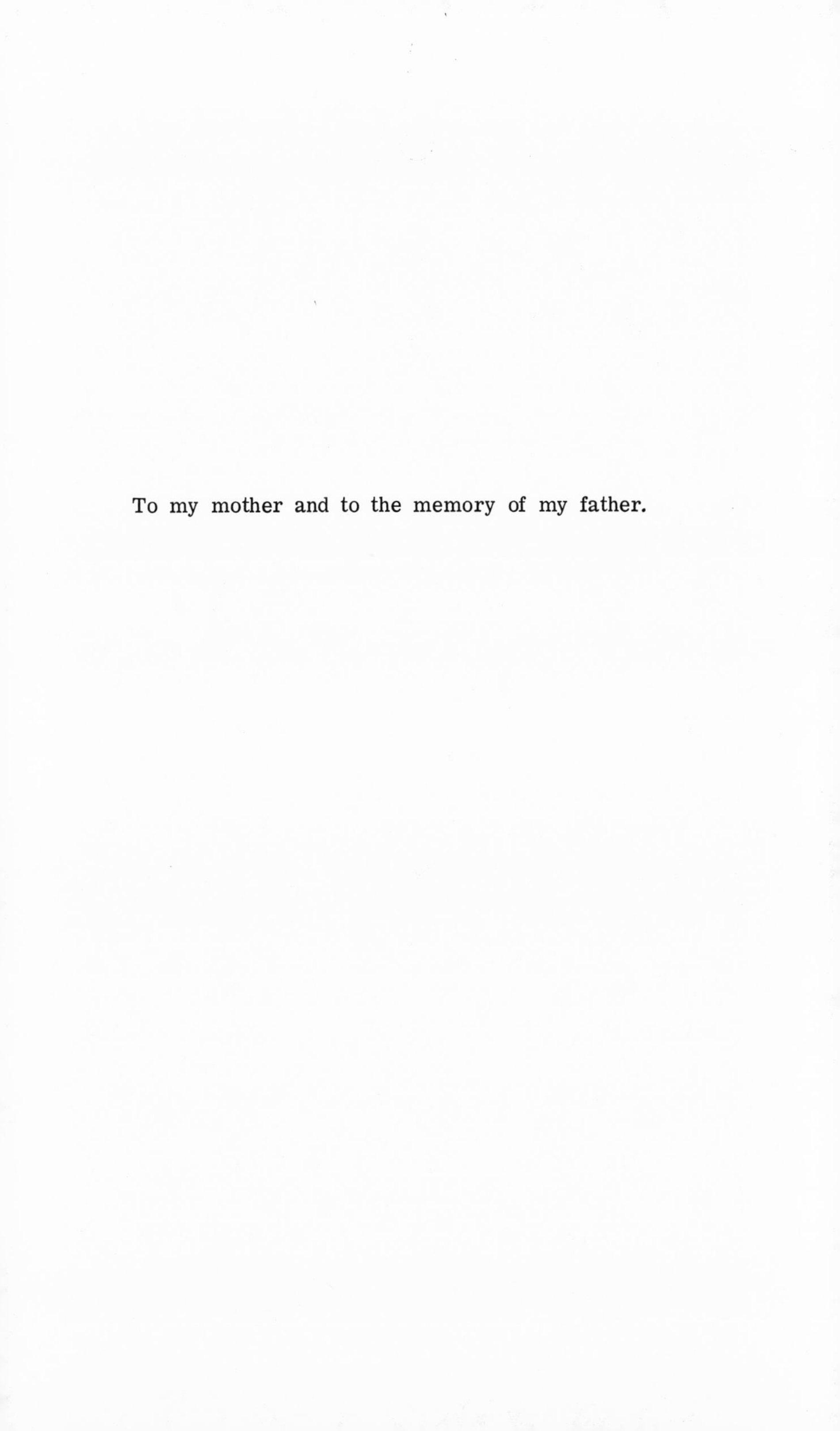

To my mother and to the memory of my father.

CONTENTS

EDITOR'S FOREWORD

Gabon, one of Equatorial Africa's most promising young nations from the start, has become even more attractive since it discovered oil. This commodity, plus major sources of iron ore, manganese, uranium, and precious woods, has given Gabon an economic boost lacking elsewhere. Due to its modest size and population, it has even assumed the dimensions of a mini-economic miracle.

Thus Gabon has aroused growing interest not only in France, the former colonial power whose relations are still very close, but in America and the Arab world. Realizing the advantages, President Bongo has taken steps to promote a more active foreign policy while encouraging greater outside participation in economic development. The numerous projects planned for the future are more ambitious than those of today. Whether all succeed or not, Gabon is a country worth watching.

However, since it remained in the shadows so long, not much is known about the country in depth. Its history is relatively obscure and its peoples have not all been studied. Those interested in learning more would find it hard enough to encounter valid reference works in French, let alone English. That is, until now.

This Historical Dictionary by Dr. David E. Gardinier fills that gap by providing, in a simple and straightforward manner, much of the general data a newcomer would like to have. In some respects, it goes much further and provides information that would be hard to obtain anywhere else. Certainly the range of leading figures, past and present, make it an exceptional "who's who" of Gabon; the entries on many of its ethnic groups offer unusual insight into its population. Those who wish to know more about Gabon will be delighted with the uniquely complete bibliography.

Dr. Gardinier, a professor of history at Marquette University, has pooled his interests in France and Equatorial Africa to write this volume on Gabon. On the basis of his studies and frequent trips to the region, he has been able not only to supply the necessary information but insert it in a clear and comprehensive framework. This will be appreciated most by those whose first introduction is through the following pages.

Jon Woronoff
Series Editor

PREFACE

My interest in Gabon originated in 1953 when, as a graduate student at Yale University in the seminar of Professor Harry R. Rudin, I prepared papers on colonial rule in French Equatorial Africa. In 1958, while a student, I published an article in Current History on the post-1945 political evolution of the Equatorial African states. After spending the subsequent decade on the political evolution of the French trusteeship territory of Cameroon and the historiography of French colonial rule throughout Africa, I returned in the 1970s to the history of the Equatorial African states, particularly to the development of western education and even more specifically to the introduction of western education in nineteenth-century Gabon. I have drawn upon material from those researches, most of which are not yet published, for this dictionary. Grants from the Marquette University Graduate School, the Hoover Institution, and the American Philosophical Society enabled me to gather materials in the U. S. A., Europe, and Gabon at various times between 1969 and 1980. A Senior Fulbright Scholarship in Paris during the fall semester of 1979 for a project on education in Francophone Africa gave me the opportunity to secure additional sources and bibliography.

In addition to these institutions, I have received assistance in locating sources and obtaining data from many individuals. In particular, I wish to express my thanks to the following: Dr. David P. Henige, Africana Bibliographer of the Memorial Library, University of Wisconsin, Madison; Rev. Philip Talmage, Mrs. Shirley Arrighetti, Mr. Jack Onufrock, and Mrs. Patricia Bohach of the Marquette University Memorial Library; Mr. Hans E. Panofsky, Mr. Daniel Britz, Mrs. Meta Schayne, and Mrs. Judith Rosenthal of the Herskovits Africana Library of Northwestern University; Professor Brian Weinstein of Howard University; Rev. Leslie King of the Christian and Missionary Alliance, Nyack, New York; Revs. Bernard Noel, Archivist, and Augustin Berger of the Holy Ghost Fathers, Paris; Abbé Jean Moreau and Mlle. Simone Robin of the O. P. F. Library and Archives, Paris; Mlle. J.-M. Léonard, Archivist and Librarian of the former Société des Missions Evangéliques, Paris; Brothers Macaire Clémenceau, Thouaré-sur-Loire, France, and André Régnier, Archivist, Rome, of the Brothers of Saint-Gabriel; Sr. Marie Damien Vallet of the Immaculate Conception Sisters, Rome; Professor Henri Brunschwig, Paris; M. Jean-Hilaire Aubame, Paris; Mlle. Edith Aujames, M. A. Salon, and M. J. Arnaud of the Ministry of Cooperation, Paris.

Dr. Christopher Chamberlin of Washington, D. C., kindly loaned me his dissertation on Gabonese economic history. Professor K. David Patterson of the University of North Carolina at Charlotte, Dr. Henry H. Bucher, Jr., of the African Studies Center at the University of Wisconsin, Madison, and Dr. David Henige read portions of the manuscript. Professor Bruce Fetter of the University of Wisconsin, Milwaukee, shared his extensive knowledge of social change and elite formation in Central Africa. Along with the three readers, he provided encouragement throughout the project. Four research assistants at Marquette University contributed to this dictionary: Lt. Robert McMahon, USN, summarized newspaper sources; Mr. Phillip Chiviges Naylor and Rev. John Steinberger, O. S. M., assembled some of the bibliography; and Mr. Jin Hee-Han typed the original draft.

My wife, Dr. Josefina Z. Sevilla, deserves special credit for suggesting some of the entries and for helping to improve others. She and our children--Kenneth, Annemarie, and Lourdes Marie--gave moral support during my absence gathering materials on three continents and during my presence writing up and typing the results. Eventually I hope to have a book on education in Gabon to dedicate to them, but I would like to dedicate this dictionary to my parents, Mrs. Velma Austin, and the late Kenneth Gardinier, whose sacrifices and encouragement aided the graduate education where my interest in the history of Gabon first developed.

David E. Gardinier
Brookfield, Wisconsin

NOTE ON SPELLING

The absence of any universally accepted system of transliteration of African names into French or English and the development of variant spellings through the centuries that Europeans have been in Equatorial Africa pose problems for any author who wishes to achieve accuracy and consistency.

Because French is the official language of Gabon, I have used the French transliteration for places and individuals. In the case of variant spellings, I have followed the usage in F. Meyo-Bibang and J.-M. Nzamba's _Notre Pays, Le Gabon_ (1975). For the names of some of the Bantu peoples, one is faced with the additional problem of whether to use the basic stem or the plural--e.g., Kota or Bakota. In this case I have chosen the form most widely used in the sources I have consulted. Thus I have found Bakèlè, Bakota, and Bapounou more frequently used than Kèlè, Kota, and Pounou, on the one hand, and Loumbou, Téké, and Vili more often than Baloumbou, Batéké, and Bavili, on the other. To aid the reader, I have given both forms in some cases--e.g., Bakota or Kota, Loumbou or Baloumbou.

ABBREVIATIONS AND ACRONYMS

ABCFM	American Board of Commissioners for Foreign Missions
AEF	Afrique Equatoriale Française
AGEG	Association Générale des Etudiants du Gabon
AGP	Agence Gabonaise de Presse
APEEG	Association des Parents d'Elèves et d'Etudiants du Gabon
BDG	Bloc Démocratique Gabonais
BEAC	Banque des Etats de l'Afrique Centrale
BEPC	Brevet d'Etudes du Premier Cycle
BGD	Banque Gabonaise de Développement
CCCE	Caisse Centrale de Coopération Economique
CCFOM	Caisse Centrale de la France d'Outre-Mer
CFA	Colonies Françaises Africaines; Communauté Financière Africaine
CFTC	Confédération Française des Travailleurs Chrétiens
CGT	Confédération Générale du Travail
CGT-FO	Confédération Générale du Travail--Force Ouvrière
CMA	Christian & Missionary Alliance
CMG	Comité Mixte Gabonais
CNTG	Confédération Nationale des Travailleurs Gabonais
COGES	Comité Gabonais d'Etudes Sociales et Economiques
COMILOG	Compagnie Minière de l'Ogooué
EDF	European Development Fund (FED in French)
EEC	European Economic Community (CEE in French)
ENA	Ecole Nationale d'Administration
FAC	Fonds d'Aide et de Coopération
FEA	French Equatorial Africa
FEANF	Fédération des Etudiants d'Afrique Noire en France
FESAC	Fondation de l'Enseignement Supérieur en Afrique Centrale

FESYGA	Fédération Syndicale Gabonaise
FIDES	Fonds d'Investissement pour le Développement Economique et Social
GEC	Groupe d'Etudes Communistes
IOM	Indépendants d'Outre-Mer
OAMCE	Organisation Africaine et Malgache pour la Coopération Economique
OAU	Organization of African Unity
OCAM	Organisation Commune Africaine et Malgache
ORSTOM	Office de la Recherche Scientifique et Technique d'Outre-Mer
PBFM	Presbyterian Board for Foreign Missions
PDA	Parti Démocratique Africain
PDG	Parti Démocratique Gabonais
PUNGA	Parti d'Union Nationale Gabonaise
RDA	Rassemblement Démocratique Africain
RGR	Rassemblement des Gauches Républicains
RPF	Rassemblement du Peuple Français
SHO	Société Commerciale, Industrielle, et Agricole du Haut-Ogooué
SME	Société des Missions Evangéliques
SNBG	Société Nationale des Bois du Gabon
SOGARAF	Société Gabonaise de Raffinage
SOMIFER	Société des Mines de Fer de Mékambo
UAM	Union Africaine et Malgache
UDE	Union Douanière Equatoriale
UDEAC	Union Douanière et Economique de l'Afrique Centrale
UDSG	Union Démocratique et Sociale Gabonaise
UDSR	Union Démocratique et Sociale de la Résistance
URAC	Union des Républiques d'Afrique Centrale
USC	Union des Syndicats Confédérés

CHRONOLOGY

1472	Portuguese arrive in the Estuary of the Gabon or Como River.
1482	Diego Cam reaches mouth of the Zaire or Congo River.
1760s to 1840s	Atlantic slave trade reaches its height.
Feb. 9, 1839 & Mar. 18, 1842	Mpongwe clan heads, Kings Denis & Louis, cede sovereignty to France.
1840s and 1850s	Fang descend northern tributaries of the Como River.
June 22, 1842	American Protestants (ABCFM of Boston) found mission at Baraka in Estuary and open schools.
June 11, 1843	French found post, Fort d'Aumale, in Estuary.
Sept. 28, 1844	French Catholic missionaries (Holy Ghost Fathers) arrive near Fort d'Aumale.
July 31, 1849	Immaculate Conception Sisters of Castres, France, arrive near Fort d'Aumale.
Aug. 1849	French found Libreville as settlement for Vili liberated from slave traders.
Sept. 18, 1852	Benga clan heads at Cape Esterias make treaty with French.
June 1, 1862	Orungu chiefs at Cape Lopez make treaty with French.

Jan. 18, 1868	Nkomi chiefs at Fernan Vaz make treaty with French.
July 27, 1870	American Presbyterians assume the missionary field of the ABCFM.
1874	Dr. Robert Nassau founds Presbyterian mission above Lambaréné in the middle Ogooué.
1875-1885	Savorgnan de Brazza explores the Ogooué and Congo Basins.
Jan. 7, 1880	Ntâkâ Truman first Mpongwe ordained a Presbyterian pastor.
Feb. 1881	Catholic missionaries found a post at Lambaréné.
Mar. 12, 1883	Vili chiefs at Loango make treaty with French; Catholic missionaries found a post there.
Dec. 12, 1885	Franco-German treaty fixes frontier with Cameroons.
Apr. 1886	French Congo established with Gabon as autonomous colony.
July 1889	Fang bring first _okoumé_ to Libreville for export to Europe.
1892-1893	Presbyterians transfer their Ogooué missions to French Protestants (SME of Paris).
1893	Société du Haut-Ogooué receives concession over vast areas.
Mar. 15, 1894	Franco-German agreement further defines frontier with the Cameroons.
1894	Jean-Rémy Rapontchombo first Gabonese to earn a _baccalauréat_ in France.
1895-1899	Catholics establish missions in the N'Gounié River Basin.

July 23, 1899	André Raponda Walker the first Gabonese to be ordained a Catholic priest.
1899	Concessionary system extended throughout Gabon.
June 27, 1900	Franco-Spanish convention defines frontier with Spanish Guinea (Rio Muni).
Oct. 1900	Brothers of Saint-Gabriel open the Ecole Montfort in Libreville.
July 1, 1904	Capital of French Congo transferred to Brazzaville.
1907	First public school opens in Libreville.
Jan. 15, 1910	Gabon becomes part of the federation of French Equatorial Africa.
1913	Dr. Albert Schweitzer begins his medical mission at Lambaréné.
1918	Loango coast transferred from Gabon to the Middle Congo.
1918	Jean-Félix Tchicaya and Hervé Mapako-Gnali sent to the Ponty School in Senegal.
1918	Libreville branch of the Ligue des Droits de l'Homme founded.
1921-1934	Forced labor for construction of the Congo-Ocean Railroad
1922	Léon Mba named Fang canton chief at Libreville.
1922	Laurent Antchouey and Louis Bigmann found _L'Echo Gabonais_ at Dakar.
Apr. 15, 1925	Haut-Ogooué Region transferred to the Middle Congo.
1928-1929	Awandji revolt against administrative and concessionary exactions.

1930	World depression hits Gabon and the okoumé industry.
1933	Léon Mba exiled to Oubangui-Chari.
1933	Americans from the Christian and Missionary Alliance enter the N'Gounié River valley.
1935	First Gabonese enroll at the Ecole Renard at Brazzaville.
1935-1936	The Great Revival throughout northern Gabon.
Oct. 1937	François-de-Paul Vané wins election to the Governor-General's Council of Administration.
Sept.-Nov. 1940	Free French defeat Vichy supporters and gain control of Gabon.
1942	Governor-General Félix Eboué creates the first public school with grades seven to ten.
Jan. 30 to Feb. 8, 1944	Brazzaville Conference considers reforms for Black Africa.
Nov. 18, 1945	Jean-Félix Tchicaya elected to the First Constituent Assembly.
Apr. 11, 1946	Forced labor abolished.
May 7, 1946	Black Africans made French citizens.
July 5, 1946	FIDES formed to make public investments in Black Africa.
Oct. 13, 1946	Gabon becomes Overseas Territory of the Fourth French Republic.
Oct. 16, 1946	Haut-Ogooué Region returned to Gabon; Gabon's international boundaries fixed.
Nov. 1946	Jean-Hilaire Aubame first elected to French National Assembly.

Dec. 1946	First elections held for Territorial Assembly.
1947	Comité Mixte Gabonais founded by Léon Mba.
Sept. 1947	Union Démocratique et Sociale Gabonaise founded by Jean-Hilaire Aubame.
Sept. 1953	COMILOG created to exploit the manganese of Franceville (exploitation begins in 1962).
Apr. 1954	Bloc Démocratique Gabonais founded by Senator Paul Gondjout.
1956	SOMIFER organized to exploit the iron of Mékambo.
Jan. 1956	First petroleum produced in Port-Gentil area.
Nov. 1956	Elections for municipal governments with African mayors.
Dec. 1956	Uranium discovered in the Haut-Ogooué (production begins in 1961).
Apr. 1957	First Executive Council with Léon Mba as its top African official.
Sept. 28, 1958	Gabon votes for membership in the French Community; federation of F. E. A. abolished.
Nov. 29, 1958	Gabon becomes an autonomous republic with Léon Mba as prime minister.
June 23, 1959	Gabon organizes a customs union with the three other Equatorial African states.
1959	Evangelical Church of South Gabon becomes independent.
July 15, 1960	Gabon signs cooperation agreements with France.

Aug. 13, 1960	Gabon becomes independent republic.
Sept. 20, 1960	United Nations admits Gabon to membership.
Nov. 15, 1960	François Ndong named the first Gabonese Catholic bishop.
1961	Evangelical Church of Gabon achieves independence.
Feb. 21, 1961	Constitution with a presidential regime adopted.
Dec. 12, 1961	Gabon organizes FESAC with the three other Equatorial states.
June 1963	Gabon joins the Organization of African Unity.
Feb. 17 to 20, 1964	Military coup leads to French intervention to restore President Mba.
Dec. 8, 1964	Gabon forms UDEAC with Cameroon and the three Equatorial states.
Sept. 4, 1965	Death of Albert Schweitzer at Lambaréné.
Mar. 19, 1967	Mba re-elected president and Albert-Bernard Bongo elected vice-president.
Nov. 28, 1967	Death of Mba elevates Bongo to the presidency.
Mar. 12, 1968	After abolishing existing parties, Bongo establishes a single party, Parti Démocratique Gabonais.
1970s	Thousands of Equatorial Guineans seek refuge from the Macias regime.
August 1970	University of Libreville created.
Feb. 25, 1973	Bongo re-elected president and a new National Assembly elected.
Feb. 12, 1974	New cooperation agreements signed with France.

Sept. 1978	First section of the Transgabonais Railroad to N'Djolé opens.
Dec. 30, 1979	Bongo re-elected president.
February 1980	Legislative elections held and government reorganized.

TABLES

TABLE 1. GABON: NATIONAL BUDGETS, 1960-1980 (in millions of francs CFA)

Year	Functioning	Equipment	Total
1960	4,072	536	4,608
1961	5,104	782	5,886
1962	5,889	1,010	6,899
1963	6,835	2,362	9,197
1964	7,957	2,554	10,511
1965	8,587	3,405	11,992
1966	10,858	1,939	12,797
1967	11,534	2,903	14,437
1968	12,116	4,484	15,600
1969	12,736	5,061	17,797
1970	14,218	5,785	20,003
1971	16,661	7,862	24,523
1972	19,227	11,776	31,003
1973	22,213	14,730	36,943
1974	27,081	20,663	48,714
1975	44,185	107,263	151,448
1976	58,717	134,396	193,113
1977	84,582	171,210	255,792
1978	226,000*	63,800	289,800
1979	238,000*	90,000	328,000
1980	221,710*	92,000	313,710

*Functioning portion of the budget includes the following amounts for debt service: 1978, 147,000; 1979, 142,900; 1980, 120,000.

Sources: 1960-1966 [408]; 1967-1973 [686]; 1974-1977 [400]; 1978-1980 [661, 680]. (Bracketed numbers refer to the Bibliography.)

TABLE 2. GABON: VALUE OF EXPORTS AND IMPORTS, 1960-1978
(in millions of francs CFA)

Year	Exports (f. o. b.)	Imports (c. i. f.)
1960	11, 826	7, 829
1961	13, 627	8, 853
1962	14, 627	10, 067
1963	18, 125	11, 875
1964	22, 540	13, 742
1965	25, 905	15, 425
1966	25, 920	16, 384
1967	29, 516	16, 585
1968	30, 714	15, 875
1969	36, 663	20, 127
1970	33, 610	22, 139
1971	51, 829	26, 810
1972	50, 297	34, 106
1973	63, 925	36, 977
1974	234, 900	85, 450
1975	201, 921	100, 529
1976	272, 449	120, 237
1977	329, 800	176, 001
1978	287, 000	125, 200

Sources: 1960-1966 [408]; 1967-72 [686]; 1972-1976 [640]; 1977-1978 [680]. Statistics after 1966 exclude gold and trade with the members of UDEAC. (Bracketed numbers refer to the Bibliography.)

TABLE 3. GABON: PRODUCTION OF FUELS AND MINERALS, 1960-1980
(in thousands of metric tons for petroleum & manganese; metric tons for uranium; kilograms for gold; & thousand cubic meters for natural gas)

Year	Petroleum	Natural Gas	Manganese	Uranium	Gold
1960	800	7,452	---	---	550
1961	774	6,700	---	969	475
1962	827	8,790	203	1,161	507
1963	890	8,612	637	1,317	1,111
1964	1,058	9,457	948	1,288	1,130
1965	1,264	10,647	1,275	1,644	1,155
1966	1,447	11,493	1,268	1,599	1,071
1967	3,444	17,422	1,147	1,452	910
1968	4,642	24,871	1,254	1,371	513
1969	5,030	25,000 (est.)	1,377	1,388	443
1970	5,364	25,000	1,453	1,077	501
1971	5,785	30,539	1,866	1,274	421
1972	6,304	34,460	1,936	523	355
1973	7,598	39,449	1,919	1,412	349
1974	10,202	45,624	2,119	1,713	227
1975	11,315	47,429	2,220	1,766	131
1976	11,325	239,417	2,280	1,297	
1977	11,070	684,277	2,080	1,850	
1978	11,000	619,000	1,661	1,407	
1979	10,000 (est.)		2,300	1,100	
1980	11,500 (est.)				

Sources: 1960-1966 [408]; 1967-1977 [640]; 1978-1980 [680]. (Bracketed numbers refer to the Bibliography.)

TABLE 4. GABON: EXPORTABLE PRODUCTION OF FOREST AND AGRICULTURAL PRODUCTS, 1960-1979
(in metric tons for okoumé, cocoa, coffee, & palm oil; in cubic meters for ozigo)

Year	Okoumé	Ozigo	Cocoa	Coffee	Palm Oil
1960	736, 673	47, 000	2, 578	655	384
1961	782, 000	45, 000	4, 022	712	307
1962	700, 000	35, 000	2, 442	540	425
1963	761, 000	54, 000	3, 742	730	555
1964	821, 000	72, 000	4, 021	847	1, 067
1965	794, 000	53, 501	3, 778	366	1, 146
1966	787, 000		3, 832	244	1, 103
1967	750, 000		4, 794	306	1, 123
1968	842, 000		4, 091	267	1, 374
1969	927, 983	59, 542	5, 050	292	1, 890
1970	922, 245	68, 326	5, 176	486	326
1971	1, 023, 939	66, 025	6, 095	485	155
1972	1, 141, 216	96, 213	5, 031	642	
1973	1, 081, 011	138, 323	3, 733	538	
1974	1, 025, 520	109, 314	5, 553	258	
1975	1, 020, 000	86, 803	4, 869	103	
1976	1, 090, 000	73, 750	2, 549		
1977	1, 100, 000	75, 000			
1978	1, 224, 924*	68, 700	3, 718		
1979			4, 532		

*cubic meters

Sources: Okoumé & Ozigo, 1960-66 [408]; 1967-1974 [710]; 1975-1979 [640, 680]; Cocoa, Coffee, and Palm Oil, 1960-1966 [408], 1967-1975 [478, 710]; 1976-1979 [640, 680]. (Bracketed numbers refer to the Bibliography.)

TABLE 5. GABON: AREA AND POPULATION OF THE NINE PROVINCES (1960 & 1970 CENSUSES)

Province	Area in km2	-1960- Population	-1960- Density per km2	-1970- Population	-1970- Density per km2
Estuary	20, 740	60, 600	2. 9	194, 976	9. 4
Ogooué-Maritime	22, 890	41, 600	1. 8	120, 371	5. 2
Woleu-N'Tem	38, 465	78, 000	2. 0	148, 287	3. 8
N'Gounié	37, 750	79, 100	2. 1	129, 859	3. 4
Haut-Ogooué	36, 547	43, 000	1. 2	127, 133	3. 4
Nyanga	21, 285	37, 700	1. 8	66, 517	3. 1
Moyen-Ogooué	18, 535	34, 100	1. 8	51, 551	2. 7
Ogooué-Lolo	25, 380	36, 800	1. 4	51, 523	2. 0
Ogooué-Ivindo	46, 075	35, 800	0. 8	59, 792	1. 2
TOTAL	267, 667	448, 564	1. 7	950, 009	3. 5

Source: [478]. (Bracketed number refers to the Bibliography.)

PHYSICAL MAP OF GABON

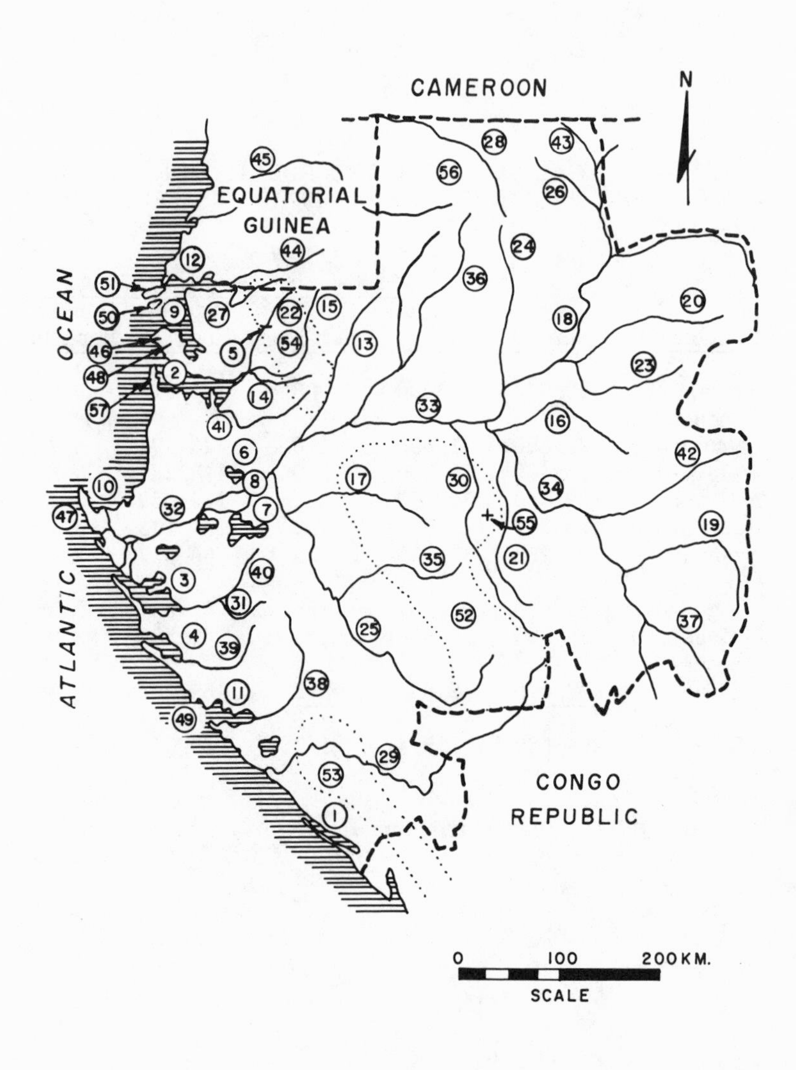

MAP DESIGN - SUSAN R. OHDE

KEY - PHYSICAL MAP OF GABON

BODIES OF WATER

1 BANIO OR MAYUMBA LAGOON
2 ESTUARY
3 FERNAN VAZ LAGOON
4 IGUÉLA LAGOON
5 KINGUÉLÉ FALLS
6 LAKE AZINGO
7 LAKE ONANGUÉ
8 LAKE ZILÉ
9 MONDAH BAY
10 NAZARETH BAY
11 N'DOGO OR SETTÉ - CAMA LAGOON
12 RIO MUNI

RIVERS

13 ABANGA
14 BOKOUÉ
15 COMO
16 DILO
17 IKOY
18 IVINDO
19 LECONI
20 LIBOUMBA
21 LOLO
22 M'BEI
23 MOUNIANGUI
24 MVOUNG
25 N'GOUNIÉ
26 NOUNA
27 NOYA
28 N'TEM
29 NYANGA
30 OFFOUÉ
31 OFOUBOU
32 OGOOUÉ, LOWER
33 OGOOUÉ, MIDDLE
34 OGOOUÉ, UPPER
35 OGOULOU
36 OKANO
37 PASSA OR M'PASSA
38 REMBO N'DOGO
39 REMBO N'GOVE
40 REMBO N'KOMI
41 REMBOUÉ
42 SÉBÉ
43 SINGOUÉ
44 TEMBONI
45 WOLEU

OTHER FEATURES

46 CAPE ESTÉRIAS
47 CAPE LOPEZ
48 CAPE SANTA CLARA
49 CAPE STE. CATHERINE
50 CORISCO ISLAND
51 ELOBEY ISLAND
52 MASSIF DU CHAILLU
53 MAYOMBE MOUNTAINS
54 MONTS DE CRISTAL
55 MONT IBOUNDJI
56 MONT TEMBO
57 POINTE PONGARA

MAP DESIGN -
SUSAN R. OHDE

INTRODUCTION

Location

Gabon is located in western equatorial Africa. It lies astride the equator between 2° 30' North latitude and 4° South latitude and between 9° and 14° West longitude. The average distance from north to south is 550 km. and from east to west 600 km. On the western side the Atlantic Ocean stretches along 800 km. of frequently indented coast. To the northwest lies Equatorial Guinea; to the north, Cameroon; and to the east and south, the Congo (the capital of which is Brazzaville). The boundaries between Gabon and these three states separate the sources of several important rivers from their outlets along the Atlantic as well as divide ethnic groups, for they were drawn by France, Germany, and Spain in the late nineteenth century without much knowledge of the geography and peoples of the interior.

Area

European competition gave Gabon an area of 267, 667 sq. km. or 103, 000 sq. mi., that is, about half the size of France or equivalent to the American state of Colorado. Gabon is three fifths the size of Cameroon and three quarters the size of the Congo Republic but it has nine times the area of Equatorial Guinea. Thus it is one of the smaller central African countries but by no means the smallest.

Climate

Gabon possesses an equatorial climate with uniformly high temperatures (averaging 26° C. or 78° F.), high relative humidities, and mean annual rainfalls from 150 to 300 cm. It has two rainy seasons (from mid-February to mid-May and from mid-September to mid-December) and two dry seasons (from mid-May to mid-September and from mid-December to mid-February).

Physical Features

Like the other western and equatorial African countries that border the Atlantic, Gabon is watered by systems of rivers and streams that empty into the ocean. Supreme among them is the Ogooué River, which with its many tributaries drains close to four fifths of the country (220, 000 sq. km.). Its largest southern tributary is the N'Gounié River, which joins it 150 km. upstream, and its largest northern tributary is the Ivindo, which enters much farther east at a point 350 km. from the coast. The two other river systems of most significance are the Como or Gabon River to the north of the Ogooué, whose broad mouth has been known historically as "the Estuary, " and the Nyanga River to the south. The far north is drained by the Woleu and N'Tem rivers, which rise within Gabon but reach the Atlantic through Equatorial Guinea and Cameroon, respectively, and the streams such as the Noya and the Temboni, which form the Rio Muni or Muni Estuary between Gabon and Equatorial Guinea. South of the several mouths or estuary of the Ogooué lie several small rivers (the Rembo N'komi, Rembo N'gove, and the N'dogo) which empty into the lagoons of Fernan Vaz, Iguéla, and N'dogo or Setté-Cama respectively. Only a very small portion of the southeast is drained by streams flowing into the northern tributaries of the Congo River system. Though Gabon has many waterways, most of them are cut at various points by falls and rapids, which make large portions of them unnavigable. For example, the Ogooué, though 1, 200 km. in length, is navigable without interruption only one-third of this distance, that is, from its estuary to the island of N'Djolé.

These rivers flow through a terrain whose relief can be separated into three regions of unequal area: plains, plateaux, and mountains. First of all, there is a low-lying coastal plain 30 to 200 km. in width that nowhere exceeds 300 meters in elevation. This plain is narrowest in the far south and broadest in the estuaries of the Como (Gabon) and Ogooué rivers. Plains also extend towards the interior through the valleys of the Nyanga, N'Gounié, and Ogooué, in the last case to within 100 km. of the frontier with the Congo Republic. Plateaux at altitudes from 300 to 800 meters cover most of the remainder of the country, in particular the north and east. Out of them rise two mountain chains, the

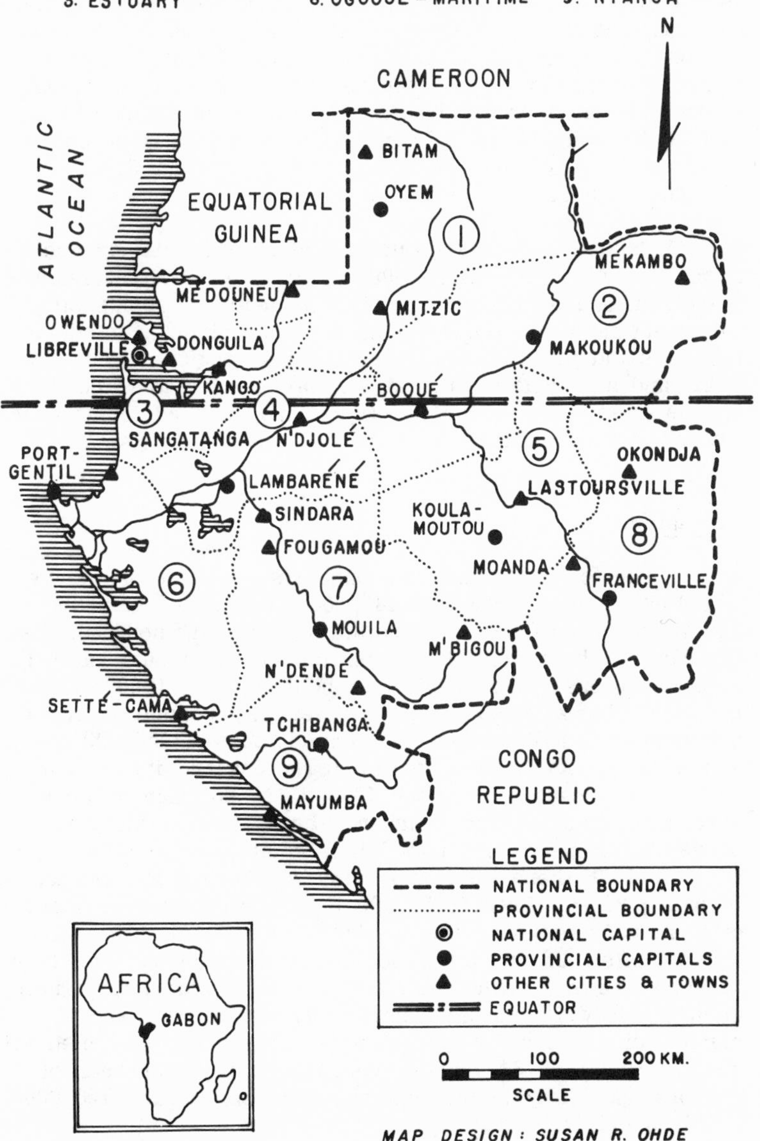
POLITICAL MAP OF GABON
PROVINCES
1. WOLEU-N'TEM
2. OGOOUÉ-IVINDO
3. ESTUARY
4. MOYEN-OGOOUÉ
5. OGOOUÉ-LOLO
6. OGOOUÉ-MARITIME
7. N'GOUNIÉ
8. HAUT-OGOOUÉ
9. NYANGA
N
CAMEROON
ATLANTIC OCEAN
EQUATORIAL GUINEA
BITAM
OYEM
MEKAMBO
MÉDOUNEU
MITZIC
OWENDO
LIBREVILLE
DONGUILA
MAKOUKOU
KANGO
BOOUÉ
SANGATANGA
N'DJOLÉ
PORT-GENTIL
OKONDJA
LAMBARÉNÉ
LASTOURSVILLE
SINDARA
KOULA-MOUTOU
FOUGAMOU
MOANDA
FRANCEVILLE
MOUILA
M'BIGOU
N'DENDÉ
SETTÉ-CAMA
TCHIBANGA
CONGO REPUBLIC
MAYUMBA
LEGEND
NATIONAL BOUNDARY
PROVINCIAL BOUNDARY
NATIONAL CAPITAL
PROVINCIAL CAPITALS
OTHER CITIES & TOWNS
EQUATOR
AFRICA
GABON
0 100 200 KM.
SCALE
MAP DESIGN: SUSAN R. OHDE

Monts de Cristal in the north and the Massif du Chaillu in the south, separated by the Ogooué river valley. The highest point in Gabon is Mount Iboundji (1, 575 meters) in the Massif du Chaillu and Mount Tembo near Oyem in the Monts de Cristal has 1, 300 meters. In the extreme southwest parallel to the coast and flanking the Nyanga River is the less elevated Mayombe chain, the bulk of which extends into the Congo Republic. The mountains are covered with dense tropical rainforest as is nearly three fourths of the country. Grasslands or savannas cover one fifth, mainly in the upper Ogooué around Franceville, the upper N'Gounié above Mouila, and in the middle Nyanga river valley--especially beyond Tchibanga. Along the coast north of the Nyanga River stretches a narrow zone of marshes and mangrove trees.

Beneath the coastal plains and offshore lie cretaceous sedimentary rocks, which south of Port Gentil have yielded petroleum and natural gas at shallow depth. Gabon's other important minerals (manganese, iron, uranium, gold) derive from the interior areas of Precambrian rocks. The heavy rains and high relative humidities have tended to leach the soil in most parts of the country, which has led to the practice of shifting cultivation.

Population

The total population of Gabon is a matter of dispute. The 1960-61 census showed 448, 564 inhabitants, including several thousand Europeans and several thousand non-Gabonese Africans. The United Nations estimated the annual natural rate of increase to be . 007 percent during the 1960s. Thus the 1970-71 census should have revealed a population of approximately a half million. Instead it showed 950, 000 inhabitants, a total which the United Nations and its agencies refused to accept. Since the 1970-71 census Gabon has undergone an economic boom which has brought many more thousands of Europeans and non-Gabonese Africans into the country. In 1978 there were approximately 30, 000 Europeans, including 21, 000 French; 60, 000 Equatorial Guineans, most of them refugees from the Macias regime (1968-1979); and approximately 20, 000 other non-Gabonese Africans. In 1978 the U. N. estimated the total population, including foreigners, at 650, 000, while the government claimed 1, 100, 000. A number of western observers, who consider that the methodology of the 1960-61 census overlooked many thousands of persons especially in the lumbering camps, regard 750, 000 to 800, 000 to be more accurate estimates.

The rapid development of Gabon's mineral resources since the late 1950s has contributed to an even more rapid urbanization. Whereas the 1960-61 census gave Libreville a population of 44,598 and Port Gentil 30,908, the French Ministry of Cooperation reported 112,000 and 45,000 respectively in September 1976. At the end of 1978 the annual survey by Europe Outremer claimed 187,000 and 85,400 for the two cities. Most of the Europeans and non-Gabonese Africans live in these two urban areas and to a lesser extent in the vicinities of Franceville and Lambaréné. An estimated 68,000 salaried persons are involved in forestry, mining, industry, and commerce, and another 8,000 in the civil service, including education. An estimated 267,000 persons are employed in agriculture, which is still mainly subsistence. They produce the staples of the Gabonese diet--manioc, plantain bananas, and other fruits and vegetables.

Peoples

Among the indigenous inhabitants there are a few thousand pygmies or negrillos who are thought to be the descendants of the oldest known inhabitants. It is possible that the various pygmoid groups may have undergone some mixing with Negroid peoples in recent centuries. The remaining 99.5 percent of the indigenous population has Negroid racial origins and has been differentiated through many centuries if not millennia into forty or more distinct peoples (a "people" being a group linked by heredity, culture--including language--and historical experience). All of these peoples speak languages belonging to the Bantu group, the large group to which most of the inhabitants of central and southern Africa belong. These peoples vary in size from a few hundred to tens of thousands. Ethnologists have been able to distribute them among ten groups, mainly on the basis of linguistic similarities. But there is evidence of genetic, cultural, and historical ties among certain groups as well so that in this sense the term "Bantu" has a wider sense than just language. To complicate matters, in the course of the past century there is evidence of peoples who have abandoned their original language and adopted or adapted the languages of other peoples with whom they had contacts. Several of Gabon's smallest peoples are in the process of disappearing, with the remnants assimilating to neighbors, who are sometimes but not always of the same group.

Largest numerically of the ten groups (on the basis of the 1960-61 census) is the Fang with 31 percent of the popula-

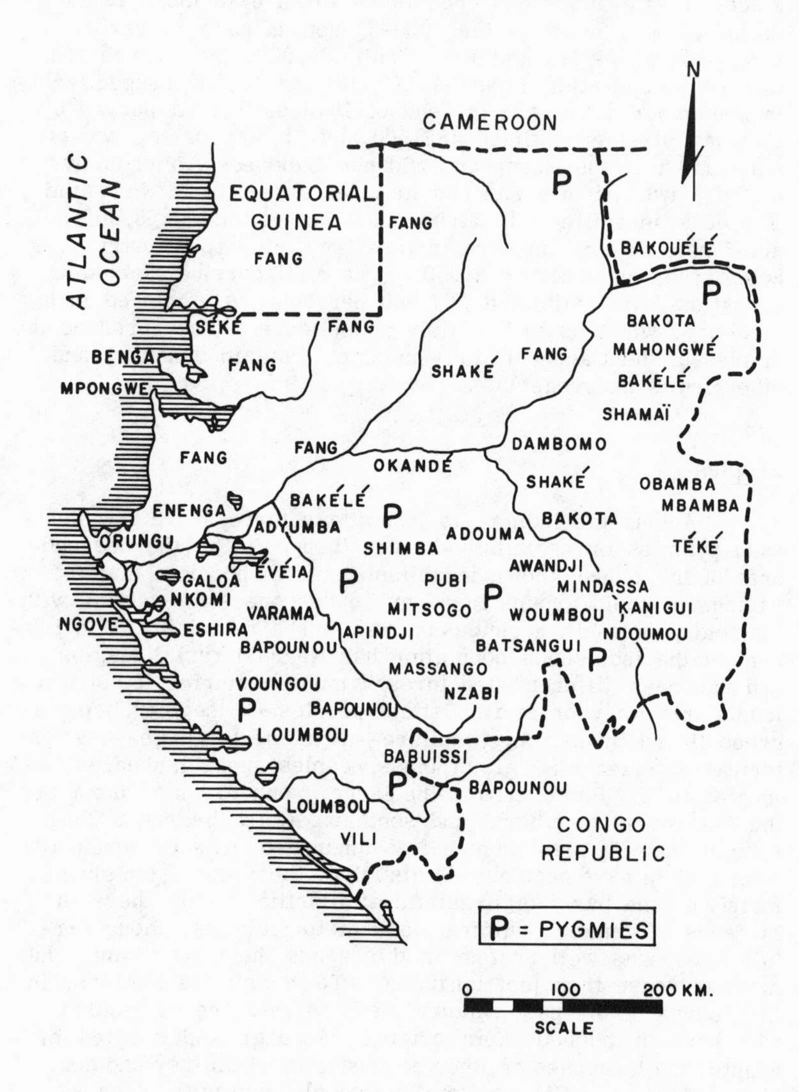

MAP DESIGN - SUSAN R. OHDE

tion, followed by the Mbédé with 25 percent and the Eshira with 22 percent. The remaining 22 percent are distributed among the other seven groups, of which two (the Vili and the Téké) have the majority of their kin in the neighboring Congo. Numerical size is not the same as historical importance, however, for the coastal Myènè group with only 5 percent has played a larger role in the development of the country than several more numerous groups from the interior.

Sources for Gabon's History and the State of Historical Knowledge

Our knowledge of Gabon's history has been shaped by the sources available and the use to which they have been put. The indigenous peoples are non-literate and their historical traditions transmitted orally. In the process these traditions have been frequently revised or transformed in the light of changing conditions. They thus reflect the interests and values of subsequent generations rather than the events themselves. Much of what has been transmitted concerns the lineage and the clan but rarely the peoples which the clans formed. Common to all of these traditions are accounts of migrations or movements and the accompanying conflicts within and among lineages, clans, and peoples. The traditions also involve genealogies, for marriages took place outside the clan and were forbidden among persons related more closely than several generations. Some genealogies extend to fifteen or twenty generations, as is the case with the Fang. But the majority, like the Bakota, go back only from five to eight generations. Oral traditions came to be recorded from time to time when literate European travellers visited the coasts and later entered the interior. But it was only from the 1840s onward when Christian missionaries from the United States and France actually lived among the Gabonese that we find very many detailed and reliable records being made. It was only after the First World War that missionaries or French administrators lived in all nine provinces and were therefore in a position to record local traditions.

It should also be recalled that the bulk of the records left by the missionaries, explorers, naval and military officers, and administrators were written for their own purposes and not too often to tell us about the history of the Gabonese. What we get in most cases is indirect evidence and much of it reflecting the interests and ethno-cultural biases of the authors. Thus most of what is known about the history of Gabon is what non-Gabonese have to tell us.

The first real historian of the indigenous peoples of Gabon was the Rev. André Raponda Walker (1871-1968), who gathered materials in the course of his long career as a Catholic priest in different parts of the country. Born in Gabon of an Mpongwe mother and a British father, Monsignor Walker knew a dozen Gabonese languages. Over many decades he assembled the histories of the peoples of the Estuary, the coasts, and the N'Gounié river valley. His sources were interviews and oral traditions supplemented by the church archives, and printed materials. Most of the results of Walker's investigations were published only in 1960 after editing by the French ethnologist Marcel Soret. By that time Hubert Deschamps (1900-1979) was undertaking the first project systematically to record the traditions of all of Gabon's peoples with the aid of local interpreters and informants. Marcel Soret continued this work in more depth and detail for the peoples adjacent to the Congo Republic a decade later as did Louis Perrois for the Bakota group and Henry Hale Bucher, Jr. for the Mpongwe.

Historical studies based primarily upon archives but using available oral data began to appear in the 1960s and increased in numbers during the 1970s. Nearly all of such studies have concerned the nineteenth century and/or earlier periods for which records were available and open to researchers. The largest collections of archival materials are located in France and the United States with less extensive ones in Britain, Holland, Portugal, Senegal, and Gabon itself. The national archives of Gabon, which were organized in the early 1970s, are most extensive for the twentieth century. Unfortunately, the works by French scholars and Africans working in France, with the exception of François Gaulme's study of the Nkomi, have not used the full range of archival resources. In particular, they have neglected the American missionary and consular records for the period 1842-1913, British official records, and printed works in English. It is only the half dozen scholars from the United States working during the 1970s who have utilized the various archival materials on three continents and the published sources in French, English, and other languages.

As yet no one has incorporated the results of the various published studies and doctoral dissertations into a history. The only existing introduction to Gabonese history is a mimeographed outline prepared for the secondary schools by Professor Frédéric Meyo-Bibang in the early 1970s. It assembles some very useful material on resistance to French penetration and the abuses of the colonial regime. But its sections on elite anti-colonialism during the 1920s and 1930s and on the country's political evolution since the Second World War omit essential data and thereby contribute to erroneous impressions. Meyo-Bibang's bibliography of printed sources in only the French language through the late 1960s further adds to the impression that the outline rests on a narrow range of materials and is now outdated.

Main Periods in the History of Gabon

The history of Gabon has been shaped by the interaction of both Africans and Europeans and by the interplay of both internal and external influences and events. On the basis of these factors, one can outline four general periods of unequal length, which can be designated by adjectives reflecting the dominant characteristics:

(1) From ancient times to 1471 A. D. (Bantu Gabon)
(2) From 1471 to 1843 A. D. (Atlantic Gabon)
(3) From 1843 to 1960 A. D. (French Gabon)
(4) Since 1960 A. D. (Independent Gabon)

Bantu Gabon

Many centuries before European peoples came along the Atlantic coasts, peoples of Negroid stock called the Bantu began their migrations into the forests which cover most of Gabon. It is believed that all of Gabon was once forest but portions were turned into grassland by human activities through the centuries. These Bantu peoples found small numbers of peoples of an older Pygmoid stock living at various points in the forest. The Bantu peoples came from the north, south, and east, and though probably all of one stock and even of one proto-Bantu language, they became differentiated in the course of their travels. It was during these centuries, both before and after their arrival in Gabon, that they developed the foundations of their societies, in which roles were assigned on the basis of sex, generations within the sexes, and kinship, as well as the material culture for survival in the forest. They were peoples of the New Stone Age, who lived from hunting, fishing, and subsistence agriculture, though the manioc and some of the varieties of bananas and plantains that would subsequently become the staples of the Gabonese diet had not yet been introduced from the New World. In this period we have called Bantu Gabon the extended family, the lineage, and the clan formed the basic social units and governance seldom extended beyond them. Only on the Loango coast, centered in the Congo Republic but extending north into Gabon, were institutions developing on a larger scale.

Atlantic Gabon

The first Europeans who came along the coasts in the 1470s and 1480s were the Portuguese. They found the Mpongwe already living along the river or estuary to which they gave the name gabão, meaning hood or sleeve. They also made contact with the Orungu at Cape Lopez and the Vili along the Loango coast. Indigenous trading networks that already extended from the interior down waterways to the ocean and along the coasts gradually acquired a new overseas dimension throughout the sixteenth and seventeenth centuries as Dutch and French traders joined the Portuguese. But the networks came to be focused upon the Atlantic coasts probably only in the late eighteenth and early nineteenth centuries as the slave trade reached its height and British industrial manufactures gained a predominance. In the meantime migrations and movements of Bantu peoples continued throughout the interior. Frequently the stronger provoked the movement of the weaker and set off a veritable chain reaction of migrations. The largest in scope would be the southward and coastward movement of the Fang in the late eighteenth century and a large part of the nineteenth century whose impact would be felt throughout most of northern Gabon. Ultimately the Fang sought to make direct contact with European traders, a goal shared by other interior peoples who were moving towards the southern coasts in these same eras. The period of Atlantic Gabon also saw the sway of the Loango kingdom extend northward into Gabon at least as far as Setté-Cama and then decline in the nineteenth century.

French Gabon

France under King Louis Philippe founded a post in the Estuary in 1843 to promote commerce and to combat the slave trade. Though the French made efforts to end the slave trade, frequently as a result of British prodding, it continued clandestinely on a reduced scale until the 1860s. On the whole, the French exhibited much greater zeal in securing recognition of their sovereignty through treaties with the clan heads of the indigenous peoples as a first step in competing with the dominant British, American, and German traders. French agents resorted to deception, threats, and finally force in 1845 to gain the submission of the Mpongwe clan head at Glass who, unlike the other clan heads, refused to consent freely to the French establishment. During the next four decades the French made treaties with all of the coastal peoples from Loango to the Rio Muni (as well as with some farther north and offshore who would eventually be assigned to Spain). In the late 1860s they penetrated the lower Ogooué river valley. Their thrust into the middle and upper reaches of the river would take place between 1874 and 1885 under the leadership of Savorgnan de Brazza as part of France's competition with Leopold II, king of the Belgians, for control of the Congo. France in 1885 and 1894 partitioned the northern and northeastern hinterlands with Germany. Then in 1900 it divided the disputed areas of the northern coasts with Spain. France would administer the Loango coast as part of Gabon until 1918, at which time most of it was transferred to the neighboring French colony of the Middle Congo.

The boundaries drawn by the colonial powers in the north and northwest divided the Fang people among Gabon, Cameroon, and Spanish Guinea as well as from the larger Pahouin group (Fang-Boulou-Beti) whose greatest numbers are located in Cameroon. The boundaries with the Middle Congo left small numbers of Vili and Téké within Gabon and split the Bakota, Bapounou, and Mbédé groups (including the Nzabi). But the fact that France controlled the Middle Congo and, after 1916, the adjacent areas of Cameroon, helped to prevent irredentist or unification movements. The inland boundaries with Spanish Guinea (Rio Muni) posed few barriers to the movement of either peoples or goods during the colonial period.

Between 1843 and 1886 Gabon was always administered by French naval officers jointly with French West African territories. France instituted customs duties on foreign trade to help pay the expenses of its establishment. The French used force when necessary to protect European merchants seeking to by-pass the coastal traders and to deal directly with the interior peoples as well as to punish Gabonese peoples who abused or attacked European traders. One of the ironies of this situation was that France was able to interest few of its own citizens to engage in commerce in Gabon. It therefore ended up providing protection for those very British, American, and German traders with whom it had hoped the French merchants would compete. In one instance in the late 1840s in which a French entrepreneur, Le

Cour, attempted to establish a commercial plantation in the Estuary, neither the Naval Ministry nor the local administration would give subsidies nor aid in labor recruitment. Later on, in the 1860s, the administration aided a private company, Victor Régis of Marseilles, to recruit so-called "free emigrants" for plantation labor in the French West Indies. The scheme deprived sparsely populated Gabon of several thousand workers who might have assisted in its own development. The French government helped Roman Catholic missionaries to establish in the Estuary in 1844 in the expectation that they would promote French cultural and political influence. Deaths and illnesses in the missionary ranks prevented them from evangelizing beyond the Mpongwe and Benga peoples or educating more than a few hundred persons at any time during their first 35 years. As far as the French government was concerned, however, the missionaries served the important purpose of providing competition to the American Protestant missionaries who had started work in the Estuary in 1842 and who entered the middle Ogooué in 1874.

In the 1880s French rule began to acquire a more typically colonialist character both in relation to the Gabonese and to other westerners. The French instituted a tax upon able-bodied persons of both sexes over ten years old and required unpaid labor for a certain number of days a year for projects deemed of public utility. In 1883 the administration closed the American Protestant schools, which had been teaching in English as well as local languages. It allowed them to reopen only after they had secured French-speaking teachers from Europe. After the Americans transferred their work to French Protestants and moved north into Cameroon, the administration showed much less zeal in enforcing the prohibition on the use of local languages for academic instruction but still vigorously encouraged the teaching of French. During the exploration and occupation of the interior, roughly from the mid-1870s through the First World War, the administration required various villages to provide foodstuffs to its posts and military units. The French paid for these provisions but generally at prices that were unattractive to both producers and transporters. The French instituted forced labor for portage and construction when free recruitment failed to yield the necessary manpower.

French colonialism saw its worst abuses and injustices as a result of the concessionary regime installed throughout the French Congo (of which Gabon formed part) in 1898-99 and not completely terminated everywhere until 1930. The regime effectively denied the land rights of the indigenous peoples. The companies systematically emptied the country of all its available resources, backed up in many cases by French-officered Senegalese militiamen. These exactions, taken together with the demands outlined above and a doubling of the head tax, caused the flight of tens of thousands of Africans in the Ogooué and N'Gounié valleys and the abandonment of food crops, with subsequent famines and epidemics. The companies and their supporters in the growing administrative machine nearly destroyed the existing commercial networks and sent the economy into a slump from which it did not begin to recover until the large-scale production of okoumé after the First World War. Concurrent with this devastation was the institution of the indigénat in 1910 at the time of the organization of the federation of French Equatorial Africa to which Gabon's interests would henceforth be subordinated, and the conscious abandonment of the cultural assimilation of the educated elite which had been official practice since the French arrival. From the institution of the federation, French educational policy aimed to create only subordinates and auxiliaries in a colonial situation where Frenchmen and French interests would be dominant for the forseeable future.

Is it therefore surprising in these circumstances to find an anti-colonialist reaction among the educated elite? Paradoxically, their numbers had increased significantly during the first two decades of the twentieth century as a result of the coming of the Brothers of Saint-Gabriel to Libreville and Lambaréné in 1900 and the establishment of public schools in the capital and other towns in 1907 and after. This agitation by educated elements from the Myènè and Fang peoples sought to curb the abuses of colonialism, which deprived them of the basic rights of liberty and property in the land of their birth, and to achieve legal and social equality with French citizens. The demands reflected elite interests almost entirely, for though the elite possessed close ties with the masses, the latter were too much in disarray and demographic decline, not to mention different in outlook, for meaningful political links to be established in this period. Members of the educated elite failed in their main objectives. But they were successful in securing appointments as chiefs among the Estuary peoples (including by this time the Fang) and as representatives in the consultative bodies established in the wake of the Popular Front regime in France (1936-37). Much of the post-war political leadership would come from these elements, plus a handful of educated Gabonese working at Brazzaville who rallied to Free France and gained advancement in the circle of Governor-General Félix Eboué between 1940 and 1944.

The Second World War generated decolonizing trends throughout the colonial empires that France tried to contain through a policy of assimilation, that is, by promoting the advancement of its Black African territories within a French Republic and Union dominated by Frenchmen. This policy, together with those of maintaining the federation of French Equatorial Africa and of treating all Black African territories alike, had the result of creating four different levels for Gabonese political activity (Gabon, FEA, all Black Africa, and the French Republic and Union). At the same time it projected some of the diverse interests and cleavages within French and Black African politics into Gabon. In addition to the opportunities for political participation, the Fourth French Republic (1946-58) saw the end of the worst abuses of colonialism and the granting of basic rights to the Gabonese. Public as well as private French investment improved and expanded the ports and roads with a view to promoting the expansion of wood production and later in the 1950s the exploitation of the mineral resources--manganese, uranium, iron, and petroleum. Primary education in French was extended to the bulk of the school-age population. Much smaller numbers benefitted from technical, secondary, and higher education. Only in the mid-1950s were a few persons receiving secondary diplomas in Gabon itself and completing university programs in France. With just a few exceptions, political life would be dominated by those educated within Gabon prior to 1945. Most influential among them were three men with similar educational backgrounds and personal ties: Jean-Hilaire Aubame (b. 1912), Gabon's deputy in the French National Assembly (1946-58); Léon Mba (1902-67), the first Gabonese mayor of Libreville in 1956 and the top African official in the first executive council in 1957; and Paul Gondjout (b. 1912), member of the French Senate (1949-58) and the leading figure in the Territorial Assembly. Though both Aubame and Mba were Fang, they drew their support from different elements from within that people and had different Gabonese and European allies. Gondjout, who came from the Myènè peoples, used his considerable political talents to promote his own career but from 1954 on allied with Mba against Aubame. On the whole, Gabonese politics were influenced by personal, regional, and ethnic interests rather than by issues or ideologies. To complicate matters, independents held the balance of power between the two political parties that formed around Aubame, on the one hand, and

Gondjout and Mba, on the other. In addition, the training of Gabonese for the highest levels of territorial administration began only in 1956.

Independent Gabon

Gabon arrived at political independence on August 13, 1960, as a result of decolonizing forces elsewhere in the French Union that had contributed first to the collapse of the Fourth Republic in May 1958 and then to the demise of De Gaulle's French Community, which had limited the African territories to autonomy or self-government. At independence Gabon possessed neither the resources nor the personnel to operate its administration and economy, much less to develop them, without continued outside aid and assistance. Much of this support was forthcoming from France and was institutionalized in the fifteen coopération agreements signed a month before independence. At the same time private investors from France, other Common Market countries, and the United States continued to develop the country's mineral resources. The early 1960s saw the first significant exports of manganese and uranium as well as the successful prospecting and construction of facilities that would lead to the exploitation of petroleum in the late 1960s and early 1970s.

In the meantime, within three years after independence, the political institutions modelled upon the Fifth French Republic had broken down, a victim of the rivalries of the politicians and parties. Central in the collapse was the determination of President Mba to provide a strongly authoritarian leadership, taken with the increasingly repressive measures necessary for him to do so. His actions provoked a military coup against his regime in February 1964. French military intervention, which restored him to power, allowed him an uncontested rule for the remaining three years of his life. It enabled him to transfer his power intact to his handpicked successor, Albert-Bernard (later Omar) Bongo (b. 1935). Bongo would face the difficult task of maintaining political stability while trying to establish a less repressive and more broadly based regime.

For this task Bongo possessed a number of assets. As a member of the numerically small Téké people of the far interior, he stood outside the ethnic rivalries (Myènè vs. Fang, intra-Fang) that had plagued political life for two decades. Though young, he possessed a good education in business administration and a decade of governmental experience, including several years in the president's office. Yet he had not been personally involved in the rivalries or repression of the Mba presidency. Responding to the wishes expressed in the National Assembly, Bongo between 1968 and 1972 released those involved in the coup and the members of the provisional government of 1964. Many of them re-entered government service while the remaining ones returned to private life in Gabon or abroad. On March 12, 1968, Bongo dissolved all the existing political parties and announced the formation of a single party, the Parti Démocratique Gabonais (PDG), which would undertake a rénovation or renewal of national political life through greater participation and by means of dialogue. Henceforth all political discussion, debate, and criticism would take place only within the framework of the PDG. During the early years of the Bongo presidency, a good deal of dialogue seems to have occurred within the regime with the chief executive ultimately making the important decisions himself.

To a much greater extent than Mba, Bongo sought to secure Gabonese control of natural resources and greater benefits to the Gabonese from their exploitation. Thus have come the requirements for greater Gabonese participation in the ownership and management of commercial and industrial enterprises. Given the paucity of private capital and its preference for investments in real estate and banks instead of industry or large-scale commerce, the state has become the leading Gabonese participant. Gabonization has advanced slowly as a result of the scarcity of Gabonese with advanced technical and managerial skills willing to work in industry instead of the civil service.

Bongo's accession to the presidency coincided with the beginnings of a decade of economic expansion based primarily on petroleum but also on manganese, uranium, and timber that multiplied the revenues hitherto available to the government. The government decided to use the bulk of the additional funds to promote the kind of development that would ultimately decrease dependence on petroleum and would create a much more diversified economy. To this end, it invested its own resources and sought foreign grants and loans to construct an infrastructure that would allow tapping of the mineral and timber resources of the interior. The cornerstone of this infrastructure is the Trans-Gabonais Railroad from the Estuary to the middle and upper Ogooué River valleys. From the early 1970s the Bongo government pursued a more active foreign policy, primarily to get more aid for development and from greater numbers and kinds of sources. While establishing relations with additional western nations, it inaugurated relations with numerous Arab and Communist states. While becoming more independent of France in terms of policy formation, as reflected in the revised coopération agreements of February 1974, Gabon became even more dependent in terms of personnel and investment capital. During the last half of the 1970s several thousand additional European technicians and managers and other thousands of non-Gabonese African laborers and employees entered Gabon to carry out the various development programs. By the time the first section of the Trans-Gabonais opened in September 1978, heavy charges on foreign loans and less than anticipated petroleum revenues were forcing cutbacks and slowdowns in the development programs. The moment when the Trans-Gabonais might reach the iron deposits of the Haut-Ogooué Province seemed more distant than ever. Expenditures which Africa Contemporary Record estimated at as much as nine hundred million dollars for a new presidential palace, beautification of the capital, and new hotels for the 1977 OAU meeting may also have contributed to the financial woes. But by the end of 1978 the government had stabilized the country's finances and had begun reduction of its debt. At the same time additional petroleum and uranium were discovered.

The financial difficulties also contributed to a political malaise, which came into the open at the Second Extraordinary Congress of the PDG in January 1979. In unprecedented criticisms of the regime, the Congress called upon the government to tackle the related problems of inefficiency and multiple office-holding, which led to neglect of duties. One resolution lambasted the economic management of the country which it stated had led to "unbridled capitalism" instead of "rational exploitation of our perennial resources" and called for agriculture to be made a priority. The Congress failed to re-elect a number of top officials to the Central Committee and urged a democratization of the process for selecting party officials and National Assembly members. President Bongo responded by reshuffling his government and announcing several democratizing measures. In November 1979 an ordinary party congress re-nominated him and on December 30, 1979, he was popularly re-elected to another seven-year term. It thus appeared that he had received mandates both to continue in office and to institute reforms that might deal with the nation's ills. Following two-stage parliamentary elections in February 1980, President Bongo reorganized the government as a step towards dealing with the current problems.

Conclusion

At the start of this historical section it was stated that the history of Gabon has been shaped by the interaction of both Africans and Europeans and the interplay of both internal and external influences and events. The summaries of the four periods indicate that Gabon came into being with its present frontiers as a result of European expansion and competition during the last half of the nineteenth century. Gabon became independent in 1960 as a result of decolonizing trends elsewhere in the colonial world, for while the country had developed anti-colonialism among its elite, it had not yet developed what one might call a nationalist movement. Ethnic diversity and rivalry, the geographic barriers to establishment of linkages between the political elite and the masses dispersed throughout the interior, the absence of economic development except for the timber industry together with the devastation wrought by the concessionary companies, the small numbers with an education beyond the early primary grades--all these factors inhibited the rise of a nationalist movement that might have mobilized popular energies for securing freedom from foreign rule, creation of national unity, and the modernization of the economy and society. Independence arrived with the vast majority of the population remaining politically unaware while retaining patterns of subsistence activity and social relations not terribly different from the previous centuries.

The development since independence with the most far-reaching consequences has been the vastly extended exploitation of the country's considerable natural resources under arrangements which, during the Bongo regime, have benefited Gabonese at least as much as foreigners. This exploitation from the late 1960s multiplied the revenues available to the government, thereby presenting unprecedented opportunities to reshape the economy and society and thus to improve national life. Clearly the elite have prospered from the greatly increased national income through lucrative public employment. At the same time the masses of people have benefited through improved health care and education. Gabon has attained near universal primary education under better trained teachers and a much larger segment of the population is receiving technical, secondary or higher education.

In the long run the infrastructure that the government has been and still is constructing may permit the exploitation of the natural resources of the interior and the building of secondary and transformation industries and thereby sustain the new levels of revenue and lead to further growth. The increased educational opportunities may enable many more Gabonese to secure productive employment in the mining and industrial sectors of the economy. But a related problem that the government has not yet tackled and to which the Secondary Extraordinary Congress of the PDG in early 1979 addressed itself is the development of a modern agriculture, which might lead to a more productive life in the countryside for the bulk of Gabon's population and stem the rural exodus. For the development of mineral resources in the late 1960s and 1970s helped to draw thousands of persons from the rural areas into urban centers in search of the kinds of employment for which many of them were neither psychologically nor educationally prepared. Urbanization has thus taken place at a much more rapid rate than industrialization. The challenge to the government of Gabon is to construct the foundations for long-term prosperity based on agriculture as well as mining and industry while at the same time providing a larger part of the educated with opportunities for meaningful participation in the political system.

THE DICTIONARY*

ADMINISTRATIVE HISTORY. France established its sovereignty in Gabon on the basis of treaties concluded with the representatives of indigenous peoples between 1839 and 1885. In the treaties the Gabonese leaders are usually identified as chiefs but they were in most cases clan heads, for only the Orungu and the Vili (and the Nkomi for a time in the nineteenth century) had chiefs who ruled an entire people. Specifically, French naval officers made treaties with the Mpongwe clan heads of the Estuary (1839-1849); the Benga of Cape Esterias (1852); the Orungu in the vicinity of Cape Lopez (1862); various peoples at the Mondah River and the Rio Muni (1845-85); various peoples of the lower Ogooué and with the Enenga, Okandé, Apindji, Bakota, and Adouma farther upstream (1867-85); the Nkomi of Fernan-Vaz, the Ngowe of Iguéla Lagoon, Loumbou of Setté-Cama, and the Vili of Loango (1867-1885). (Between 1842 and 1885 the French also made treaties with peoples along the coast of Equatorial Guinea and the Cameroons in areas eventually assigned by negotiation to Spain and Germany.) Recognition of French sovereignty was generally accompanied by the cession of a plot of ground for a French post. The first French post was Fort d'Aumale established on the northern shore of the Estuary in 1843. While the French Navy patrolled the coasts, rivers, and streams of the areas under French sovereignty, the establishment of permanent posts was a slower and later process. French occupation of much of the interior took place only in the late nineteenth and early twentieth centuries, either as a result of competition with other colonial powers or in the wake of boundary agreements with them. Thus France made agreements with Portugal and the Congo Free State of King Leopold II concerning the southern boundaries (areas that in 1918 were trans-

*Numbers in brackets appearing at the ends of entries refer to items in the Bibliography.

ferred to the Middle Congo) and with Spain and Germany defining the northern ones. In 1911 as a result of a Franco-German agreement giving France a free hand in Morocco, Germany was ceded portions of northern Gabon extending south of Equatorial Guinea, which was consequently bordered on the three land sides by German territory. France re-occupied these areas in 1914 and regained them formally through the Treaty of Versailles of 1919.

Throughout nearly all of the period of French colonial rule, Gabon was attached administratively to other French territories--between 1843 and 1886 to various possessions in West Africa, and from 1886 to 1958 to others in Equatorial Africa. The administrators from 1843 to 1886 were naval officers under the authority of the Ministry of the Navy in Paris. The *commandant-supérieur,* who had responsibility for various West African settlements in addition to Gabon, also headed a Naval Division --up to 1860 covering the area from Senegal to Gabon and after that from the Gulf of Guinea to Gabon. Under the *commandant-supérieur* was a *commandant-particulier* charged with the administration of Gabon.

In the wake of French expansion into the interior, in February 1883 the explorer Savorgnan de Brazza (q. v.) was named government commissioner for the upper Ogooué and the Congo. In 1886 the colonies of Gabon and Congo were placed under Brazza as Commissioner-General with a Lieutenant-Governor under his authority having charge of Gabon. These territories would be known collectively as the French Congo, a name formally adopted in 1891. Further French expansion produced several re-organizations and ultimately the formation in 1910 of the federation of French Equatorial Africa (q. v.). Gabon was headed by a Lieutenant-Governor under the authority of the Governor-General, who from 1903 resided at Brazzaville. (The name French Congo would henceforth be restricted to the French colony next to the Congo Free State or Belgian Congo; after 1903 the colony was formally called the Middle Congo and is today's People's Republic of Congo.)

In the meantime responsibility for the French colonies had passed in March 1894 from the Ministry of the Navy to a separate Ministry of the Colonies. Between 1882 and 1894 there had been an Under-Secretary of State for the Colonies, a position held by a civilian politician drawn from the Chamber of Deputies. Within the Ministry of the Colonies a single bureau handled matters concerning both French West Africa and French Equatorial Africa, which encouraged the already present tendency to consider the latter as a less populated and poorer version of the former. In the mid-1930s the Popular Front changed the name of the Ministry of the Colonies to the Ministry of Overseas France.

After the Second World War the Lieutenant-Governor of Gabon was retitled Governor, a designation that would be retained throughout the Fourth French Republic. Within Gabon from the 1880s the Lt.-Governor or Governor was assisted by territorial administrators, who at first were often naval or military officers and later, after organization of the Colonial School in Paris, professionally trained civilians. Gabon was divided into a number of regions (also called circonscriptions in the early period and prefectures later), which were subdivided into districts. The boundaries within Gabon and between Gabon and the Middle Congo were frequently redrawn between the 1880s and 1946. For example, the Loango coast formed part of Gabon between 1883 and 1918 while the Upper Ogooué Region was attached to the Middle Congo between 1925 and 1946. Gabon acquired its present international boundaries and nine regions only in 1946.

In 1975 Gabon began an administrative reorganization. The regions and districts were renamed provinces and prefectures with the latter divided into sub-prefectures. (This usage of prefecture differs from the usage above where prefecture was the equivalent of a region.) Governors appointed by the president head each province with prefects and sub-prefects in charge of their constituent units. There are nine provinces and 37 prefectures.

In addition to this territorial organization, Gabon has eight cities with elected mayors and municipal councils (communes de plein exercice). They include Libreville, Port-Gentil, Oyem, Bitam, Mouila, Lambaréné, Moanda, and Franceville. The officials of these cities are responsible to the territorial administrators of the units of which they are geographically a part.

The Parliament in the late 1970s was studying the reform of local collectivities that have heretofore existed in the rural areas, the communes. See GOVERNORS. [251, 125, 96, 60, 213, 701]

ADOUMA. A people of the Mbédé-speaking group who occupy the left bank of the upper Ogooué in the area of Lastoursville. Expert canoemen, they played an important role at the time of Brazza (q. v.). According to their traditions, they arrived from the east or south-east, travelling down the Sébé River to the Ogooué and then down it to the Doumé rapids where they encountered pygmies. They made canoes of okoumé. They sold slaves to the Okandé (q. v.) for transmission down the Ogooué. In exchange they received salt, guns and powder, fabrics, matches, and copper utensils. Lastoursville was an Adouma village before De Lastours established a French post there. The SHO (q. v.) opened a factory there and purchased rubber, ivory, and ebony. The Adouma traders purchased various products (mats, raphia thread, gourd seeds, groundnuts, palm oil) and went to sell them at Lambaréné. In the past two decades many Adouma have been settling down river towards Port-Gentil (q. v.). [189, 182]

ADYUMBA. The Adyumba people are part of the Myènè (q. v.) linguistic group of the Bantu. They were originally an Mpongwe (q. v.) clan that inhabited the banks of Nazareth Bay near the mouth of the Ogooué River. Their activities included canoe-making and weaving but their speciality was ceramics. After initially friendly relations with the Ombéké or Orungu (q. v.) immigrants to their region, misunderstandings developed in the late eighteenth century which expanded into war. An Adyumba remnant, including Chief Repéké, fled to the region of Lake Azingo, where they became by the 1810s an important link in the trading network between the Agulamba clan of the Mpongwe on the lower Remboué River and the Lambaréné sector of the Ogooué River. [251, 232]

AGRICULTURE. Perhaps as much as three quarters of Gabon's active population work at agriculture, most of it for subsistence and much of the rest for local markets. Farmers still use traditional methods and hand tools. Manioc (cassava) and plantains are the two most important staples, supplemented by yams, sweet potatoes, taro, maize, groundnuts, sugar cane, pineapples, and cucumbers. Mountain rice is grown only in the southwestern savannas around N'Dendé and Tchibanga. Fruit trees such as the mandarin, orange, mango, papaya, and _atangatier_ are most common in the northern half of the country. Dairy products and meat have to be imported.

Only one half of one percent of Gabon's area is under cultivation given the poor quality of the soils, the rapid leaching when tilled, and the unremunerative prices of agricultural produce. Roughly one quarter of this small area falls in Woleu N'Tem Province and is devoted to commercial crops, above all, cocoa. Smaller amounts of coffee, palm oil and kernels, groundnuts, and rice are also produced commercially. The palm products and rice are raised by companies and the other crops by peasant producers. In the late 1970s commercial crops contributed less than one percent of Gabon's export earnings. The Third Development Plan (1976-80) devoted about 3 percent of its investments to increasing agricultural output in the face of rural labor shortages and the stagnation of subsistence production. The government also sponsored expensive capital-intensive truck gardening schemes to supply Franceville and Libreville. [478, 483, 11]

ALAR AYONG. Alar ayong in Fang means "to unite the clans." It was a movement among the Fang of the northern Woleu N'Tem in the late 1940s and early 1950s to revitalize their traditional structures and values by a regrouping of the 150 or so Fang clans. Alar Ayong originated among the Ntumu and Boulou recipients of American Presbyterian mission education in southern Cameroons in the late 1930s and early 1940s. These peoples, like the Fang, belonged to the Pahouin group of peoples. Their researches into the Pahouin past as contained in clan genealogies, legends, and myths revealed an unexpected degree of organization in the clan relationships of the peoples under colonial rule which had heretofore thought to have been extremely scattered and disorganized. Their findings encouraged the Fang to find similar linkages, which they did and on the basis of which they undertook a regrouping of their clans. While the French administration favored a regrouping of the populations for convenience in providing services and securing revenues, it was suspicious of any movement with links to the trust territory and American missionaries. It also feared that the Alar Ayong leaders might try to displace the chiefs recognized by the French. In these circumstances the movement did more to restore Fang self-esteem by affirming the relevance of the ancestors and of the clans than it did to modernize society along western lines. [261, 283]

ALLISON, FRANCIS. Allison was the first bookbinder in Gabon. A Grebo from Cape Palmas, he learned bookbinding in New York City and served the ABCFM mission in Gabon as binder and teacher from 1843 to 1846 and from 1849 to 1856. [517]

AMOGHO, EUGENE (1918-). Politician. Amogho was born at Franceville on June 17, 1918. A civil servant, he was elected to the Territorial Assembly from the Haut-Ogooué Province in March 1952 and re-elected in March 1957. He served as one of Gabon's councillors in the Grand Council of French Equatorial Africa from 1957 to 1959. Amogho entered the first Gabonese executive in March 1957 and subsequently held various ministerial posts while serving in the Territorial and then National Assembly. He was a member of the short-lived provisional government of February 1964. In January 1969 he became president of the Caisse Gabonaise de Prévoyance Sociale. [694, 642, 686, 682]

ANGUILE, ANDRE-FERDINAND (1922-). Monsignor Anguilé was the first Gabonese to be named Roman Catholic Archbishop of Libreville in July 1969. A relative of the Mpongwe clan head, King Quaben (q. v.), and a member of a prominent *métis* family, Anguilé was ordained a priest in July 1950 and became pastor of the main church in Libreville, St. Peter's, in October 1956. [487, 488]

ANGUILE, ANDRE GUSTAVE (1920-). Civil servant. Anguilé was born at Libreville on March 3, 1920, into a prominent *métis* family. His father was the wealthy lumberman, Augustin Anguilé. André-Gustave was one of the three Gabonese who obtained a *baccalauréat* in France between the two world wars. After secondary studies at Bordeaux and Sens, he specialized in forestry engineering in Paris, where he was active in African politics. On his return to Libreville, he directed a forest exploitation from 1946 to 1952. With Léon Mba (q.v.) and Paul Gondjout (q. v.) he was involved in the Bloc Démocratique Gabonais (q. v.). From 1952 to 1957 he served as Secretary-General of the Territorial Assembly. Between 1957 and 1964 he held various ministerial posts concerned with the economy, and particularly industrialization. He was involved with the formation of UDEAC (q. v.) in 1964. With Jacques David, a French customs expert, he published *L'Afrique Sans Frontières* (1965) on the background and functioning of the UDEAC and questions of industrial development in Equatorial Africa. Since June 1973 he has been director-general of the Société Nationale des Bois du Gabon (until October 1975 called Office des Bois). Anguilé has been regarded as one of Gabon's most talented and able administrators. [694, 682]

ANTCHOUEY, LAURENT (1897-1926). Mpongwe critic of colonialism and defender of elite interests. Antchouey and his cousin Louis Bigmann (q. v.) graduated from the Ecole Montfort (q. v.) at Libreville. They served as non-commissioned officers in a Gabonese regiment of the French army which fought in the Cameroons against the Germans during the First World War. In 1920 they became clerks for a shipping company in Dakar. There, with the protection of the French law that existed in the four communes of Senegal and with financial backing from the Mpongwe and Vili elites and the Ligue des Droits de l'Homme, Antchouey in 1922 founded a monthly newspaper, L'Echo Gabonais: Organe d'Union et de Défense des Intérêts Généraux de l'A. E. F. After three issues and until his death he edited the paper from Nice, France. His articles, based on steady correspondence with Mpongwe at Libreville and Brazzaville, made sophisticated attacks on the colonial administration at both territorial and federal levels. In addition to criticizing the indigénat, (q. v.), native courts, forced labor, and various forms of discrimination, Antchouey accused European merchants and the SHO (q. v.), Gabon's largest trading company, of attempting to instill a feudal regime. Antchouey and his paper sought reforms, above all, that would benefit the Estuary peoples and those assimilated to European culture. He sought the assimilation of these elements into the French nation as a means of political and social advancement. He was sympathetic to Pan-Africanism, hostile to Marcus Garvey's Back-to-Africa movement, and opposed to ties with the Communist Party. By including news of all French territories in L'Echo, he enlarged the horizons of the Estuary elite. Through his work in the Nice chapter of the Ligue and his contacts with leading French politicians and colonial ministry officials, he provided Gabon with a spokesman in the metropole. In April 1925 Antchouey returned to Gabon and encouraged the formation of a cooperative among African foresters, the Association Organisatrice du Progrès Economique du Gabon. The association gained recognition from the administration, which favored such economic activity, but confined its activities to a defense of African lumbering rights. Antchouey accidentally drowned on October 26, 1926, shortly before the Libreville branch of the Ligue gained official recognition. [335]

ANTINI, SISTER HYACINTHE (1878-1952). The first Gabonese to become a Catholic sister. The explorer Savorgnan de Brazza (q. v.) found her as an eight-year-old Ndoumou orphan on the upper Ogooué in 1896. He placed her with the Immaculate Conception Sisters at Libreville where she became a novice under the direction of Mother Louise Raynaud. She took vows on May 15, 1890, in the presence of Brazza. Sister Hyacinthe served at Donguila between 1894 and 1919 and thereafter at Fernan-Vaz until her death on July 16, 1952. President Mba dedicated the social center of Nomb-Akèlè to her memory. [530]

APINDJI. People of the east side of the middle N'Gounié River north of Mouila belonging to the Okandé linguistic group. Essentially a river people, they were excellent navigators and fresh-water sailors. They provided expert canoers which facilitated the expeditions of Brazza (q. v.). It is believed that they came originally from the banks of the upper Ogooué River and were a numerous people at one time. Their ranks were decimated by the epidemics of 1877 and the famine of 1922. In addition to making iron goods and canoes, they produced a raphia cloth of high quality which was their main export towards the coast. They sold palm oil to the Eshira (q. v.) and later to the SHO (q. v.) when it acquired a concession over their lands. It is their religious cult, Bwiti (q. v.), which was taken over and adapted by the Fang during the twentieth century. A Roman Catholic mission located among them in June 1900. By the time of independence few Apindji still inhabited their home region, most of them having resettled at Lambaréné, Sindara, and Fougamou. [251, 189, 182, 136, 453]

ARMED FORCES. The armed forces of Gabon in 1978 numbered 1,250: 950 belonged to the Army, 100 to the Navy, and 200 to the Air Force. These forces were French-trained and are Gabonese-directed. France has a force of 650 paratroopers stationed near Libreville under terms of the defense cooperation agreement.

The President has direct authority over the armed forces as head of the armies and minister of national defense. The national police or gendarmerie, numbering 2,000, were directly attached to the Ministry of National Defense in June 1977. [637, 684]

ART. The traditional art of several of Gabon's peoples has been sufficiently studied to relate them to broader artistic traditions. The art of the Mpongwe (q. v.) belongs to a geographic area extending northward along the West

African coast into Yorubaland (Nigeria) while the art of the Vili (q. v.) reflects, in addition, influences from the Congo Basin. At the same time the art of both the Fang (q. v.) and the Bakota (q. v.) adheres to traditions developed in the grasslands farther north and north-east. All four of these peoples have created objects of wood, stone, and metals that form an intimate part of their religious and social lives. Masks are used in traditional religious ceremonies and statuary serves as the tombs and tomb decorations of the ancestors. At the same time other decorated objects from these same materials are employed in everyday life.

Among the most notable artistic creations in Gabon for ritual use are the Mpongwe polychromed, soft-wood masks; the Fang dark-lacquered hard-wood and metal statuettes; and the Bakota sculptured faces of wood covered with brass and copper. The traditional art of the Vili was a sumptuary art analogous to that of the Benin kingdom of western Nigeria in its great variety of richly decorated objects for both ritual and daily use. Several peoples of the southern Gabon interior (e. g. the Mitsogo (q. v.)) developed dyed raphia cloth of high quality as well as great beauty. [700, 652, 620, 605, 608]

ASSOCIATION GENERALE DES ETUDIANTS DU GABON (AGEG). An organization of Gabonese university students in France, important in the 1950s and 1960s. The first Gabonese scholarship holders arriving in France in 1949 organized the AGEG to promote and defend the interests of Gabonese students in higher education. The AGEG was modelled after the general African students' organization, the Fédération des Etudiants d'Afrique Noire en France (FEANF), with which it was affiliated. The FEANF was usually Marxist and militant in its support of anti-colonialist and left-wing political causes but the AGEG tended to limit its activities more to student matters. Until 1960 it received a subsidy from the government. Politically active Gabonese students formed a separate organization, the Mouvement Gabonais d'Action Populaire, which published irregularly a newspaper, La Cognée (The Hatchet) and political tracts. While its members pursued their activities in relative freedom under the Fourth Republic, they ran into trouble after Gabon acquired its own government, which moved against its student critics. The activities of the Mouvement led to the suppression of the scholarships of some of its leaders and legal actions against them in 1960. Though the movement continued to exist until 1967, it was in 1960 that the AGEG became more active politically. For the next decade it would provide a permanent external opposition to the government in power. In January 1961 its president, Xavier Onde-Ndzé, and a member of its executive bureau, N'Dong-Obiang, were arrested at the Cité Universitaire of the University of Paris and expelled from France at the request of the Gabonese government. Subsequently the AGEG strongly criticized the French military intervention of February 1964 and called for revolutionary action to bring down the Mba government. Its monthly newspaper, _L'Etudiant du Gabon_, was thereafter banned in Gabon. In 1965 its president, Marc Mba-N'Dong, was expelled from France. Continued criticisms by the AGEG and other student groups of the decisions and policies of the Bongo government led to legal restrictions on their activities. On July 18, 1971, the Gabonese Council of Ministers dissolved all corporative associations of Gabonese students both at home and abroad. It authorized the students of the national university to create a representative movement which alone would have the right to speak and act in their name. Every student receiving financial aid must belong to this movement. Action was taken among the governments of overseas countries which receive Gabonese students, especially the French government, to ensure execution of these requirements. Thus weakened, the AGEG for all practical purposes ceased to operate. [372, 448]

ASSOCIATION PROFESSIONNELLE DES AGENTS INDIGENES DES CADRES LOCAUX DU GROUPE DE L'AFRIQUE EQUATORIALE FRANCAISE. With the bureaucratization of the colonial administration in the late nineteenth century and the growth of discrimination against Africans, the civil service was divided into a European cadre and a "local" one. Only Africans who held the _baccalauréat_ were henceforth admitted to the European cadre (one Gabonese received the _bac_ at Rennes in the 1890s and three others at Nice and Bordeaux in the 1930s) and the local cadres received considerably lower salaries than their metropolitan equivalents and fewer fringe benefits. After the First World War, higher Myènè and West African civil servants at Libreville, who shunned activity in the Ligue des Droits de l'Homme for fear of reprisals by the administration, formed the Association to ensure their representation on a commission sitting at Brazzaville to determine salaries. They delegated a Gabonese working there to represent them and spurred formation of branches at Brazzaville and Bangui. The Association gained satisfaction on some issues because of their moderation and fear by the Government-General of loss of trained functionaries to the Belgian Congo, which often raided the cadres at Libreville. After a dormant period, the Association revived in the late 1930s in the more favorable climate of the Popular Front. At that time the Gabonese elite at Brazzaville maintained an Association des Fonctionnaires, which was dominated by three young civil servants who had studied together at the Catholic seminary--Jean-Hilaire Aubame (q. v.), René-Paul Sousatte (q. v.), and Jean-Rémy Ayouné (q. v.). In June 1940, after the fall of France, the Association's leaders told Governor-General Pierre Boisson that they supported continued resistance to the Germans. They later established close links in August 1940 with the Free French. After the Second World War the Association Professionnelle itself was transformed into an Association des Fonctionnaires with branches at the federal capital and in each of the four territories of French Equatorial Africa. [335]

AUBAME, JEAN-HILAIRE (1912-). Gabonese politician (1946-64) and French deputy (1946-58). Aubame was born into a Fang family near Libreville on November 10, 1912. Left an orphan at an early age, he came under the care of the Abbé Jean Obame (d. 1934), who arranged for his education in a Catholic primary school and at the minor seminary. When Aubame left the major seminary, Father Obame's brother, Léon Mba (q. v.), helped him to obtain a position in the customs service. Transferred to Brazzaville in 1936, he founded a branch of the Mutuelle Gabonaise in cooperation with a brother of Louis Bigmann (q. v.). He became involved along with Jean-Rémy Ayouné (q. v.) and René Sousatte (q. v.) in various Catholic and _évolué_ organizations and activities. He was among those who rallied to the Free French movement (q. v.) and was therefore sent by its leadership in November 1940 to Libreville to win over the Fang to the Free French cause. Back in Brazzaville, in February 1942 he became a protégé of Governor-General Félix Eboué (q. v.) and his main informant on African affairs. In February 1943 Eboué promoted him, along with several other Africans, into the European section of the civil service. In 1944 Eboué named Aubame as president of the new municipal commission of the Poto Poto section of the capital, to which he also named three other Gabonese. Aubame was among the évolués who helped to prepare position papers for the Brazzaville Conference of January-February 1944. After Eboué's death, Aubame became an adviser to Socialist Governor-General André Bayardelle and to his Secretary-General André Soucadoux. With their encouragement and support, he returned to Gabon to seek election as the second electoral college's deputy to the French National Assembly. Within Gabon he had the support of the administration and the missions. Aubame was elected in November 1946 and then re-elected in June 1951 and January 1956. He thus served until the end of the Fourth French Republic in September 1958. In Paris he affiliated at first with the Socialists but then with an African parliamentary group, the Indépendants d'Outre-Mer, which was led by Léopold Sédar Senghor of Senegal and Dr. Louis-Paul Aujoulat of Cameroon. Aubame played an important role in several Assembly committees dealing with overseas matters. He purchased a home in Paris and established his family there to facilitate the education of his many children. At the same time he made annual tours of all the provinces of Gabon.

In Gabon itself Aubame was active right after the war in the efforts to revitalize the Fang and was influential in the movement to regroup the clans (the alar ayong) (q. v.) to this end. In 1947 he organized the Union Démocratique et Sociale Gabonaise (q. v.), a party centered upon regional notables throughout the interior but drawing its leadership from the Fang of the Woleu-N'Tem Province. In March 1952 Aubame was elected to the Territorial Assembly from the Woleu N'Tem and was re-elected in March 1957. Though his party received 60 percent of the votes cast in that election, it won only 18 of the 40 seats. The Bloc Démocratique Gabonais (q. v.) and independents, backed by some of the wealthy Europeans in the Assembly, selected Léon Mba by a vote of 21-19 as the vice-president of the first government council. Aubame's party accepted four of the twelve ministerial posts but Aubame himself did not enter the government. After independence Aubame cooperated with President Mba by accepting nomination on a single slate of candidates for the National Assembly selected by the latter. Elected to the National Assembly in February 1961 from the Moyen-Ogooué Province, he thereafter joined a coalition government as Minister of Foreign Affairs. He served until May 1962 when, as a result of conflicts with the president, he was demoted to Minister of State for Foreign Affairs. Early in 1963 he was dropped from the cabinet after his refusal to join a single party headed by Mba. Mba thereupon appointed him president of the Supreme Court in the expectation that he would have to abandon his Assembly seat and thereby lose his parliamentary immunity. But on January 10, 1964, Aubame resigned instead from the court. When Mba dissolved the National Assembly and announced new elections with arrangements that favored the BDG, Aubame and his party declared their intention to abstain from participation. Soon thereafter occurred the coup of February 1964 against Mba by elements of the army and gendarmerie and their establishment of a provisional government, to which they called Aubame as head. After the intervention of French troops and the restoration of Mba, Aubame was arrested. Though not considered by most observers to have been a party to the organization of the coup or to have had foreknowledge of it, he was placed on trial at Lambaréné in August 1964. On September 10 he was condemned to ten years hard labor and ten years banishment. On Independence Day 1972 President Bongo released him. Since that time he has lived in Paris and is no longer active in politics. See COUP OF FEBRUARY 17-20, 1964; POLITICS. [335, 372, 364, 347, 694]

AVARO, PIERRE (1911-). Politician. Avaro was born on March 15, 1911, at Port-Gentil among the Orungu (q. v.) people. He was one of the handful of Gabonese to earn the higher primary diploma before the Second World War. Keenly interested in education, he organized the Association of Parents of Pupils and Students of Gabon (Association des Parents d'Elèves et d'Etudiants du Gabon). (Elèves is the term for the primary level, étudiants for the secondary). Avaro gained eminence as the president of the labor union which grouped the workers on Gabon's plantations and forest enterprises. He himself headed the administration of a national forestry enterprise dealing in okoumé. From 1960 to 1963 Avaro served as secretary-general of the BDG (q. v.), which earlier he had helped to organize. He sat in the National Assembly from February 1961 and headed six different ministries at various periods between November 1960 and December 1966. [694]

AWANDJI. The Awandji are an Mbédé-speaking people south of Lastoursville in the upper Ogooué and are closely related to the Adouma (q. v.). Traditionally they exchanged their meat for the Adouma's fish. In 1928-29 they revolted against the exactions of the colonial administration.

The revolt resulted from the increasing demands of the French administration upon a population already victimized for three decades by the commercial monopoly of the SHO (q. v.). The French instituted a capitation or head tax among the Awandji in 1923 and prestation or unpaid required labor in 1926. In December 1927 they demanded that the Awandji bring provisions regularly to the market at Lastoursville for the benefit of the French post. Not only were the prices paid unattractive but appearance at market made the Awandji more liable for enforcement of the capitation and prestation, not to mention recruitment for construction of the Congo-Ocean Railroad (1921-34). Starting in January 1928 Chief Wongo led twelve other chiefs and about 1500 villagers in resisting French demands for bringing foodstuffs to Lastoursville. French attempts at repression encountered a guerrilla warfare, which was not suppressed until May 1929. At the Awandji surrender the African militia (tirailleurs) executed scores of resisters and took 150 prisoners. Chief Wongo and another leader, Chief Lessibi, died three months later aboard a steamer in transit to Bangui for trial. [189, 182, 206, 211]

AYOUNE, JEAN-REMY (1914-). Civil servant and intellectual. Ayouné was born in an Nkomi (q. v.) area, at Assewe near Fernan-Vaz in the Ogooué-Maritime Province on June 5, 1914. He received his early education in the Catholic school at Lambaréné. His studies for the priesthood at the Catholic seminaries of Libreville (1927-1931) and Brazzaville (1931-1933) made him one of the best educated Gabonese of his day. Ayouné joined the federal civil service in 1934 at Libreville. There with François-de-Paul Vane (q. v.) he founded the Mutuelle Gabonaise (q. v.) of which he served as secretary. Thereafter in July 1937 he was assigned to Brazzaville, where he held senior posts in the financial and personnel departments of the Government-General.

In February 1942 he became the Secretary-General of the Union Educative et Mutuelle de la Jeunesse de Brazzaville, an organization led by young educated Gabonese. In 1943 Governor-General Félix Eboué (q. v.) promoted him, along with other Gabonese, into the European cadres of the civil service, provoking lawsuits by European co-workers and strikes by Congolese employees. In January 1944 Eboué named him to the municipal commission of the Poto-Poto district of Brazzaville. At the same time a paper he prepared for the Brazzaville Conference on the respective roles of African and western cultures in an evolving Africa revealed him as a talented social philosopher. The essay, "Occidentalisme et Africanisme" was later published in Renaissances (1944). Between 1946 and 1960 Ayouné held various positions in the civil service at Libreville except for 1956-57 when he served in the Délégation de l'AEF in Paris. In September 1957, he was named an administrator of Overseas France, that is, a member of the top-level of the civil service, heretofore occupied by Europeans. With the arrival of independence, he held several ambassadorial posts (1960-1964) and high administrative positions (Secretary-General of the Government, 1964-1966; Minister of the Civil Service, 1966-1968; Minister of Foreign Affairs & Cooperation, July 1968 to June 1971; Minister of Justice, June 1971-September 1972). Since July 1976 Ayouné has been President of the Chamber of Commerce, Agriculture, Industry, and Mines. [580, 116, 335, 682, 4, 5]

- B -

BABUISSI. A people who are linguistically part of the Eshira group. They live inland in the upper Nyanga River Basin. Part of them inhabit the Congo Republic. [189]

BAKELE. The Bakèlè were important hunters, especially of elephant tusks, and traders over large areas in northern Gabon during the nineteenth century. They are better known historically under their Myènè name, Bakèlè or Akèlè, than by their own name, Bongom or Bougom. Bakèlè traditions indicate their presence many centuries ago throughout vast areas of the forests and savannas from Booué on the middle Ogooué River west to the lower Como, and from the Monts de Cristal to the lower N'Gounié and to the various lakes on both sides of the lower Ogooué to the northwest and southwest. At their arrival they found only pygmies, with whom they sometimes lived in symbiosis. Though they established farming villages, their hunters continued to range far and wide in search of elephants and other game. In the process they came into conflict with other peoples who were entering these areas. By the early nineteenth century they had become parts of the trading networks that fanned out from the Estuary and Ogooué River delta. On the upper Como and Bokoué (a Como tributary) rivers, from the Fang they obtained ivory, which they exchanged along with their own ivory, with the Séké on the lower Como, who exchanged it with the Mpongwe of the Estuary. On the Ogooué and N'Gounié rivers they were involved in a more linear type of network in which they controlled sections of the rivers and therefore all trade going either upstream or downstream. In the wake of the increased demand for slaves between the 1760s and 1860s the Bakèlè became more active in slave raiding. They were the only Gabonese people, in fact, to indulge in large-scale slave raiding of their neighbors in addition to purchasing slaves and to selling some of their own people. In the middle third of the nineteenth century the Bakèlè were believed to number at least 25,000 persons, a total double that of the largest Myènè (q. v.) people. They were nowhere so numerous, however, as the Fang peoples whose southward and westward migrations began by the late 1840s to force them to move down the Como and the Bokoué towards the Estuary and ultimately to disperse for the first time into the upper Ogooué and Ivindo rivers and their eastern tributaries where several thousands of Bakèlè still live. Though the Bakèlè were fierce warriors, they were sent into retreat by the equally intrepid Fang (q. v.), who were better organized for warfare.

During the 1870s the Bakèlè on the middle Ogooué were almost the sole suppliers of rubber to the European traders who were penetrating the region. From these locations they also continued to export dyewood and ebony.

Some Bakèlè chiefs on the Como River along with some Séké chiefs made a treaty on December 2, 1846, recognizing French sovereignty but the absence of central authority, the wide dispersion, and the semi-nomadic life of many Bakèlè made it impossible for the French to deal with most of them. It also hindered American Protestant missionary efforts among them. The ABCFM of Boston, which had its headquarters at Baraka east of Libreville, in 1849 established a mission 25 miles to the east and twelve miles up the Ikoi Creek at Olandebenk, among the Bakèlè. Missionaries transcribed Dikèlè into the Latin alphabet, prepared some school booklets and tracts, and translated portions of the Scriptures. Unsettled conditions in the area resulting from conflicts among the Bakèlè and between them and other peoples, forced the closing of the post by the end of the 1850s. Later, American Presbyterians, who had taken over the work of the ABCFM in 1870, opened up a station among the Bakèlè on the middle Ogooué at Talagouga. This station would be transferred to the French Protestants in 1892.

Independence in 1960 would find the Bakèlè the most widely dispersed of any people in Gabon and numbering around ten thousand. Though now absent from the Como and Remboué rivers as a result of Fang pressures, they have settled in the Lambaréné prefecture and in ten other prefectures from the Atlantic to the eastern frontiers. Those in the extreme east live among the Bakota (q. v.) to whom they are gradually assimilating. [251, 178, 232, 170, 154]

BAKOTA (or KOTA). The Bakota of northeastern Gabon are one of the country's most numerous peoples. Other thousands of them inhabit adjacent regions of the Congo Republic. According to their traditions the Bakota came from the upper Ivindo region along the Singoué and Nona rivers (its western tributaries) in the nineteenth century to their present locations farther south and east in the face of Bakouélé invasions. These invasions were known as the War of Poupou after a ferocious cannibalistic Bakouélé warrior. The Bakouélé (q. v.) themselves were being forced south and east by Fang (q. v.) invaders. Enroute the Bakota encountered the Chiwa (q. v.) with whom they established friendly relations and who were also being down river. On the southward trip some Bakota headed westward where they eventually became the Benga. Others descended to the junction of the Ogooué where they were attacked by another Bakouélé warrior, Mékomba, following Poupou's death. Finally, some of the Bakota were able to defeat the Bakouélé and kill Mékomba. They assimilated the Bakouélé remnants. Other Bakota settled on the eastern tributaries of the Ivindo River and along the upper Ogooué towards Lastoursville. Arrival of the Fang around Booué forced the Bakota there to move east beyond the Ivindo. Those who settled around Mékambo used the iron of the vicinity to make high quality weapons and tools. These traditions suggest that the present Bakota are quite a mixture of peoples swept together by the various Bakouélé and Fang invasions. The presence of some of the same clans among the Bakota and other peoples of the east and even among the Fang gives further evidence of this mingling.

The SHO (q. v.) concession in the 1890s encompassed the Bakota areas. The Bakota exchanged ivory, rubber, goats, and chickens for guns, axes, matches, knives, and fabrics. With the arrival of the French military, Booué became a commercial center for the Bakota areas and porters were required to a greater extent. Companies based in the Congo Basin such as the Tréchot Brothers and the Compagnie Ngoko-Sangha also traded in the Bakota regions. [235, 313, 189]

BAKOUELE. The Bakouélé people occupy the upper Ivindo River as far as Makokou as well as adjacent areas of the Middle Congo and Cameroon. They also have several villages north of Mékambo. Their traditions relate that they migrated to these areas from the sources of the Ivindo under pressures from the Fang (q. v.). At the arrival of the French, they had advanced along the Ivindo as far as Mipemba but thereafter regrouped above the French post at Makokou. From there they exchanged ivory and rubber for various manufactures and salt. [318, 189]

BANKING. The organization of the country's banking reflects its French colonial past and continuing ties with France and other capitalist countries. The largest bank, the Banque Gabonaise de Développement (BGD), has a capital of four billion CFA francs of which 54. 5 percent represents the participation of the state. It was organized as a public institution in 1960 as the successor to the Société Gabonaise de Crédit to provide both financial and technical assistance for economic development. It undertakes operations on its own account and on behalf of the government and public institutions. It can make loans of up to ten years to private enterprises and subscribe capital to them for the same maximum period. There are four important commercial banks in which the state and private citizens hold between 10 and 40 percent of the capital but French, Dutch, and other European banks have the majority. [408, 401a, 684]

BANTU SETTLEMENT. All of the forty or so peoples native to Gabon, other than the pygmies, belong to the Bantu group. Bantu peoples today inhabit the southern half of the African continent. The origins and movements of the Bantu have been sources of much investigation and speculation during the past two decades. It is believed that at a distant time, perhaps several thousand years ago, there was a single Bantu people defined by its common heredity, culture, and language. During movements that covered many hundreds of years, the original people divided and sub-divided and became differentiated culturally and linguistically. At the same time various Bantu absorbed and incorporated elements from non-Bantu groups while some non-Bantu groups adopted elements of Bantu culture and language. As a result of these several processes, the term Bantu has come to refer primarily to language and only secondarily to culture and heredity.

Recent research by German scholars has produced evidence for the possibility of Bantu speakers, particularly of the Myènè (q. v.) group, in the Estuary as long as two thousand years ago. More certain is that the movements of Bantu peoples into Gabon occurred throughout many centuries and that once within Gabon they transferred to new locations as a result of pressures from or conflicts with other peoples. The oral traditions of practically all the Bantu peoples tell of such developments as well as of encounters with groups of pygmies (q. v.), who often served them as guides and who moved farther into the dense forests to pursue their own way of life. When the Portuguese arrived along the northern coasts and the Estuary in the late fifteenth and sixteenth centuries, they encountered groups that well may have been the ancestors of the Mpongwe, Séké, and Nkomi (qq. v.). The populations they found south of Fernan-Vaz as far as Loango (q. v.) may have been the ancestors of the Vili (q. v.). Of other peoples, it is difficult to speak with certainty about much more than the general directions from which they came. Thus it is believed that the Bakèlè, Benga, Bakota, and Okandé group (Mitsogo, Shimba, Pove [qq. v.]) came from the north and northeast; the Eshira, Bapounou, and Loumbou (qq. v.) from the south and southeast; the Téké and Mbédé group (Obamba, Ndoumou, Awandji, Adouma [qq. v.]) from the east.

In the late eighteenth century and early nineteenth century, the Fang (q. v.) left the north and northeast and moved towards the south and southwest, generating new movements among most of the peoples they encountered and leading to a new wave of conflicts. The Fang eventually spread out over the northern half of the country, except for the extreme northeast, and into the southern coastal regions as far south as Setté-Cama. The Fang were seeking to make direct contact with European traders along the coasts and rivers, which is the same reason that had moved other peoples in a coastal direction in the previous three centuries. [251, 189, 227]

BAPOUNOU (or POUNOU). The Bapounou are numerically

one of the most important peoples. They inhabit inland areas of southwestern Gabon in the mountains and grasslands in the upper N'Gounié and Nyanga River systems. In earlier periods, the name Bayaka, which they consider to have a pejorative sense, was applied to them. Other Bapounou inhabit the adjacent Divénié and Mossendjo Districts as well as Kibangou District north of the buckle of the Niari River in the Congo Republic. Until 1925 Divénié District formed part of Gabon. Bapounou traditions indicate a migration in the wake of wars to their present areas prior to the nineteenth century from the south, from regions as far away perhaps as the Congo or as close as the Niari-Kwilou Rivers. During the nineteenth century the Bapounou sent slaves from their own ranks or acquired from inland peoples to Loango and Fernan Vaz. They also gathered rubber for export. Like the neighboring Eshira (q. v.), to whom they are linguistically related, they produced a fine cloth of palm fibers as well as arrow heads, spears, and sabers of high quality iron. [296, 298, 314, 189, 247]

BATSANGUI (or TSANGUI). An Mbédé-speaking people, closely related to the Nzabi. They inhabit an enclave within Nzabi lands in the southeast. Other Batsangui live in the Congo Republic.

BENGA. The Benga people of Cape Esterias on the northern coast are fishermen who accepted French rule in 1852. Part of the Benga inhabit Corisco Island and the coast of Equatorial Guinea.

Benga traditions suggest distant origins in the grasslands of Cameroon north of the rainforests from which they began to migrate as a result of pressures from other peoples, quite possibly in the eighteenth century. The migrants travelled southward along rivers until, at the Ivindo River, they separated into several groups. One group remained there and became the Bakota (q. v.). Other groups, which became the Benga, followed the rivers and streams that enter the Atlantic north of the Estuary in Gabon, Equatorial Guinea, and Cameroon. These latter groups located near the mouths of these rivers and adjacent coasts, and on offshore islands. By 1800 they had become important middlemen in the ivory and redwood trade north of the Estuary. Thus in the late 1840s at the arrival of Christian missionaries the Benga were inhabiting Cape Esterias, Corisco, and the Elobey Islands, as well as Cape San Juan (St. Jean). They lived mainly from fishing, agriculture, and trading. Corisco and the portions of the mainland where the American Presbyterians evangelized from 1850 later became part of Spanish Guinea or Rio Muni (the mainland portion of today's Equatorial Guinea). The French Catholic mission at Cape Esterias came under French sovereignty in 1852 as a result of a treaty with several Benga clan heads. In 1855 the French navy had to intervene to rescue the Holy Ghost Fathers (q. v.) and some of their converts, whom traditionalists had captured and threatened with death, and to evacuate the Sisters of the Immaculate Conception (q. v.). In 1859 the Catholic missionaries decided to withdraw completely when disputes with the traditionalists again threatened their safety and that of the Christian community, which by this time numbered several hundred persons. Some Benga children continued to pursue their education in the Catholic schools of Libreville. The missionaries returned between 1878 and 1904, at which time they withdrew definitively because the population they served had dwindled to only two hundred. During the twentieth century some Benga moved into the Libreville area where they assimilated with the Mpongwe (q. v.). Among the most notable Benga in public life was François-de-Paul Vané (q. v.), who played an important role in politics in the 1920s and 1930s. He was a descendant of Chief Vané of Venje, one of the early Catholic converts, who had moved his family to Libreville in 1859. On the Protestant side, the first Presbyterian convert on Corisco, Ibea J. Ikenga (q. v.), was later ordained a pastor in 1870. Rev. Ibea's influence for several decades extended to some of his fellow Benga on the mainland in French territory. [189, 251]

BESSIEUX, JEAN-REMY (1803-76). Founder of French Roman Catholic mission in Gabon and first bishop. Monsignor Bessieux was born on December 24, 1803, at Villieux in the Montpellier diocese. He served as a parish priest and minor seminary teacher before entering the Holy Heart of Mary Congregation in August 1842 which François Libermann had founded to evangelize the black race. (In 1848 it merged with the older Holy Ghost Fathers (q. v.) and retained that name.) Bessieux arrived in Gabon in September 1844 in the company of Brother Grégoire Say. He founded a post at Okolo in the territories of the Agekaza-Quaben clan of the Mpongwe people not far from the French fort. Bessieux learned Mpongwe well enough to publish a grammar (1847).

He founded a boys' school and St. Mary's Church and arranged for the arrival of the Immaculate Conception Sisters of Castres (1849). His attempts to found other posts in the Estuary in the early 1850s proved unsuccessful. Except for brief visits to Europe to restore his health, he labored in Gabon, after December 1848 as bishop, until his death on April 30, 1876. Bessieux's experiences in Gabon influenced the missionary doctrine of his congregation, which in its comparative lack of ethnocentrism was far ahead of its time. Bessieux's determination to remain in Gabon, even without official support if necessary, on several occasions when the government was thinking of withdrawing, quite likely influenced the French decisions to remain. [538, 498, 497, 201, 157]

BIFFOT, LAURENT-MARIE (1925-). Sociologist. Born at Nkovié in the Moyen-Ogooué Province on February 25, 1925, into a prominent Mpongwe (q. v.) family, Biffot was sent to the Ecole Montfort (q. v.) in Libreville for his early studies and thereafter entered the Catholic seminary for several years. He completed his secondary education at Rennes, France, where he later received a doctorate in sociology. In December 1957 he became a researcher for the Office de la Recherche Scientifique et Technique d'Outre-Mer (q. v.) in Paris and then after December 1959 at Libreville. He has made important studies of the rural populations, youth, and labor. After the opening of the university as Libreville in 1970, Biffot became a professor there as well as dean of letters and social sciences. [580, 682]

BIGMANN, LOUIS (1897-). Journalist and politician. Bigmann was born at Libreville on October 18, 1897, into a prominent Mpongwe (q. v.) family. His family name is a translation of the Mpongwe name Onom'mpolo or "big man" given to an Agwempónó clan ancestor who was a highly successful trader. Bigmann is also descended from Toko (q. v.), the leading trader at Glass in the mid-nineteenth century and is a nephew of the wealthy lumberman, Paulin Auleley. After studies at the Ecole Montfort (q. v.), Bigmann served as a non-commissioned officer, along with his cousin, Laurent Antchouey (q. v.), in the Cameroons campaign, 1916-1919. After the war the two became active in the Ligue des Droits de l'Homme. Together they went in 1921 to work as shipping clerks at Dakar where they founded the anti-colonialist paper, L'Echo Gabonais which Antchouey thereafter edited at Nice, France. Bigmann served in the French army again during the Second World War, this time on the western front, where he was wounded and taken prisoner in the battle of the Somme at the same time his colleague Captain Charles N'Tchorere (q. v.) was assassinated by a German officer. After release in 1942 Bigmann joined the Resistance. In October 1944 he founded the journal l'Empire. Repatriated to Gabon in May 1946, he thereafter worked as a journalist and was frequently an unsuccessful candidate for office, between 1948 and 1953 as representative of the Gaullist movement, the Rassemblement du Peuple Français. From 1953 to 1955 Bigmann headed the association of war veterans. As an ally of Léon Mba (q. v.), he became administrative secretary of the BDG (q. v.) and editor of its paper, L'Union Gabonaise. In February 1961 he became president of the National Assembly and later in 1966 president of the Supreme Court. [335, 170]

BLOC DEMOCRATIQUE GABONAIS. The BDG was a political party founded by Senator Paul Gondjout (q. v.) in April 1954 to oppose the UDSG (q. v.) of Deputy Jean-Hilaire Aubame (q. v.). Aubame had succeeded in replacing René-Paul Sousatte (q. v.) with Jean-Jacques Boucavel (q. v.) in 1953 when the Territorial Assembly elected its representative to the Assembly of the French Union. Gondjout feared that he would not be re-elected to the Senate if he did not organize Aubame's opponents. Gondjout served as Secretary-General of the BDG and Léon Mba (q. v.) became its Secretary. Between June 1954 and 1961 the BDG edited a paper, the Union Gabonaise. Though the UDSG won a majority of the popular votes in the April 1957 Assembly elections, the BDG with the aid of Independents and French allies was able to name the first government under the Loi-Cadre reforms. The party thereafter controlled the legislative and executive branches of the government. After independence, Mba quarreled with Gondjout over the form of the government with Gondjout favoring a parliamentary regime and Mba wishing a presidential one. Mba jailed Gondjout and replaced him as Secretary-General of the BDG. After Mba's death in November 1967, President Bongo dissolved the BDG and other parties on March 12, 1968, and replaced them with a single party, the PDG. [335, 336, 381]

BLUE SISTERS see IMMACULATE CONCEPTION SISTERS

BONGO, OMAR (1935-). President since November 1967; re-elected in 1973 and 1979. Bongo, who had the first names of Albert-Bernard until 1973, was born on December 30, 1935, at Lewai, the Lekoni Prefecture, Haut-Ogooué Province, among the Téké (q. v.) people. He was the youngest of nine children and his father died when he was seven. The Haut-Ogooué formed part of the Middle Congo at that time so young Albert was sent to a public school in the Bacongo section of Brazzaville where relatives lived. He completed secondary studies in commerce at the technical lycée in the capital and in 1958 entered the posts and telegraphic services of the administration. Between July 1958 and October 1960 he served as a second lieutenant in the French Army of the Air, during which time he earned the baccalauréat at Brazzaville. While still serving as a lieutenant, he was assigned to the Ministry of Foreign Affairs of Gabon (1960-62). Between 1962 and 1965 he served as Assistant Director and then Director of the president's cabinet, that is, top assistant to President Mba (q. v.). At the same time he had responsibility for information and tourism (February 1963-April 1964), and then for national defense (April 1964-September 1965) in the wake of the February 1964 coup. In September 1965 he became Minister-Delegate to the Presidency responsible for national defense and coordination. In November 1966 Mba named him Vice-President of the Government responsible for defense, the plan, information, and tourism. By that time Mba was aware of his own serious illness and the necessity of providing for a succession. He thus advanced the date of the presidential election and established the position of vice-president of the republic. In a national election on March 19, 1967, Bongo was elected vice-president and Mba re-elected president. At Mba's death on November 28 of that year, Bongo became president.

Upon his succession, Bongo responded to the urgings of the National Assembly for a policy of reconciliation with the opponents of Mba but without altering the authoritarian regime with its strong presidency. Thus between 1968 and 1972 he released or reduced the sentences of the coup-makers and the members of the provisional government sentenced at the Lambaréné trial in 1964. The capable and cooperative among them were reintegrated into the civil service, and, in several cases, given ministries or lower cabinet positions. The exception was Jean-Hilaire Aubame (q. v.), whom Bongo criticized in 1968 as "having brought the country to the brink of catastrophe through his reckless ambition." Bongo released Aubame from solitary confinement on the Ile des Perroquets in August 1972 and permitted him to leave the country.

As a part of reconciliation under authoritarian rule, President Bongo dissolved all existing parties and on March 12, 1968, created a single party, the Parti Démocratique Gabonais (q. v.), of which he is the secretary-general. He urged a rénovation or renewal that would invigorate national life through greater participation and zeal and that would involve greater dialogue. This would take place within the PDG, which is the only legal forum for political discussion and criticism.

In addition to being president and party head, Bongo heads the government (the prime minister is the vice-president of the government) and directly heads several ministries. Among them are defense, information, planning and development (since March 1969), territorial management (since February 1972), national guidance (since July 1974), postal services and telecommunications (since April 1975). At times Bongo has served as minister of foreign affairs. He reshuffles some of the nearly forty cabinet posts (ministers and secretaries of state) three to four times a year to secure greater efficiency and continued loyalty. Members of the government and party leaders are required to take a loyalty oath to Bongo as head of state and party. Bongo personally takes charge of the civic service and specialized organisms of the party.

In his life style the president has followed a policy of grandeur. He reportedly spent as much as three hundred million dollars for the new presidential palace which contains his residence and the executive offices. It was built on the site of two historic buildings, the colonial governor's residence and St. Peter's Catholic Church, both of which were razed to secure a large enough space. The president also maintains other residences at Libreville, Port-Gentil, Franceville, and abroad. Bongo is believed to have spent vast sums to host the 1977 meeting of the Organization of African Unity, some of them for hotel construction of permanent use and on the beautification of the capital.

After his marriage to Josephine Kama in 1959, Bongo showed an interest in the Catholic religion of his wife but did not become a Christian. In September 1973 he announced his conversion to Islam, which he stated was a personal decision, and took the name of Omar, later calling himself El Hadj Omar after a pilgrimage to Mecca. In this period Bongo undertook increased contacts with Arab countries in North Africa, some of which, as in the case of Libya, did not produce the expected results in terms of development aid. The ties with Morocco knotted at this time proved to be more durable.

In the area of foreign relations, Bongo in 1973 announced a policy of non-alignment, which was followed by the establishment of diplomatic relations with the Arab and Communist nations as well as additional western ones. At the same time, while remaining closely linked with France, Bongo secured an adaptation of the cooperation agreements of 1960 which governed their relations to permit greater Gabonese independence in policy-making and use of resources as well as less overt dependence on France.

Bongo's accession coincided with a wave of economic expansion based primarily on petroleum but also on manganese, uranium, and woods. To a much greater extent than Mba, he has sought to secure Gabonese control over natural resources and greater benefits to the Gabonese from them. This has involved the requirement for greater state participation in the ownership of enterprises and Gabonization of their senior personnel. State participation has been necessary in view of the paucity of private capital. Gabonization has advanced slowly as a result of the scarcity of Gabonese with advanced technical and managerial training. To promote the long-term development of the country, the president sought to use the increased revenues to construct an infrastructure that would decrease the dependence on petroleum products and would create a more diversified economy. To this end he undertook the construction of the Trans-Gabonais Railroad, the first section of which opened in September 1978. By that time heavy charges on foreign loans for development and less than anticipated petroleum revenues were forcing cutbacks and slowdowns in the development programs.

The government's success in stabilizing the country's finances and reducing its debt during 1978 did not head off criticism of its policies at the Second Extraordinary Congress of the PDG in January 1979. The unprecedented criticism of the leader of the sole party by the delegates revealed a serious erosion of his authority. It remained to be seen whether the various measures he undertook in response would succeed in restoring confidence. In November 1979 an ordinary party congress renominated

Bongo for another seven-year term as president to which he was popularly elected on December 30, 1979. Following the legislative elections of February 1980, Bongo reorganized the government.

In January 1980 the Paris semi-monthly Afrique-Asie alleged that misuse of funds and corruption were a major source of the country's financial difficulties. It claimed that the president, his wife, and her brother, Jean-Boniface Assele, director of the national police and Minister of Public Works, had acquired vast real estate holdings as well as majority interest in a score of companies involved in industry, construction, air transport, insurance, and banking. The same magazine claimed that the regime had used violence to intimidate or to silence its critics. It listed a dozen of the most extreme examples. In interviews in the European press President Bongo rejected the charges of corruption and personal excesses but admitted the existence of police brutality, which he was seeking to curb. See DECOLONIZATION; FOREIGN RELATIONS. [682, 343, 372, 344, 341, 373]

BOUCAVEL, JEAN-JACQUES (né Boukakad; 1923-). Politician. Boucavel was born on February 21, 1923, into a Bapounou (q. v.) family at Kibangou, Congo Republic, just across the frontier from southern Gabon. He was educated to be a primary school teacher at the Ecole Renard in Brazzaville and thereafter taught at Mouila. He was active in politics throughout the Fourth Republic. He allied with the Union Démocratique et Sociale Gabonaise (q. v.) of Jean-Hilaire Aubame (q. v.) at that time. He served in the Territorial Assembly from 1952 to 1957, in the Grand Council of the federation during the same period, and in the Assembly of the French Union from 1953 to 1958. In August 1958 he allied with René Sousatte (q. v.) in organizing a new party, PUNGA (q. v.), to represent southern peoples and to campaign against Gabon's joining the French Community in the September 1958 referendum. Thereafter he held various posts in the administration and since September 1964 has been president of the Economic and Social Council. [642, 335]

BOUET-WILLAUMEZ, EDOUARD (1808-1871). As a young naval officer from Britanny and then governor of Senegal,

Bouët played a significant role from 1838 on in securing and implementing the policy that led to the establishment of a French post on the Estuary in June 1843. Bouët personally negotiated the treaties with King Denis (q. v.) (February 9, 1839) and King Louis (q. v.) (March 18, 1841) that provided the legal bases for the French installation. The French decision of December 1842 to establish a naval station and trading post (comptoir) implemented a policy of the Orleanist regime to compete more actively in the commercial sphere in the Gulf of Guinea with the British, the dominant traders who seemed to be on the verge of further expansion. Bouët in 1849 was involved in the establishment of the settlement of freed slaves at Libreville. He wrote an important work, *Commerce et traite des noirs aux côtes occidentales d'Afrique* (1848). [188, 246, 216, 174]

BOUMAH, AUGUSTIN (1927-). Career civil servant. Boumah was born at Libreville on November 7, 1927. He received his secondary education there at the Collège Moderne (1942-1945) and professional training at the Ecole des Cadres Supérieurs in Brazzaville (1945-1948). He later attended the Ecole Nationale de la France d'Outre-Mer, the school which trained the highest level of overseas administrators, in Paris. As a career civil servant from 1949, he held important posts under the French and several high offices since independence. Among them have been head of the National School of Administration (1963-1967) and since April 1975 President of the Supreme Court. [682]

BRAZZA, PIERRE SAVORGNAN DE (1852-1905). Explorer and creator of the French Congo. An Italian-born aristocrat, Brazza became a French citizen in August 1874 while serving as a career officer in the French navy in Equatorial Africa. During his three expeditions under Naval Ministry auspices (1875-1878, 1880-1882, 1883-1885) he founded the French post at Franceville in June 1880, made a treaty with the *makoko* of the Téké (Tyo) at the Stanley Pool on September 10, 1880, and played a role in securing a treaty with the Maloango on March 12, 1883. His explorations helped to establish the bases for French sovereignty in the middle and upper Ogooué River system, on the Loango coast and the Kwilou-Niari River, and in the Congo River system north of the Pool. Brazza brought into being the colony of French Congo in 1886 of which an enlarged Gabon and Middle Congo formed the components. Further additions of territory, including some by him, would lead to the reorganization of the French Congo as the federation of French Equatorial Africa in 1910. Thus his activities had the effect of linking the evolution of Gabon to the three other territories (Middle Congo, Oubangi-Chari, Chad). Most Gabonese consider that this connection ultimately drew away their revenues and hindered their development.

Brazza's explorations added significant geographic information. He showed that the Ogooué River was not part of the Congo River system and there was no direct water route from Gabon into the Congo interior. At the same time he found out that the headwaters of the M'Passa River, an Ogooué River tributary, rose only a few miles from the headwaters of the Alima River, a northwestern tributary of the Congo.

Brazza served as commissioner-general of the French Congo from 1886 to 1897. He spent much of his energies in extending French control and claims, especially in relation to Germany. In 1905 Brazza was summoned from retirement to head an inquiry into the abuses of the concessionary regime which the French government had installed in 1899 to promote economic development by private companies. He was overwhelmed by the injustices and brutalities of the system, to which his exaggerations about the riches of Equatorial Africa had inadvertently helped to give support. Though his report was never published and colonialist elements tried to discredit him, his inquiry resulted in the mitigation of some of the worst abuses and scaling down of many of the concessions. Moreover, Brazza retained his reputation among the peoples of the Ogooué and Congo as a peaceful explorer and friend. Brazza died at Dakar enroute to France in September 1905. [117, 164, 181, 94]

BROTHERS OF SAINT GABRIEL. The Brothers of Saint Gabriel are a French congregation of professionally trained primary school teachers founded by St. Louis Grignion de Montfort (1673-1717) and reorganized in the nineteenth century by Gabriel Deshayes. Brothers arrived in Gabon on October 7, 1900, to assume direction of the boys' schools at Libreville and Lambaréné. They withdrew from Lambaréné in October 1910 for financial reasons and from Libreville in July 1918 for lack of staff but returned in November 1924. At their Ecole Montfort (q. v.) in Libreville they provided an education of high quality to a large portion of the Gabonese elite during the first half of the century. Perhaps the best known member of the congregation is Brother Macaire Clémenceau (1905-), who headed the Ecole Montfort from 1936 to 1963 and who sat in the Territorial Assembly. He is the author of many primary-level texts used throughout Equatorial Africa and Cameroon. Today the Brothers of Saint Gabriel direct primary schools for boys at Libreville, Lambaréné, Port-Gentil, and Oyem. [509, 487, 488]

BUSHNELL, ALBERT (1818-79). American missionary in Gabon, 1844-79. The Rev. Albert Bushnell was born in Rome, New York, on February 9, 1818, and educated at Lane Theological Seminary in Cincinnati, Ohio. After ordination as a Presbyterian minister, he was sent as an ABCFM missionary to Gabon; after 1870 he served under the Presbyterian Board for Foreign Missions. He became an expert in Mpongwe and translated portions of the Scriptures. But his major work was a ministry to young men who were former pupils of the Baraka boys' school for whom he maintained a Bible class. With his second wife, Lucina Boughton (1834-87), he also directed the girls' boarding school there. Bushnell died in Sierra Leone on December 2, 1879. [517, 505]

BWITI. Originally a masculine secret society of the Mitsogo and Apindji, now a syncretic cult of the Fang (q. v.). Practically all Gabon's peoples traditionally had secret societies of both men and women which sought protection and benefits from the spirits of the ancestors and natural forces. These societies also served to strengthen and enforce group solidarity. Bwiti, a masculine secret society of peoples along the N'Gounié River, was spread to various non-Myènè peoples on the middle Ogooué and to the coasts from the Estuary to Setté-Cama as a result of the slave trade, in particular. The Fang who arrived in new locations throughout northern Gabon in the last half of the nineteenth century were by the early twentieth century finding Bwiti attractive. For its rituals and beliefs were much more elaborate and dramatic than those of the bieri and other traditional Fang secret societies. The Fang used various elements from the original Bwiti to fashion a new cult that reinterpreted traditional Fang rituals and beliefs in the wake of the new situations arising from their migrations and contacts with Europeans. Between the late 1930s and the early 1950s, Fang Bwiti further incorporated Christian elements into its rituals and beliefs in response to missionary advances among them. The creator God of the Bantu peoples, formerly considered to be aloof, now was regarded as concerned with the affairs of human beings. A female deity, who blends the qualities of St. Mary in Catholicism with the female river spirit Mboumba characteristic of African religions south of the Ogooué, has an importance equal to her brother, the creator God. Men and women hold equal importance in the cult, a departure from the separate societies of the past and male dominance. Taken as a whole, Fang Bwiti can be seen as an attempt to adjust to the situations emanating from their migrations and acculturation. Léon Mba in the Estuary in the 1920s sought to spread Bwiti as a means of restoring solidarity among the fractionated clans there. At independence there were five different branches of Bwiti, which had constructed one hundred cult chapels to which an estimated 8 percent of the Fang belonged (perhaps twenty thousand persons). But the influence of Bwiti extended well beyond formal membership, often with attendance by Christians who were not particularly fervent or devoted. Given the equalitarian character and loose social organization of Fang society, Bwiti has never developed into a Messianic movement, that is, one led by a single influential leader who elaborated rituals and beliefs. Rather there have been several figures, all of only local importance. [286, 283, 261, 381, 501, 543]

- C -

CAISSE CENTRALE DE COOPERATION ECONOMIQUE (CCCE). The official agency through which the government of the French Fifth Republic has since 1958 channeled, banked, and administered its aid to Francophone Africa. It also handles the funds dispersed by the European Economic Community's Economic Development Fund. The CCCE succeeded the Caisse Centrale de la France d'Outre-Mer (CCFOM) of the Fourth Republic (1946-58) which administered the aid of FIDES. The CCCE handles the grants from the Fonds d'Aide et de Coopération (FAC) and also carries out credit operations on its own account. Thus it extends medium- and long-term loans to African governments, public corporations, and private concerns. But it has sought whenever possible, to work through the development banks of the African states such as the Banque Gabonaise de Développement (BGD) which was established in 1960 as the successor to the Société Gabonaise de Crédit. [408, 406]

CATHOLICISM. Between 1766 and 1776 French priests based at Loango reached the southern coasts of Gabon. Though numerous deaths and illnesses forced their withdrawal, some of their influence persisted. For when Admiral Linois visited Mayumba in 1802, he found Africans who knew French and elements of the Roman Catholic religion. In 1777 Italian Capuchins based on São Tomé and Príncipe briefly operated a mission at the mouth of the Gabon Estuary. But they had to withdraw when the Portuguese authorities of the islands refused to permit foreign missionaries to be based there or to offer hospitality to members of their congregation working on the mainland.

Roman Catholicism was permanently introduced into the Estuary region in September 1844 by French missionaries who belonged to the congregation of the Holy Heart of Mary. The order had been founded only a few years before by F. M. X. Libermann (1802-1852) to minister to black people. The Holy Heart of Mary group merged in 1848 with the older Congregation of the Holy Ghost (Spiritans) (q. v.) whose name was retained for the unified organization. In July 1849 Sisters of Our Lady of the Immaculate Conception (q. v.) or Blue Sisters of Castres, France, arrived to work with women and girls. After the failure of early attempts at expansion, the Catholics limited their work until 1878 to the Mpongwe communities of the northern shore of the Estuary, except for a brief mission (1849-58) among the Benga at nearby Cape Esterias. In the late 1870s, concurrent with a new wave of French expansion into the interior of Gabon linked with the expeditions of Savorgnan de Brazza (q. v.), the Holy Ghost Fathers made new efforts to reach other peoples of Gabon. In 1878 they resumed their work among the Benga and established a post among the Estuary Fang at Donguila. In 1881 they sought to compete with the American Presbyterians in the Lambaréné area among the Galoa, Bakèlè, and Fang. Between 1881 and 1897 they extended their work successively to the Vili of Loango, the Adouma of Lastoursville, the Séké near the Rio Muni, the Nkomi at Fernan Vaz, the Loumbou at Mayumba and Setté-Cama, the Eshira of the southwest interior, and to various peoples of the middle and upper Ogooué and N'Gounié rivers. But they arrived at Port-Gentil only in 1927 and established posts in the Fang areas of the far north only between 1929 and 1935.

The sisters located in many of these places and the Brothers of Saint-Gabriel (q. v.) arrived in 1900 to operate primary schools for boys.

Throughout the nineteenth century the Catholic missions received aid from the French government, which hoped that the missionaries would spread French culture and promote French influence. The missionaries preferred to evangelize in the indigenous languages and prepared catechisms and other materials in fifteen of them. They taught French above all in order to enjoy official support. The missionaries made little headway among adult Africans for several decades because of their opposition to polygamy, which was an important aspect of African economic and social structures. Most of the missionaries' early converts came from the boarding pupils in their schools. Catholics began to make numerous converts among the general population from the 1880s when they were able to train catechists who lived in the interior villages among peoples less involved in overseas trade. The Catholic population of Gabon has grown as follows:

1870: 1,105
1900: 12,500
1930: 29,234
1960: 186,607 plus 27,828 catechumens
1977: 399,453 plus 16,632 catechumens

From the earliest days the Catholic mission sought to prepare an indigenous clergy and for most of the time after 1856 operated a minor seminary where Latin was taught. But the first Gabonese priest, André Raponda-Walker (q. v.), was ordained in 1899 and the next three in 1919. Between 1895 and 1963 Catholics in northern Gabon ordained 39 priests and professed 32 brothers. Between 1879 and 1938 the Mayumba seminary, which served the Loango coast as well as southern Gabon, ordained fifteen priests. The first African brothers were Dominique Fara (1876-1922) (q. v.) and Jean-Marie Ogwaruwé (1874-1955), both professed in 1895. At first the brothers were auxiliaries to the Holy Ghost Fathers. In 1952 they were organized as the Brothers of St. Joseph. Their novitiate from 1959 was placed under the direction of the Frères Auxiliaires du Clergé. The first African sisters including Hyacinthe Antini (1878-1952) (q. v.) made professions in 1890 as auxiliaries of the Blue Sisters. In 1911 a separate congregation for them was organized, the Sisters of St. Mary of Gabon, which in 1977 had 49 professed members in six convents. Implementing the Vatican's policy of Africanization, the first Gabonese bishop was appointed in 1960. Today the archbishop of Libreville and the bishops of Oyem, Mouila, and Franceville are all Gabonese. They direct a church that has 22 Gabonese and 87 foreign priests; 10 Gabonese and 27 foreign brothers; and 32 Gabonese and 108 foreign sisters. The scarcity of new vocations among Gabonese men suggests that the Gabonese church will be dependent upon foreign clergy for a long time to come. Catholic schools, which receive government aid, educate one-third of the primary and one-fifth of the secondary pupils. Sisters are also involved in health care and social work, fields in which they pioneered from the middle of the nineteenth century. See ROMAN CATHOLIC BISHOPS. [487, 518, 528, 530, 488, 497]

CHAMBER OF COMMERCE, AGRICULTURE, INDUSTRY AND MINES. A semi-official body of representatives from the private sector of the economy which advises the government. During the colonial period it was the organism through which French interests formally had access to the territorial administration and brought influence to bear upon it. Since independence it has continued to represent all individuals and companies, whether Gabonese or foreign, conducting business in Gabon.

CHIWA (or BICHIWA). These people are celebrated in the history of exploration under the Okandé name of Osyéba, that is, the people who blocked the passage of Marche and Compiègne up the Ogooué because they were guided by the Okandé (q. v.). The Europeans called them the Fang Makina. Today the remnants of the Chiwa inhabit several villages on the Ogooué downstream from Booué. Linguistically the experts classify Chiwa as a Fang dialect. Some of the Chiwa state that their language most closely resembles that of the Ngumba of the Kribi Region of Cameroon, and after that, the Bakouelé, and only then the Fang.

Chiwa traditions declare a common origin with the Ngumba in an unknown area to the north from which they reached Gabon by descending the Ivindo River. Some settled along the lower Ivindo near the junction of the Ogooué and others along the Ogooué downstream towards Booué. Thereafter the Danbomo and the Shaké arrived in these same areas. At the granting of the SHO (q. v.) concession, the French administration forced the relocation of the Chiwa villages at the Ivindo-Ogooué junction in order to use the land for the company. [189, 132]

COMITE MIXTE GABONAIS (CMG). A political party organized by Léon Mba (q. v.) early in 1947 in the wake of the disintegration of the PDA (q. v.) from personal rivalries and administration pressure on its members who were also active in the GEC (q. v.). It included some members from the Estuary elite who were not Fang but the majority came from the Comité Fang, which had been organized by Mba's supporter, Edouard N'Guéma in 1944 to promote Fang interests. The main Fang members were Mba's nephew, Paul N'Guéma, Jean-Baptiste Obiang, and N'Dong-Mebale at Libreville and two primary school teachers, François Meye (q. v.) and Philippe Ndong (q.v.), at Oyem. The "Mixte" in the name referred to the goal of surmounting tribalism and of including all peoples of Gabon. At a later time the CMG became known also as the Comité Mixte Franco-Gabonais in order to emphasize that it was anti-colonialist but not anti-French. The two names seem to have been used interchangeably after 1949. The CMG replaced the PDA as the local branch of the inter-territorial RDA (q. v.), which until 1949 had ties with the French Communist Party and the Communist-dominated labor confederation, the CGT. In the course of 1947 the administration transferred from Libreville all those civil servants who had been active in the GEC and thus removed an important segment of the CMG from the capital. After François Meye was transferred to Libreville in June 1949, he became the CMG's secretary and contributed most of the group's articles to the Brazzaville RDA paper, AEF Nouvelle. The CMG also became a focus for opposition to the Fang deputy, Jean-Hilaire Aubame (q. v.) and his UDSG (q. v.), which had the support of the Christian missions and, until 1956, the sympathy of the administration. Further it became a vehicle for the political career of Léon Mba after Senator Paul Gondjout (q. v.) helped him to secure the restoration of full civil rights, including the right to seek office, of which his conviction on a criminal charge in 1933 had deprived him. In 1954 most of the CMG membership followed Mba into Gondjout's BDG (q. v.), which replaced the CMG as the main opponent of the UDSG and became the local affiliate of the RDA. [335]

COMITE MPONGWE. Founded officially in January 1936 after two years of informal activity by Mpongwe leaders to defend and to regain their traditional rights, especially land rights in the Estuary. The Comité was led by Amaka-Dassy, Frédéric Moreau, and François-de-Paul Vane (q. v.), the last named of Benga ancestry but assimilated to Mpongwe society. The Comité sought the creation of a single superior chief, a position which they wished vested in a member of the educated elite. The Comité successfully supported Vané for election as Gabon's delegate to the Governor-General's council of administration in October 1937. Vané was instrumental in securing a ministerial decree of February 10, 1938, recognizing traditional land rights, previously weakened by the concessionary regime and other legislation, and providing a more equitable basis for compensation. The Comité secured the nomination of its candidates for chefs de groupes de quartier in the Libreville sections of Louis and Glass, and its president, Amaka-Dassy, as chef de groupe of Glass. Vané and Prince Félix Adandé (q. v.) from the Comité became the first African members named to the Libreville municipal commission. These measures strengthened the Mpongwe people in relation to other peoples and the Europeans as well as the younger educated elements within the Mpongwe clans in relation to the rest.

The Comité unsuccessfully supported Mpongwe candidates for the French Constituent and National Assemblies in 1945-1946 and saw two Fang elected to represent Libreville in the Territorial Assembly in December 1946. During 1946-1947 Governor Roland Pré attempted to settle the Mpongwe problems. He made a settlement with the leaders of the Comité Mpongwe which provided for election of an Mpongwe chief and council. The council was to control most of the land in the quartiers of Louis & Glass and to decide judicial disputes among Mpongwe. But the governor-general at Brazzaville vetoed the agreement. In 1950 the administration gave the Comité the task of dividing twenty million CFA francs to indemnify Mpongwe land-holders (roughly eighty thousand U. S. dollars at that time). In 1955 a delegation to Paris composed of Princes Félix Adandé and Louis Berre (q. v.), Vané, and Louis Bigmann, (q. v.) failed to get a second grant for this purpose. [335]

CONCESSIONARY COMPANIES. In the aftermath of the European scramble to partition Africa, France sought ways to exploit and to develop its vast territories in French Equatorial Africa (q. v.), including Gabon, with as little expense to the French taxpayer as possible. It turned over economic control of most of the equatorial areas in 1899 to over forty chartered companies who were given monopolistic privileges in trade and/or exploitation of natural resources other than minerals for thirty years. The government, imitating the policy of Leopold II in the neighboring Congo Free State, hoped that the companies would make the investments in infrastructure (roads, ports, telecommunications) which the French state was unable or unwilling to make. France also hoped that the concessionary system would transfer the trade of its territories from English and German merchants in the case of Gabon and Dutch and Belgian ones in the case of the Middle Congo to French ones. But matters did not work out as planned. Most of the concessionary companies were family enterprises which lacked the capital and technical skill to undertake the huge tasks assigned them and who sought quick return on short-term commercial investments. The companies encountered a lack of manpower and many barriers to transportation and communication in the vast, sparsely populated equatorial regions. These situations contributed to an often brutal exploitation of the population and to many abuses. The European merchants of the previous trading system, which was long established in the Estuary and the Loango coast and more recently (the 1870s) on the Ogooué and Congo rivers, resisted and protested, the British ones with the support of their Foreign Office. Following an official inquiry by Savorgnan de Brazza (q. v.) in 1905, the half dozen companies in Gabon other than the SHO (q. v.) abandoned their vast concessions in exchange for outright title to thousands of hectares (two acres = one hectare) of rich and accessible forest lands or the right to cut trees over even larger areas. These new arrangements provided the basis for profitable European development of okoumé (q. v.) and other woods during the 1920s and after. In general, the concessionary companies during the years of their functioning contributed to the displacement of African populations and the disorganization of agricultural production with disastrous consequences throughout subsequent decades. They helped to keep Gabon's total population stationary at 389,000 from 1921 to 1955 and to create patterns of underdevelopment that are being altered only in our own times. [182, 180, 73, 143]

CONSTITUTION. The present constitution was adopted on February 21, 1961. It was modelled closely upon the Gaullist constitution of the Fifth French Republic, which established the president as a strong executive and a parliament with legislative powers. The constitution was amended by the law of February 15, 1967, instituting a vice-president of the republic, and by the law of April 15, 1975, suppressing this position and instituting the positions of prime minister and vice prime minister. The president is the sole holder of executive power. He is directly elected for seven years by universal suffrage and is eligible for re-election. He names the prime minister. The members of the National Assembly, called deputies, are directly elected by universal suffrage. Beginning in 1980 their terms of office were reduced from seven to five years and their numbers increased from 70 to 89. The constitution provides guarantees for civil liberties.

Earlier, between 1946 and 1961, Gabon was governed by the provisions of two French constitutions and two short-lived ones of its own. As an Overseas Territory of the Fourth French Republic from October 1946 to September 1958, Gabon came under the provisions of its constitution of October 13, 1946. With the establishment of the Fifth French Republic in September 1958, Gabon became an autonomous republic within the French Community. Its place in the community was regulated by the French constitution of September 1958 and it acquired its own constitution of February 19, 1959, for internal matters. With the transformation of the Community, Gabon became an independent republic with a new constitution of November 14, 1960, which established a basically parliamentary system. By the end of 1961, most of the provisions concerning the Community were no longer implemented or enforced but Gabon formally remained a member. [377, 329, 328, 10]

COUP OF FEBRUARY 17-20, 1964. The coup reflected dissatisfaction by young Gabonese officers, trained at St. Cyr, with the regime of President Léon Mba (q. v.). The coup took place in the wake of conflicts between Mba and opponents in the National Assembly, which had led Mba to dissolve that body on January 21, 1964, and to call for new elections on February 23. The opposition refused to participate because the revised arrangements discriminated against them. On the night of February 17-18, 1964, 150 soldiers led by Lt. Valère Essone and Lt. Jacques Mombo seized the presidential palace and other government buildings. They captured Mba and Louis Bigmann (q. v.), president of the National Assembly, and thereafter arrested all the cabinet except the respected technician André-Gustave Anguile (q. v.). A committee of six junior officers, including Lt. Essone and Second Lt. Ndo Edou of the First Army; Lt. Jacques Mombo and Second Lt. Daniel Mbene of the National Police (gendarmerie), announced that the revolution was taking place to prevent disturbances during the elections. After cancelling the elections, declaring martial law, and forcing Mba to broadcast a resignation and an apology for authoritarian rule, the committee handed power to a ten-member Provisional Government. The government, which was headed by Jean-Hilaire Aubame (q. v.), included two other prominent UDSG politicians, Jean-Marc Ekoh (q. v.) and Eugène Amogho (q. v.), leading opponents of Mba within the BDG such as Paul Gondjout (q. v.) and Philippe Ndong (q. v.), the editor of Réalités Africaines; Eloi Chambrier, M. D. , Gabon's only physician; and Philippe Maury, the country's only actor. The provisional government announced it would respect Gabon's treaties and other obligations. The overthrow of the Mba regime produced no popular reactions or manifestations in its defense.

On the evening of February 18, six hundred troops under command of French General Kergaravat, flown into Libreville from Brazzaville and Dakar on the orders of General de Gaulle after notification by French Ambassador Cousseran, intervened to restore Mba. The French-led troops captured the headquarters of the provisional government in the palace without resistance. But the military camp in the Baraka section held out against air and surface attacks until late on the 19th. Two Frenchmen and 25 Gabonese were known to be killed, including Lt. Edou, and possibly some additional civilians hit in the air attacks. President Mba was located at Lambaréné, where the rebels had taken him, and was returned to the palace. The French intervention provoked popular outbursts and daily protests against the regime at Libreville in the following three weeks, including some counter-manifestations by Mba supporters.

On February 26 the French Minister of Information announced that the intervention had resulted from an appeal by the legitimate authorities for help against the coup-makers. It appears likely, however, that the French attack on Baraka took place before the actual appeal of Vice-President Paul-Marie Yembit (q. v.) later on the 19th, for at the time of the coup he was touring in the N'Gounié Province and was out of contact with the capital. The De Gaulle government may have intervened out of friendship for Mba. But it definitely did so to protect French interests, particularly the uranium, which was essential for securing an independent atomic force, and investments in petroleum, manganese, iron, and wood. The De Gaulle regime incorrectly regarded Aubame as less friendly to French involvement in Gabon and more favorable to increased American involvement, a claim which Aubame denies. In this same vein, elements in the French government and among the settlers in Gabon sought to make the United States the scapegoat for the coup. They refused to recognize that some Gabonese by themselves had sufficient grievances and initiative to undertake a revolt against the regime. It appears that the coup-makers were concerned about the state of the country under Mba and the luxury-living of the ruling class. Some of them may have harbored personal grievances against the regime.

In the aftermath of the coup, Mba promised vengeance for his opponents but Ambassador Cousseran privately urged him to be more conciliatory and apparently persuaded him to hold the Assembly elections on April 12 under fairer arrangements than contemplated for February 23. Cousseran also influenced the decision to establish a special commission of inquiry to investigate the coup. For his pains Mba had him recalled. Unfortunately, Mba prevented the commission from undertaking anything resembling an unbiased inquiry. Mba's arrest of the members of the provisional government and 150 other opponents and critics contributed, along with the French intervention and continued hostility to his regime, to a wave of demonstrations in several regions. A demonstration by several hundred Mba supporters on February 23 at Libreville led to a counter-demonstration on March 1 by five hundred workers and students and one thousand others shouting for "an end to dictatorship." A similar manifestation the following day was accompanied by a strike of _lycéens._ Government repression of the demonstrations involved brutality and many arrests. The demonstrations spread to the lycées of Port-Gentil and N'Dendé. At the latter town national police fired on the students killing one and leading to the death of a gendarme.

The elimination of the opposition leaders from the electoral campaigns, along with numerous irregularities, prevented fair elections. Even then Mba's party only narrowly won the populous Estuary and N'Gounié Provinces, possibly by falsifying the results in the latter case, and lost the Woleu N'tem to the opposition. With only 50.38 percent of the popular vote, it still acquired two thirds of the assembly seats. Announcement of the results brought a nationwide strike by opponents on April 16. Additional student disorders led to the early closing of the schools for annual vacation. After police operations in July eliminated open manifestations of opposition, the government proceeded with the trials of the military rebels and provisional government under strict security at Lambaréné in August. The special court condemned Aubame to ten years at hard labor and ten years banishment, and lieutenants Essone and Mbene to twenty years at hard labor. It confirmed the internment of Gaston Boukat, Marcel Rahandi, Dr. Eloi Chambrier, Philippe Maury, and Philippe Ndong. But it released Lt. Mombo and acquitted Paul Gondjout. It appears that despite Aubame's conviction, he had no foreknowledge of the coup. Rather he seized the opportunity offered to him by the rebels to assume power. There are indications that other civilians, including Aubame's nephew Pierre Eyeguet, who received a sentence of twenty years at hard labor, had some foreknowledge of the coup or were in contact with the plotters.

President Bongo (q. v.), in order to promote national reconciliation, beginning in 1968 pardoned or reduced the sentences of the civilians sentenced at Lambaréné and gave many of them positions in his government. The last to be released was Jean-Hilaire Aubame, who in August 1972 left his solitary confinement on the Ile des Perroquets in the Estuary. [371, 347, 344, 346]

CURRENCY. The currency is the franc of the Communauté Financière Africaine (CFA). The CFA franc is equal to 0.02 French francs so that 50 CFA francs equal one French franc and approximately 200 CFA francs equal one U.S. dollar.

In the aftermath of the Second World War France established a colonial franc for its Black African territories, the CFA franc. (CFA at that time stood for Colonies Françaises Africaines; in 1962 it was renamed the Communauté Financière Africaine.) The colonial franc was tied to the French franc. For the four Equatorial countries and Cameroon, France established the Institut d'Emission de l'Afrique Equatoriale Française with a capital of 250,000,000 CFA francs, which issued a single currency in both notes and coins for all five countries. At independence the five states remained in the franc zone and continued their monetary union with the Banque Centrale des Etats de l'Afrique Equatoriale et du Cameroun issuing a common currency but with separate notes for Cameroon and distinctive serial numbers for each state. This central bank was reorganized in November 1964 as a multinational institution.

The broad principles governing the functioning of the monetary system are contained in the five states' cooperation agreements with one another and France. France guarantees the convertibility of the CFA franc into French francs and is represented on the board of directors of the central bank. These agreements also provide for coordination of commercial and financial policies vis-à-vis countries outside the franc zone.

In 1977 the headquarters of the central bank, now called the Banque des Etats de l'Afrique Centrale, were transferred from Paris to Yaoundé, Cameroon, paralleling the move of the bank for the West African states to Dakar several years earlier. On April 3, 1978, a Gabonese, Casimir Oye Mba, became its first African director-general or governor, all the previous heads having been French. [408, 9, 684, 680]

- D -

DAMAS, GEORGES ALEKA (1902-). Public figure and composer of the national anthem, La Concorde. Damas was born at Libreville on November 18, 1902, and was educated at the Ecole Montfort (q. v.). He served as a bank clerk from 1924 to 1939 and then as head bookkeeper for the Compagnie Maritime des Chargeurs Réunis from 1939 to 1959. As a young Mpongwe working at Brazzaville in 1934, he wrote a series of letters to the Etoile de l'AEF attacking the creation of special rights for métis. The Free French appointed him to represent Gabon on the Governor-General's council of administration between 1943 and 1946. He also served as an adviser to the governor of Gabon from 1948 to 1954 and as a member of the governor's council of administration. He was active after the Second World War in the formation of labor unions affiliated with the French Socialist confederation, the CGT-Force Ouvrière, and in territorial politics. From November 1956 to 1963 he served on the municipal commission of Libreville, his first elective post. In 1959 he represented Gabon on the Economic and Social Council of the French Community. Between 1961 and 1964 he served as ambassador to the Common Market and the Benelux countries and later to West Germany. In April 1964 he was elected to the National Assembly, which selected him as its president, a post he held until 1975. On May 29, 1968, he was named president of the Bureau of the Parti Démocratique Gabonais (q. v.), the country's new single party. He later served as the party's treasurer-general for several years. Between April 1975 and his retirement in February 1977 he acted as an adviser to President Bongo. [682, 580, 335]

D'ARBOUSSIER, GABRIEL (1908-1976). Civil servant and RDA leader. Gabriel d'Arboussier was born on January 14, 1908, at Djenne, French Sudan (now Mali), son of the French governor, Henri d'Arboussier, and an African mother. He graduated in law from the University of Paris and from the Colonial School for overseas administrators. He was assigned to Brazzaville late in 1944, where he served as interim director of political affairs and chef de cabinet for Secretary-General André Soucadaux in the administration of Governor-General Charles-André Bayardelle. Bayardelle encouraged and supported his successful candidacy for the first college (European) deputy to the First Constituent Assembly in October 1945 from Gabon and Middle Congo. In that assembly he allied with the nine African deputies in Lamine Guèye's Bloc Africain and developed a close working relationship with the Communists, which antagonized his European electors and led to his defeat in the elections of June 1946 for the Second Constituent Assembly. He stayed on in Paris to coordinate the work of the Rassamblement Démocratique Africain, a movement in which all the territories of Black Africa were represented. In Gabon the local RDA branch was at first the Parti Démocratique Africain (q. v.) and then the Comité Mixte Gabonais (q. v.) (1947) and later the Bloc Démocratique Gabonais (q. v.) (1954). D'Arboussier published the monthly newspaper AEF Nouvelle at Brazzaville, which contained party and political news from Gabon and the rest of the federation. In 1947 he was elected a councillor of the Assembly of the French Union from the Ivory Coast. The RDA's branch in Gabon in 1951 opposed D'Arboussier's position on maintaining ties with the Communists in the face of administrative pressures and repression. They sided with Félix Houphouet-Boigny in abandoning these ties and seeking an accommodation that might allow them to come to power. D'Arboussier, who died in 1976, is remembered as one of the finest political orators of his day. [335]

DARLINGTON, CHARLES F. A career diplomat and one-time international businessman, Darlington was the first full-time American ambassador to Gabon. He worked in Libreville from October 1961 to July 26, 1964. His eye-witness account of Gabon's political evolution is critical of President Mba. It contends that de Gaulle betrayed the Gabonese people by his intervention on behalf of Mba and his support for Mba's repressive policies. [347]

DECOLONIZATION. Decolonization may be defined as the process by which Africans and Asians have achieved emancipation from western control. In a narrow sense it refers to the political aspects which led to self-government and/or independence. In a broad sense it refers to the elimination of all forms of external control--economic, cultural, psychological as well as political.

Between the mid-nineteenth century and the Second World War Gabon was a French colony and its indigenous inhabitants subjects of the French Empire. The Second World War undermined the ideological and political foundations of western colonial rule in Asia and Africa. France, which did not wish to relinquish control of its overseas possessions for fear of losing its rank as a great nation, nevertheless realized that it had to reform the colonial system to permit the advancement of the Africans and Asians. In the case of Black Africa, the Free French government sponsored the Brazzaville Conference of colonial administrators and officials in January-February 1944 to plan post-war reforms. The Conference, while reasserting the attachment of the African territories to France, advocated representation of the Africans in decision-making as well as publicly-funded programs to promote economic, social, and educational advancement. The French provisional government headed by General De Gaulle (1944-46) and the two Constituent Assemblies (1945-46) abolished many of the oppressive aspects of colonial rule such as forced labor, the <u>prestation</u> (labor tax), travel controls, and the <u>indigénat</u> (q. v.) (administrative justice). Whereas the draft constitution defeated by the French electorate in the spring 1946 would have permitted the Black African territories the long-range possibilities of self-government or independence within the French Empire (now called the French Union), the constitution finally adopted in October 1946 denied them these options. It offered them only a greater degree of participation in their own administration under the continued domination of metropolitan France. Thus the Constitution made Gabon and the other territories of French Equatorial Africa (q. v.) and French West Africa overseas territories of the Fourth French Republic. As such, Gabon and the others each acquired a territorial assembly comparable to a general council (_conseil général_) of a metropolitan department, which treated many local matters in cooperation with French administrators. While the Constitution gave the Africans the protection of the French law and most of the same rights as the citizens in Europe, it left the important matters of representation and voting to legislation. Voting at first was restricted to a tiny fraction of the African population (e. g. primary school graduates, notables, war veterans), nearly all of whom were men. A system of two electoral colleges was established which gave the Europeans living in the African territories about one-third of the representation.

Thus in the case of Gabon, the few thousand Frenchmen held one third of the seats in the Territorial Assembly at Libreville and 400, 000 Africans two thirds. Gabon's delegation to the French National Assembly, Council of the Republic (Senate), and Assembly of the French Union in Paris contained a similar proportion. While these arrangements had the effect of over-representing French interests, they also provided the Gabonese with a valuable political education. Many of them quickly became adept questioners during the discussions of the territorial budget and the implementation of the various five-year development plans under FIDES (q. v.). Gabonese representatives in Paris established ties with the representatives from other African territories. At Brazzaville, where Gabon had five representatives in the Grand Council of the federation of French Equatorial Africa, they acquired an understanding of the problems of the three other territories and Gabon's place in the federation.

While the Gabonese thus obtained some political representation in institutions dominated by Frenchmen, they were unrepresented until the late 1950s in the administrative corps which ran Gabon. Not until the mid-1950s did any Gabonese enter the Ecole Nationale de la France d'Outre-Mer in Paris which trained the top overseas officials such as heads of the nine regions and thirty-seven districts. By that time a few Gabonese were graduating from French universities and could be assigned to technical and supervisory positions in the bureaus of the central administration in Libreville.

Between 1946 and 1956 France, in response to African pressures, extended the suffrage in stages to include all adults of both sexes and even the illiterate. In 1956 it abolished the special representation of the French residents, some of whom would subsequently be elected on lists with Africans, and it established municipal government in the larger towns. Although these reforms represented an advancement in terms of African participation, it did not alter the basic constitutional and political arrangements which centralized the government of the entire republic in Paris and placed legislative and executive power in metropolitan hands. Responding to African demands for the transfer of decision-making to the territorial level, France under the Loi-Cadre or Enabling Act of June 23, 1956, and the decrees of April 1957 implementing it, created a legislative assembly and an executive council in each territory. These changes, which resulted from developments in Indo-China and North Africa at least as much as in Black Africa, were quickly superseded as a result of the collapse of the Fourth Republic in the wake of the revolution at Algiers on May 13, 1958.

Under the constitutional arrangements of the Fifth Republic, the African territories became self-governing but not completely independent states. No longer part of the French Republic, they became in March 1959 autonomous republics within the French Community in which metropolitan France still had the final word on matters of foreign policy, defense, higher education, and monetary arrangements. Given the decolonizing currents emanating from the other African countries, including the British and Belgian ones and the former French trusteeship territories of Togo and Cameroon, General De Gaulle permitted the revision of the constitution to allow the African states to accede to independence and yet remain in the Community. Gabon, like the other French African states, opted for independence on August 13, 1960. By the end of 1961 the Community had ceased to function. Gabon's relationship with France would be governed by the cooperation agreements negotiated in 1960 and then revised in 1974.

Decolonization in the economic sphere occurred in the 1970s as Gabon took steps to gain greater control over its natural resources and a greater share of the benefits from them. In the cultural sphere, Gabon has voluntarily decided to retain French as its national language and medium of instruction. These policies were reaffirmed by the First Extraordinary Congress of the PDG (q. v.) in 1973. [364, 381, 215, 336, 118, 80]

DENIS, KING or ANTCHOUWE KOWE RAPONTCHOMBO (c. 1780-1876). Most eminent of the nineteenth-century Mpongwe clan heads, first to accept French sovereignty and to promote French influence in Gabon. Antchouwé Kowe was known to the French as King Denis and to the British as King William. Denis headed the Asiga clan of the Mpongwe (q. v.) from 1810 to 1876. The Asiga occupied the peninsula at the extreme western tip of the Estuary and along the Atlantic. There in the last third of the 1700s and first half of the 1800s, they actively engaged as middlemen in a slave trade with the interior and Cape Lopez to the south. Denis personally profited from the trade. He himself possessed 300 to 400 domestic slaves and 40 to 50 wives. Though non-literate, Denis could speak English, French, Spanish, and Portuguese as well as several African languages. He impressed European and American visitors to his court by his keen intelligence and cultivation. He acquired a reputation for wisdom and honesty and enjoyed great respect and influence. His assistance to European seamen and traders on many occasions led to a medal from Queen Victoria in 1839. The same year he was named a Chevalier of the Legion of Honor and later received a medal from Pope Gregory XVI for his aid to the Roman Catholic mission. Throughout his lifetime he continued to serve as an intermediary in conflicts between European and African traders and in disputes among the Gabonese.

However, Denis's actions in regard to the establishment and extension of French rule contain inconsistencies and contradictions that lend themselves to different interpretations. Denis was the first Mpongwe clan head to make a treaty recognizing French sovereignty and ceding a site for a French establishment (February 9, 1839). He encouraged other clan heads to make similar treaties and served as an intermediary between the French and them to this end. Yet he successfully maneuvered to prevent the French from establishing their post on his lands as he had agreed. He prevented European traders from residence in his lands and withdrew active support from the Holy Ghost Fathers (q. v.) mission (St. Thomas) which he had allowed to be established in 1851. It failed and was closed in 1853 in part also because of a lack of personnel and resources. At the same time Denis sent several of his children, including his son and successor Louis Félix-Adandé (q. v.), to the Catholic mission schools at Libreville and maintained cordial relations with the French priests. As a polygynist, Denis could not receive baptism without renouncing all but one of his wives, so his entrance into the Catholic Church was postponed until just before his death on March 9, 1876.

Given the fact that Denis's relationships with Europeans were essentially commercial, he may have thought of the treaty with France as formalizing this situation. He may have hoped that acceptance of French sovereignty and the cession of a plot would lead to the establishment of a commercial post that would promote trade in commodities other than slaves without interfering in the latter. The post would give him advantages over his Agekaza rivals on the northern shore who were allied with English and American traders. For the treaty made no mention of the slave trade or its suppression. When Denis became aware of French intentions to establish a degree of political control and to suppress the slave trade, he used diplomacy to prevent a post on his lands. He took measures in cooperation with the Spanish traders who operated barracoons at his capital to protect the slaving operations from French surveillance. Having failed to interest his subjects in commercial alternatives to the slave trade, he may have sought to perpetuate and profit from the nefarious business as long as he could. At the same time he maintained good relations with the French authorities, who were far more interested in the 1840s-1860s in establishing and extending French control and in gaining commercial supremacy over British rivals than in suppressing the slave trade. In 1862 he helped the French to secure treaties with the Orungu chiefs of the Cape Lopez area. Throughout his lifetime he refused to permit American Protestant missionaries to operate schools or preaching stations on his territories. It is his clear preference for the French, above all, at a period in which, despite their treaties, their commercial and cultural influence was very much secondary to the British, American, and later the Germans, that has endeared him to them. Denis is more responsible than any other Mpongwe ruler, including King Louis (q. v.), for attaching Gabon to France and promoting French influence. [170, 251, 232, 219]

DORSEY, JOSIAH (d. 1860). Dorsey was an Afro-American from Baltimore, Maryland, who taught in the schools of the ABCFM mission at Cape Palmas (1838-42) and in Gabon (1842-55). He learned Mpongwe well and taught in it as well as in English. In 1846 Dorsey married Mary Clealand, a Grebo, whose uncle was King Freeman of Cape Palmas. Their son, William or Guillaume Dorsey (1849-69), became a Catholic seminarian and studied at Ngazobil, Senegal, prior to his death. [517]

DU CHAILLU, PAUL (1831-1903). Nineteenth-century Franco-American explorer and author. Du Chaillu was born on July 31, 1831, possibly in Paris but more likely on Reunion to a French father and a mulatto mother. While living in Gabon from 1848 to 1852 with his trader father, he resided with the American missionary John Leighton Wilson (q. v.) and attended the school of the Holy Ghost Fathers (q. v.). He learned several Gabonese languages in the course of his journeys with his father. Between 1852 and 1855 he studied natural history in Philadelphia, where he may have become an American citizen. He returned to Gabon in 1855 with modest support from the museums of Philadelphia and Boston to explore and to collect fauna and flora. During the next four years he was the first European and literate observer to explore many parts of Gabon. He went inland 100 miles from the Rio Muni through Séké (q. v.) country to Fang (q. v.) areas at the edge of the Monts de Cristal. With Nkomi (q. v.) help, he went up the Rembo Nkomi as far as the Ofoubou River among the Bakèlè and thereafter visited the Eshira (q. v.) and Apindji (q. v.) peoples enroute to the N'Gounié River. During a second voyage between 1863 and 1865, he collected museum specimens, including the gorilla. He travelled east from the N'Gounié into the Massif du Chaillu, which still bears his name, through the territories of the Bapounou, Mitsogo, and Obongo pygmies of so-called Ashango land (Massango) (q. v.) as far as Mouaou Kombo, a bit east of modern M'Bigou.

Despite exaggerations in his first book and some sensationalism, his works are valuable sources for the life and customs of various peoples of Gabon at this time. They have more value for the coastal peoples than the ones of the interior but in both cases Du Chaillu was a keen and sympathetic observer. [231, 250, 117, 167]

DURAND-REVILLE, LUC. Long-time director of the most important concessionary company, the Société du Haut-Ogooué (q. v.), Luc Durand-Réville represented Gabon in the French Senate from 1947 to 1958 and in the Senate of the French Community from 1959 on. In the French Senate he affiliated with the Rassemblement des Gauches Républicains and maintained friendly relations with the Gaullists of the Rassemblement du Peuple Français. He ably represented European lumbering and commercial interests and promoted the economic development of Gabon. [335]

- E -

EBOUE, FELIX (1884-1944). Black French colonial governor and Free French leader. Born in French Guyana and a graduate of the Colonial School for career administrators in Paris, Eboué served mainly in Oubangui-Shari before becoming governor of Chad in January 1939. In that position he was instrumental in rallying Chad to the Free French movement in late August 1940, which in turn aided the Gaullists to gain control of the other territories of French Equatorial Africa (q. v.), including Gabon. As Free-French governor-general (1940-1944) Eboué granted a special status of _notable évolué_ to two hundred educated Africans, which freed them from some of the burdens of the ordinary colonial subject (e. g. the _prestation_ or labor tax). Eboué integrated several Gabonese civil servants into the European cadres and did not retreat when there was a furor among some whites and Congolese. He encouraged the formation of discussion and cultural groups among the _évolués_ and civil servants. He took a personal interest in the careers of some Gabonese civil servants at Brazzaville; among them were the future deputy (1946-1958) Jean-Hilaire Aubame (q. v.), the future foreign affairs minister Jean-Remy Ayouné (q. v.), and future councillor of the Assembly of the French Union René-Paul Sousatte (q. v.). In 1944 Eboué named Aubame president of the new municipal commission of the Poto Poto commune of Brazzaville, which he had established to permit greater African participation.

Despite the problems of wartime, Eboué tripled expenditures for education, including important subsidies to the Catholic and Protestant mission schools, which had previously been receiving only token amounts. Though himself a socialist and freemason, Eboué was determined to enlist all available forces to promote educational progress. The government of the Fourth French Republic would make Eboué's practice a policy, thus enabling the mission schools to continue to play a major role in education in the post-war period (and since then in Gabon). In 1942 Eboué opened an _école supérieure_ (grades seven to ten) in each territory, including one at Libreville. This school provided the first secondary education in

Gabon outside the missions' seminary and Bible schools. Together with the increased primary enrollments, it permitted the expansion of the numbers of Gabonese in middle-level positions in the administration and upper-primary teaching.

Eboué favored the promotion of the French language and culture but advocated the revitalization of traditional African institutions in his circular, La Nouvelle Politique Indigène (The New Native Policy) of November 8, 1941. He played an important role in organizing a conference of French administrators at Brazzaville in January-February 1944 to plan the post-war reform of the colonial empire. [116, 191]

ECOLE MONTFORT. The Ecole Montfort refers to the boys' primary school at Libreville directed by the Brothers of Saint Gabriel (q. v.) which played a vital role in educating the elite, especially between 1900 and the end of the Second World War. The Holy Ghost Fathers (q. v.) operated schools for boys from their arrival in the Estuary in 1844. But they were not a teaching order and in 1900 gained the assistance of the Brothers of Saint Gabriel, a congregation of professional teachers, to upgrade the instruction in some of their schools. The first brothers arrived on October 7, 1900. Led by Brother Fulgent Boisdron (1853-1903) they assumed direction of the school near St. Peter's Church at the center of Libreville to which the boarding pupils at St. Mary's Church two miles away also came daily. The brothers were aided by African monitors and seminarians. They were able to provide several hundred boys an education of higher quality and more advanced level than hitherto had been available. Specifically, they gave their most advanced pupils instruction in French equivalent to the French brevet élémentaire, that is, several years beyond the certificat d'études primaires indigènes which was granted locally after approximately six years of study. The brothers also took direction of the boys' school at Lambaréné between December 1901 and October 1910 where the Catholics were facing strong competition from the Protestants who had preceded them into the area. The termination of state subsidies in 1907 in the wake of the separation of church and state in France contributed to their withdrawal from Lambaréné. Immediately after the First World War those at Libreville went on leave and were not replaced. Their departure brought forth a strong reaction from the Gabonese elements who had been benefitting from their instruction.

The brothers had drawn their pupils from all over Gabon and a few from other territories of French Equatorial Africa. Their former students were holding important positions in the administration, commerce, education, and religion in Gabon and throughout West and Equatorial Africa and the Belgian Congo. The elite elements accused the administration of eliminating the means for their entrance into the higher levels of the civil service and commercial management and for the achievement of equality with Europeans. The departure of the brothers indeed meant that Gabon could no longer produce enough personnel locally and had to recruit African staff from Senegal, Dahomey, Togo, Cameroon, and even Nigeria. From being an exporter of educated staff, Gabon was transformed once more into an importer. In November 1924 the Brothers of Saint Gabriel returned to Libreville at the request of the French Spiritan bishop and resumed direction of the boys' school. But apparently they no longer attempted to provide instruction beyond the local primary certificate. In 1927 a new Ecole Montfort in central Libreville was once more giving an education to 700 boys. It thus provided instruction for a large segment of the educated elite throughout the rest of the interwar period during which public education was little developed. The graduates of the Ecole Montfort would form an important part of Gabon's politicians and civil servants during the Fourth French Republic and the 1960s. [509, 335]

ECONOMY. The economy of Gabon has always contained both subsistence and market sectors. From prehistoric times the inhabitants of the equatorial forests, savannas, and coastal marshes hunted, fished, gathered fruits and nuts, and raised food stuffs and livestock. The presence of the tsetse fly in most regions usually made herding all but impossible. The poor soils, which leached rapidly under rainstorms, led to shifting cultivation and gradual but regular population movements. The introduction of new food staples from the Americas in the sixteenth and seventeenth centuries, particularly manioc (cassava), new varieties of plantains, bananas, yams, and the sweet potato, made the forests much more viable homes for the various peoples entering them from the neighboring savannas. Iron deposits in both the north-east and south-west made possible the manufacture of tools and weapons. In the south-west palm fibers, including raphia, were woven into cloth and mats of often high quality.

The salt of the Loango (q. v.) coast, including from

Mayumba and Setté-Cama, which was evaporated from sea water, was especially desired by the peoples in areas of heavier rainfall and damper climate. The salt was being sent inland and north along the coasts as far as the Bight of Benin even before Europeans first appeared on the coasts late in the 1400s.

The coming of the Europeans led to the establishment of additional coastal markets, especially at the mouths of the rivers, which gave access to the interior, for water transportation was a necessity in a sparsely populated country like Gabon. Porterage was an expensive supplement ordinarily employed to circumvent the sandbars at river mouths as well as the falls and rapids upstream. In these circumstances, much of Gabon's foreign trade centered upon the Estuary or Gabon River (considered now part of the Como River) and the Ogooué River, whose watershed encompassed nearly four-fifths of the country. Trade with the Europeans included such items as dyewood (padouk), beeswax, gum copal, palm oil, ivory, and, by the nineteenth century, rubber. The fine-quality palm cloth and matting of southern Gabon were much sought after until gradually replaced in the nineteenth century by inexpensive mass-produced British textiles. Copper reached the Loango coast from the inland area around Mindouli in today's Congo Republic. From Europe and North America traders brought such items as cloth strips, rum and other strong alcoholic beverages, firearms, gunpowder, knives, and iron bars. Trade in goods was frequently accompanied by trade in slaves but the slave trade did not achieve importance until the late eighteenth century and trade in goods never ceased even during its height between 1760 and 1860.

Between the sixteenth and mid-nineteenth centuries coastal peoples served as commercial middlemen between European and American traders and inland peoples. Trading routes and networks developed which were tiered or layered, as in the Estuary, or basically linear, as in the Ogooué where each people controlled a portion of the river and all traffic both upstream and downstream. Each people involved in the network thus profited from the transmission of goods.

Trade in northern Gabon up to about 1840 depended upon informal understandings between a clan head or chief trader and an individual captain or supercargo, on the one hand, and between the coastal leader and the network of inland chiefs, on the other. In the aftermath of the French establishment on the Estuary and northern coasts, European trading companies founded permanent posts and under French protection penetrated inland and eliminated the various middlemen. These processes transformed the former middlemen into European agents and employees and transferred a greater share of the profits to the companies. Prior to 1860 most of the traders and trading firms in northern Gabon were British, American, and German rather than French. 95 percent of the commercial shipping was either British or American. Most of the expansion into the Ogooué in the late 1860s and 1870s, first at Fernan Vaz and then at Lambaréné, was undertaken by British and German firms. In 1900 out of 224 trading posts in Gabon (of which 80 were in the Estuary, 9 at Cape Lopez, 15 at Fernan Vaz, and 120 up the Ogooué), Hatton & Cookson of Liverpool (in Gabon since 1851) had 78; John Holt of Manchester 59; and Adolph Woermann of Hamburg 20. The only major French company was the recently organized SHO (1893), which had been given a commercial monopoly over vast areas of the upper Ogooué.

Though the steamboat came into use in the 1870s, it could not be employed farther than eighty miles up the Como River or beyond N'Djolé on the Ogooué. The SHO (q. v.), whose territories lay above N'Djolé, was obliged to depend on local canoers and porters for much of its transport of rubber and other commodities. It encountered somewhat the same kind of labor shortage which had doomed French attempts at commercial plantations in the Estuary in the 1840s.

In the late 1890s the administration of the French Congo of which Gabon had become a part sought to develop its natural resources through the kind of concessionary regime previously installed in the neighboring Congo Free State. The regime installed by these monopolistic companies, which extended to all of Gabon except the Estuary, disrupted the existing trading networks without replacing them with viable alternatives. In the face of growing abuses and injustices, the companies were phased out by the time of the First World War except on the upper Ogooué where the commercial monopoly of the SHO persisted until 1930.

From the 1890s Gabon began to export okoumé (q. v.), used for plywood, and various hardwoods, first to German and Dutch markets, and in the twentieth century to French ones. French industrial firms became dominant in logging after the First World War. The woods were obtained from an area that extended from Spanish Guinea south to Setté-Cama and that encompassed the Estuary, the lower and middle Ogooué, and the lower N'Gounié. Woods remained Gabon's leading export until the late 1960s when petroleum (q.v.) products, which had been developed since the late 1950s, surpassed them in importance. The late 1950s also saw the exploitation of Gabon's manganese (q.v.) and uranium (q.v.) as well as the location of important reserves of iron (q.v.) ore and other metals and minerals.

In the 1920s and 1930s the administration sponsored commercial agriculture, in particular in the Woleu N'Tem Province where peasants produced cocoa and coffee for export. Though the government became more active in promoting economic development, imports and much of the exports remained in the hands of the large European companies. In the late 1970s these firms (e.g. Gaboma, Cie. Française de l'Afrique Occidentale, Hollando, and Hatton & Cookson) continued to handle most of the imports of consumer goods such as food and beverages, textiles and clothing, and household goods. These enterprises control all wholesale and much of the retail operations as well as the transport of the goods.

In the late 1970s over half of Gabon's active population continued to engage in agriculture, mainly for subsistence, but the market economy rested primarily on the exploitation of mineral resources and timber. The increased output of manganese, uranium, and above all petroleum brought Gabon three to four times the annual revenues in real terms that it possessed prior to independence. Though the life of the oil reserves is uncertain, the impending exploitation of important iron deposits offers other alternatives for revenue, probably much smaller annually but of much longer duration. Though timber production has declined with the depletion of the coastal forests, the revenues from this source remain important with the increased exploitation of the interior forests. The government of President Bongo, while maintaining a basically liberal economic policy, has taken steps to give Gabonese cutters a much larger share of the output. At the same time, while encouraging foreign investment (by the EEC countries and the USA in particular), in the mid-1970s it has instituted measures to give Gabon greater control of its natural resources and a greater share of the revenues from them. With the greatly increased income, it has invested in transport facilities and has encouraged the development of processing industries and manufacturing. But the agricultural sector from which the majority of the population still earns its living has not been directly touched, except for the creation of capital intensive truck gardens to supply the growing populations of Libreville and Franceville.

Gabon's economy is a kind of enclave economy, linked more with world markets, especially European ones, than with neighboring states or the rest of Africa. It also shares some of the characteristics of other African economies that have recently achieved political independence: strong links with the former metropole, a large degree of foreign investment and control; dependence on foreign technicians; persisting underdevelopment. Gabon differs from other tropical states in its reliance on thousands of wage laborers from other African countries to supplement its own sparse supply of workers. See AGRICULTURE; FORESTRY; GOLD; IRON; LABOR UNIONS; MANGANESE; OKOUME; PETROLEUM. [11, 478, 214, 178, 182, 108]

EDUCATION. Education among the indigenous peoples of Gabon, who were non-literate, was always informal. Formal education was introduced by Christian missionaries in the mid-nineteenth century. Congregational and Presbyterian missionaries sponsored by the ABCFM of Boston opened the first schools in the Estuary region in 1842. They taught religion, reading, writing, arithmetic, other elementary subjects, and the domestic arts (the latter only to girls), using both Mpongwe and English as the media of instruction. The missionaries sought to prepare teachers, Bible-readers, catechists, and preachers as well as Bible-reading laymen. In early 1845 members of the Congregation of the Holy Ghost (Spiritans) (q. v.) from France started a similar kind of instruction for boys in the vicinity of present-day Libreville employing French and Mpongwe. The Sisters of Our Lady of the Immaculate Conception (q. v.) of Castres, France (Blue Sisters), who arrived in 1849, taught domestic and literacy skills to girls. The Spiritans by 1856 were teaching Latin to the most talented boys in an attempt to prepare an indigenous clergy as well as catechists and teachers. They also began apprenticeship programs in gardening, agriculture, woodworking, masonry, and other skilled trades. The pupils of the schools included orphans, recaptives, and _rachétés_ (slaves whose freedom the missionaries purchased) from the entire Gabon and Congo areas and the Portuguese islands of São Tomé and Príncipe in addition to the Mpongwe of the Estuary. In the 1850s the Protestants opened schools among the Bakèlè and the Catholics among the Benga. Presbyterian missionaries sponsored by the PBFM of New York, based on Corisco Island since 1850, also educated some mainland Benga north of Cape Esterias. In the 1870s, these Presbyterians, having assumed the work of the ABCFM, undertook instruction of the Fang farther up the Estuary and of Fang, Galoa, and Bakèlè on the middle Ogooué River at Lambaréné and Ndjolé. During the decades in which the American Protestants operated schools, several hundred boys and several scores of girls learned to read and write in English and in Mpongwe, Dikèlè, Benga or Fang. Many of the young men became employees of the British, American, and German trading firms which dominated the export trade until late in the 1800s.

The French government, which subsidized the educational work of the Catholic missions but did not regulate it, became increasingly nationalistic in the aftermath of the Franco-Prussian War (1870-1871). In April 1883 it instituted a primary school curriculum based on Jules Ferry's recent metropolitan one in which at least half of the program involved teaching the French language and culture. It forbade the teaching of other languages, including indigenous ones. The American Protestants secured French-language teachers from France and Switzerland but then transferred their work on the Ogooué in 1892-1893 to French Protestants sponsored by the SME of Paris. The SME missionaries added instruction in various trades and established separate programs to prepare catechists and preachers. After the departure of the Americans, the government still pushed for the teaching of French but tolerated religious instruction in local languages. It granted small subsidies to the French Protestant schools. In the wake of the anti-clerical legislation and the separation of Church and State in France (1905), the government withdrew all support from the mission schools and used the funds to open a public school at Libreville in 1907 to compete with the Ecole Montfort (q. v.) established seven years earlier there by the Brothers of Saint Gabriel (q. v.). In 1922 the federation of French Equatorial Africa resumed the granting of small subsidies to mission schools teaching the official programs but reserved the bulk of expenditures for the handful of public schools it had founded in the main towns. Between the two world wars the government devoted less than one percent of its budget to education. During the Second World War the Free French administration under Governor-General Félix Eboué (q. v.) increased educational spending to 4.75 percent of the budget and granted important subsidies to the mission schools, which the war had cut off from their French supporters.

Until after the Second World War the numbers who attended school were always tiny. For example, in 1882 the American Presbyterians taught 90 boys and 55 girls and the French Catholics 216 boys and 79 girls, all of them in the Estuary or along the Ogooué. In 1898 the Catholics had 1,118 pupils and the American and French Protestants 430, now including the upper Ogooué, the N'Gounié, and the southern coasts. During 1929-30 the Catholics had 2,100 primary pupils, the Protestants 680, and the public schools 457, for a total of 3,237. During the interwar period the school programs were adapted to emphasize practical skills and more material on Africa added. Only local diplomas were given, which inhibited further education abroad for even those whose parents might be able to afford it. In these circumstances the only Gabonese who earned the baccalauréat in France during the 1930s were three sons of wealthy lumbermen. In Gabon itself the only education beyond the six primary grades was in the seminaries and Bible schools of the missions. In 1935 the government opened a higher primary school and a one-year teaching training course at Brazzaville to which several Gabonese were sent.

Prior to 1945 only a minority of those who entered school stayed long enough to achieve literacy or to learn a skilled trade. Yet it was this small group which permitted the colonial institutions to function. Its members served as the employees of the administration and commerce and as teachers, pastors, and priests. Some of them later would sit in the territorial and federal assemblies created in 1945-1946 and in the representative institutions of the Fourth French Republic. It is they who would be most responsible for transferring the metropolitan programs into Gabon after 1945, thus giving Gabon an educational system more closely modelled after the French in both form and content than at any previous period and permitting Gabonese to continue their education in France. For the educated Gabonese saw education identical with that of France, not one adapted to Gabon, as the only effective means of securing equality and advancement.

Gabon as an Overseas Territory of the Fourth Republic received aid under FIDES (q.v.) for construction and equipment of schools and assistance in staffing the newly opened secondary schools. Primary enrollments increased from 9,082 in 1945-46 to 50,545 in 1959-60 but most pupils were enrolled in the early grades and remained only two to three years. The consequences of the situation were illustrated by a survey taken in mid-1963. It indicated that 48.6 percent of all Gabonese over fifteen years of age could speak French but that only 12.3 percent could read or write it. Much larger percentages of men than women knew French. In 1959-60 the secondary schools enrolled 2,036 students, double the number only two years earlier. Small numbers of Gabonese received government scholarships for secondary programs not available in the federation and for higher education in France. In 1957-58 87 Gabonese were studying in French universities, 60 of them on scholarships. But on the eve of independence in August 1960, only a handful of Gabonese had completed the full secondary program or programs in higher education. This situation meant that independent Gabon continued to depend upon French personnel to staff the higher levels of the bureaucracy and economy. At the same time, Gabon with French aid, undertook an expansion of enrollments at all levels of the existing system.

Today the educational system of Gabon still closely resembles that of France. Material about Gabon and Africa is included in the courses in geography, history, literature, and science but the heavy emphasis on the French language and culture remains. The primary level has six grades, one more than in France, to enable the children to spend their first year adjusting to instruction in French. The possibility of the introduction of indigenous languages as the instructional media in the early primary grades, as has been undertaken in other Francophone states, seems remote. Secondary education has both general and technical programs with long cycles of seven years leading to the baccalauréat and short cycles of four years leading to the brevet d'études du premier cycle (BEPC). Holders of the baccalauréat are eligible for the university while BEPC holders may enter programs for primary and lower secondary teachers, middle-level positions in national administration, and a variety of professional and para-professional positions such as medical-social assistant, nurse, accountant, and forestry technician. Since the late 1960s the requirements for entering various programs have been upgraded from the primary level to the BEPC level, on the one hand, and from the BEPC to the baccalauréat, on the other. The government since the mid-1970s has devoted even greater attention to technical education than previously with the aim of preparing increased numbers of Gabonese for technical and managerial careers. Traditionally such careers have proved less attractive than those in public administration, law, and education.

Gabon continues to subsidize the schools of the Catholic and Protestant churches in which European and American missionaries provide a large part of the secondary staff. The government pays most of the operating expenses of the church schools and the salaries of the African staff, including the Gabonese sisters in the Catholic schools. Religion is taught in addition to the official programs. The church schools enroll close to half of all primary pupils and a third of secondary ones.

Enrollments of Gabonese in all schools in September 1979 were 140, 632 at the primary level and 21, 814 at the secondary level. For general secondary education there were 4, 899 in the short cycle and 14, 369 in the long; for technical secondary education, 960 in the short cycle and 1, 586 in the long. Girls form nearly half of the primary enrollments and two fifths of the secondary. Most of the teaching staff at the primary level is Gabonese but non-Gabonese, particularly French staff provided through the cooperation agreements, form a majority of the secondary teachers and nearly all of those in technical fields. In addition to the Gabonese students, there are 3, 000 French children enrolled at the primary level and 1, 100 at the secondary level. Gabon and the Ivory Coast are the only former French states in which most French nationals still attend the local schools. Elsewhere, French residents have established separate schools with the metropolitan programs in the wake of modifications in the local programs to meet national needs and goals.

Higher education in Gabon has recent origins. After more than a century of primary education in the French language, Gabon in the late 1940s acquired its first secondary schools. Their graduates had to go abroad for further study until the organization of the Fondation de l'Enseignement Supérieur en Afrique Centrale (FESAC) in 1961 by the four Equatorial states and France. Gabonese students attended three- to four-year programs in law and economic sciences, letters and social sciences, physical sciences and mathematics, and secondary teaching at Brazzaville, People's Republic of the Congo; agronomy at Mbaïki, the Central African Republic; animal husbandry at Ndjamena, Chad; and polytechnics in Libreville. Students in other programs and advanced students continued to go to France. The growth of the number of secondary school graduates, political tensions in the Congo Republic, inter-state rivalries, and Gabon's desire to educate its future leaders at home all contributed to the dissolution of FESAC in April 1971. Early in August 1970 Gabon with French support and encouragement created its own national university at Libreville, which during 1970-71 enrolled 168 holders of the baccalauréat. In September 1979 approximately 1400 students, four fifths of them Gabonese, were enrolled in the university and other higher institutions. They are following two- to three-year programs in law and economic sciences; letters and social sciences; physical sciences and mathematics; medicine; engineering; forestry management, juridical science, and national administration. Gabon is also the seat of the inter-state Institut Africain d'Informatique which in 1976-77 enrolled 12 Gabonese among its 108 students. In 1976-77 1,366 Gabonese holding scholarships were enrolled in higher education abroad, including 831 in France, 148 in Romania, and many of the remainder in Francophone African countries. A majority of the staff in higher education is French but the rector of the university and other top administrators are Gabonese.

The structure and programs in higher education remain nearly identical to those adopted in France in implementation of the Law of November 12, 1968. They contain the modifications made during the late 1960s by the fourteen Francophone states (excluding Guinea but including Madagascar) of Black Africa jointly with French assistance, which added African content. Gabonese diplomas are valid in these fourteen Francophone countries of Africa, France, Belgium, and Canada. Current Gabonese thinking about the reform of education appears to focus on the further professionalization of higher and technical education rather than upon any fundamental changes in the French-derived system. [446, 448, 449, 455, 451]

EKOH, JEAN-MARC (1929-). Politician. Ekoh was born on November 12, 1929, at Bitam in the Woleu N'Tem Province into a family prominent in the French Protestant mission. He was one of the first Gabonese after the Second World War to receive a secondary education and to attend French universities. He became active in the Union Démocratique et Sociale Gabonaise and its youth movement from 1947. In March 1957 he was elected to the Legislative Assembly from the Woleu N'Tem and later to the National Assembly. He held ministerial posts from the first government council in March 1957 through the end of the government of national union in 1963, including the post of Minister of National Education after independence. As a member of the short-lived provisional government in February 1964, Ekoh was arrested and sentenced to detention. He was later pardoned by President Bongo and rejoined the cabinet in 1968. Then in September 1970 he was accused of masterminding the kidnapping of a civil servant, Bernard Eyi (q. v.), and his wife. He was sentenced to ten years in prison and ten more under house arrest. Released early, he today teaches in a Protestant secondary school in his home area. See EYI AFFAIR. [681, 371, 361, 364]

EMANE TOLE (d. 1914). Emane Tole was a Fang (q. v.) chief who resisted French attempts to achieve economic control of the middle Ogooué. He organized thirteen Fang clans in the area of N'Djolé Island in the middle Ogooué between February 1901 and September 1902 to resist the exactions of the SHO (q. v.), a chartered company which had been given a commercial monopoly by the French government in 1897. In reprisal for increased prices, the Fang clans used force to block the river for many months. Emane Tole and his son Tole Emane were exiled to Grand Bassam in the Ivory Coast in 1904 after the SHO's militia had suppressed the resistance in 1903. [182, 223, 243]

ENENGA. The remnants of the Enenga, a Myènè-speaking (q. v.) people, today inhabit the area around Lake Zilé, a widening of the middle Ogooué River between Lambaréné Island and the junction with the N'Gounié River. According to their traditions the Enenga came to this area from the upper Ogooué and later ceded some of their new territory to the Galoa (q. v.) after the latter's arrival. The Enenga gradually became Myènè speakers to the point that by 1900 only the older people knew their original language, which belonged to the Okandé group. In the nineteenth century the Enenga controlled trade on portions of the middle Ogooué and N'Gounié rivers. They purchased slaves from the Adouma (q. v.) and Okandé (q. v.) for transfer downstream to the barracoons of Cape Lopez. In the 1870s and 1880s the Enenga were headed by three blind co-rulers--King Ranokè and Queens Evindo and Mbumba. Ranokè, who possessed many slaves, aided the Marquis de Compiègne and Alfred Marche in 1873-1874, and Brazza in 1875 and after, to obtain the expert canoemen that allowed them to pass the various rapids and heavy currents of the middle and upper Ogooué. Queen Evindo ceded the plot at Lambaréné that became the site of the Roman Catholic mission in 1881. [251]

ESHIRA. The Eshira people appear to have migrated into the grasslands and gallery forests south of the Ogooué River, west of the lower N'Gounié River, and on both banks of the Rembo Nkomi in the mid- or late eighteenth century in the wake of wars with the Bakèlè (q. v.) or others. In the nineteenth century they exchanged slaves from the interior with the Nkomi (q. v.) of Fernan Vaz. They raised a popular tobacco and produced a fine cloth of raphia that was much sought after by other Africans. Though they still rank as an important people in numbers, their ranks were decimated by smallpox epidemics in 1865 and 1898. The Holy Ghost Fathers (q. v.) established a mission among them in 1895 and transcribed their language in the Latin alphabet.

When the explorer Paul Du Chaillu (q. v.) passed through Eshira areas in 1858 and 1864, each clan controlled its own affairs. The most important chief, Mulenda of the Kamba clan, possessed three to four hundred slaves. He died of smallpox in 1885. At Du Chaillu's visit, the raphia textiles were losing ground to inexpensive British fabrics, which ultimately destroyed the local industry. [189, 251, 247]

EVEIA. The Evéia people are part of the Okandé linguistic group. They inhabit the middle N'Gounié River in the vicinity of Fougamou. According to their traditions, they came from the sea, where they had Mpongwe (q. v.) neighbors and spoke a Myènè (q. v.) language. They moved inland to escape slave raiders and traders. It is likely that they relocated because of Orungu (q. v.) control of the main mouths of the Ogooué, which dislocated their economy. During the nineteenth century they moved into the Ogooué valley near Lambaréné to escape pressures of the Bakèlè and Fang (qq. v.); from there they migrated up the N'Gounié River. On the right bank of the N'Gounié where they settled, they were divided into river clans and mountain clans. In 1866 British firms established trading posts among them, including at their main village of Bwali. At the time the French established their post at Sindara in 1899, their main village was Mokandé. [272, 189]

EXPLORATION. Various explorations between the 1470s and the early 1900s made the geographical features and peoples of Gabon known to the western world and, often, to the Gabonese themselves. In the 1470s and 1480s Portuguese navigators came along the coasts of Gabon in their search for the routes to India, China, and the Indies. To various geographical features they gave the names that are still in use today, including the name Gabon itself. In 1471 Vasconcellos discovered the island of São Tomé (St. Thomas) off the coast. The following year the Portuguese discovered the Estuary or Gabon River to which they gave the name gabão (hooded cloak). Later in 1472 Lopo Gonçalves (called Lopez Gonzalves in Spanish) reached the cape to which he gave his name, Cape Lopez. In 1475 Ruy de Sequiera reached Cape St. Catherine 100 miles farther south. In 1480 Fernan Vaz attained the coast near the lagoon that still bears his name. Two years later Diogo Cão (Diego Cam in Spanish) reached the mouth of the Zaire River, which he named the Congo for the Kongo people on its banks.

While a number of later travellers and merchant adventurers have left useful accounts of the coastal peoples (particularly the Dutchman Willem Bosman in 1705 and the Englishman T. Edward Bowdich in 1815), increased knowledge of the interior peoples would have to await the second period of exploration between the 1840s and the early 1900s. Though these explorations would involve missionaries, merchants, and adventurers from France, Britain, the United States, and Germany, French naval officers and officials tended to predominate as did the desire to reach the heart of central Africa and the French wish to extend their control and influence.

Between 1844 and 1860 a number of expeditions by various French naval officers collectively revealed that the Estuary or Gabon River was really a bay into which flowed the Como River and its tributaries from the east/northeast and other rivers such as the Remboué from the east/southeast. Specifically, in 1844 Lt. Darricau explored up the Como as far as Cobangoi; in 1846 Lt. Pigeard and Engineer Deschamps reached Kango; and later the same year Lt. Mecquet arrived at the junction of the Bokoué. The Como was explored farther upstream in 1857 by Rev. G. du Mesnil and between 1857 and 1859 by Lt. Jules-Edouard Braouëzec. In 1860 the surgeon Roullet and Lts. Touchard and Genoyer identified the sources of the Como.

In 1856 the Franco-American adventurer, Paul du

Chaillu (q. v.), who claimed he had been commissioned by the National Academy of Sciences in Philadelphia, Pennsylvania, to explore and collect fauna and flora, explored the Rio Muni inland to the Monts de Cristal. There he made contact with the Fang and saw a live baby gorilla. Between 1857 and 1859 French lieutenants Braouëzec and Genoyer reconnoitered in the Rio Muni and the Mondah River. Taken as a whole, these explorations indicated that the Rio Muni and the Mondah River did not lead into the heart of the continent. Later in 1873 an expedition sponsored by the Geographical Society of Berlin and headed by Dr. Oscar Lenz further explored the region of the Rio Muni and the Temboni River.

In 1854 two American Protestant missionaries, the Reverends Ira Preston (q. v.) and William Walker (q. v.), made a pioneering exploration up the Nazareth mouth of the Ogooué River half way to the site of Lambaréné. In two expeditions, 1855-59 and 1863-1865, Du Chaillu explored inland at various points from Sangatanga, north of Cape Lopez, south as far as Cape St. Catherine. He was the first European to travel up the Mpoulounié mouth of the Ogooué and near Lake Anengué. After extensive explorations in the area of Fernan-Vaz, he went up the Rembo Nkomi and overland to the N'Gounié River without realizing it was a tributary of the Ogooué. East of the N'Gounié River he reached the mountainous terrain that still bears his name, the Massif du Chaillu. His descriptions of the various peoples he encountered were the first accurate and detailed accounts to reach the western world. In June 1862, after the signing of a treaty with the Orungu chiefs who controlled the known mouths of the Ogooué River, two French naval officers, Lt. Serval and the surgeon Dr. Griffon du Bellay, attempted to ascend the river. But they were forced to turn back by other Orungu upstream. In December 1862 they sought to reach the Ogooué by travelling southeast up the Remboué and then overland. Though illness forced Serval to abandon the trip midway, Dr. Griffon du Bellay reached the Enenga village of Orongo, not far from Lambaréné. In 1865-66 Robert Bruce Walker, English agent for the Hatton & Cookson firm, took the Remboué route to Enenga territory, and after being delayed for six months by Chiefs Rempolé and Ranokè, finally advanced upriver into Okandé territory at the junction of the Lopé River in July 1866. In 1867 Lt. Aymes travelled up the Ogooué itself to Enenga territory and in 1871 the German merchant Schultz followed the same route to the Lopé River junction.

In 1873-1874 the Marquis de Compiègne and Alfred Marche ascended the Ogooué as far as the junction of the Ivindo, its chief northern tributary where in June 1874 the hostility of the Osyéba (possibly a Fang clan) and the Okandé forced them to turn back. In 1876 Dr. Lenz, with aid from Marche and Brazza, reached the junction of the Sébé River, where ill health forced his return.

By this time, exploration of the Gabon interior had become part of the European competition and scramble to control and eventually to partition and to occupy Africa. Within this context took place the three expeditions of Pierre Savorgnan de Brazza (q. v.) (1875-1878, 1880-1882, 1883-1885) under the auspices of the French Navy. His first expedition proved that the Ogooué River system was distinct from the Congo River system. At the same time he found out that the headwaters of the M'Passa River, an Ogooué tributary, rose only a few miles from the headwaters of the Alima River, a north-western tributary of the Congo. Unfortunately, the hostility of the Apfourou people prevented his descent down the Alima. During his second expedition he founded the post of Franceville at the junction of the M'Passa and Ogooué in June 1880. Thereafter he crossed overland and followed the course of the Lefini River down to the Congo River. The following year he explored the Kouilou-Niari River valley, which linked the area of the Stanley Pool with the Loango coast. Brazza's third expedition served more to establish French authority on the upper Ogooué than to explore new territory.

The portions of northern Gabon between the Como and Ivindo Rivers were explored in the wake of agreements between France and Germany, on the one hand, and France and Spain, on the other, delimiting the frontiers of Gabon, the Cameroons, and Spanish Guinea (Rio Muni). Paul Crampel and Alfred Fourneau in 1888-1889, Dr. Cureau in 1900 to 1903, and Captain Cottes in 1905 to 1907 all explored in these areas as part of the process of delimitation. [251, 632, 16, 117, 196]

EYI AFFAIR OF 1970. A dispute between a high-ranking civil servant, Jean Bernard Eyi, and Monsignor Camille Nziboe, vicar-general of the archdiocese of Libreville, had repercussions in both the Catholic and Evangelical Protestant churches and in the government. Details on some aspects of the affair are lacking despite the government's issuance of a White Paper. But it appears that after Eyi accused Monsignor Nziboe, who belonged to the same Fang clan as his wife, of employing her without his permission and maintaining a personal relationship with her, three clansmen of the Monsignor on August 19, 1970, kidnapped Eyi and his wife and beat Eyi. He was detained in the residence of Nziboe with the prelate's knowledge. In the police investigation that followed upon Eyi's complaint, a noted cabinet minister, Jean-Marc Ekoh (q. v.), was adjudged as an accomplice and the brains behind the kidnapping. Ekoh was a brilliant Fang intellectual from the Woleu N'Tem Province who had held high government office in the late 1950s and early 1960s. He was also a person of high standing in the Evangelical Protestant Church. He had only recently been restored to a cabinet post by President Bongo after being pardoned for his role in the provisional government of February 1964. Ekoh was removed from office as a result of the trial of the five accused. He received a sentence of ten years in prison and ten more in forced residence. Monsignor Nziboe was sentenced to eight years in prison and five in residence. One of the three kidnappers received a sentence identical to Ekoh and two received sentences of six years in prison and three of residence. Collectively the five were required to pay damages of one million CFA francs (about $5,000 at the time) to the Eyis. The official White Paper gives no real information on Ekoh's alleged motives or role in the affair so that the matter is still clouded with mystery. Ekoh and Nziboe were released from prison early and were allowed to assume positions in secondary teaching and the parish ministry, respectively, in the Woleu N'Tem Province. [361]

- F -

FANG. The Fang today form nearly one third of the population of Gabon. The Fang are part of a larger group, called the Pahouin by French scholars, that includes the Beti and Boulou of southern Cameroon. Nearly as many Fang live in Cameroon and in eastern Equatorial Guinea as in northern Gabon.

During the eighteenth century the Fang were living in the grassy plateaux north of the Sanaga and Lom rivers in Cameroon. Their traditions relate that at mid-century horse-borne raiders and invaders caused their movement southward and westward into the forests. By about 1800 they had made a rapid and apparently successful adaptation to the new environment of the forests. Fang traditions contain a symbolic account of a compact with the pygmies, who taught them to survive and to thrive by hunting, especially for the elephant. The Fang gradually became involved in the trading networks that sent ivory from the hinterland to the coastal markets. The Fang brought with them a superior technology for iron working. While learning how to raise such forest crops as cassava, bananas, plantains, and oil palms, they retained cultivation of such savanna crops as peanuts, gourds, and tobacco. Once in the forest, the dynamic of further migration was the exhaustion of the elephant herds and the soil around their villages. Villages seemed to uproot themselves quite regularly every ten to fifteen years and to relocate in the sparsely populated country beyond the last Fang settlement. In the northern Gabon forests east of the Monts de Cristal, the Fang by the 1840s encountered the semi-nomadic Bakèlè (q. v.) hunters with whom they exchanged their ivory. When the Fang learned that their ivory was being sold to European traders on the Estuary for ten times the price they received as a result of its transmission through a network of Bakèlè, Séké, and Mpongwe (qq. v.) middlemen, some of them accelerated their efforts to contact the Europeans directly. While many Fang remained in the forests of the Woleu-N'Tem Province, others began migrations that carried them into the upper Como River by 1846, the Estuary in the early 1860s, the Ogooué in the late 1860s, and the northern coasts by the 1870s. Dispersing or absorbing the peoples in their path, by 1900 they had become the most numerous people in northern Gabon. Fang success derived from their superior social organization, which reduced internal fighting among the Fang and mobilized large numbers of villagers for warfare against the clans of other peoples.

During these migrations, leadership tended to be based more on prowess and wealth than on kinship, which enabled the Fang clans to benefit from the best talent among them in the task of expansion. Most of the peoples upon whom the Fang encroached fled. The remnants were usually absorbed into Fang ranks, the children by adoption, the women by marriage, and the men by consent or by slavery. The Fang ordinarily did not possess slaves and did not sell any until the 1860s, that is, during the last gasp of the trade in the Estuary and on the Ogooué.

The first Fang who made contact with European

traders and their representatives on the Como River began to seize European merchandise, attack the ships of European firms, and take prisoners for ransom. French efforts at repression were largely unsuccessful because the Fang fled into the forest. Eventually the French succeeded in capturing and hanging a few Fang chiefs and notables and taking some hostage to ensure the good behavior of their kin. Gradually under missionary influence the Fang in the Estuary abandoned their violence. The first Fang boys entered the Catholic schools at Libreville in the 1860s, all of them at first in the apprenticeship programs rather than in the academic ones. In 1879 the Holy Ghost Fathers (q. v.) opened their first mission among the Fang on the Estuary at Donguila. The American Presbyterians, who were already working with other Fang at Bokoué in the Estuary, in the mid-1870s established posts just above Lambaréné and farther upstream among the Fang and other peoples. French Protestants and Catholics entered the Woleu-N'Tem mainly after the First World War. By the mid-twentieth century a large majority of the Fang had become Christian, though a minority retained their ancestral religion and around ten percent adopted the syncretist cult Bwiti. It was also among the northern Fang that the Great Revival of 1935 had its greatest impact, leading to the organization of the Pentecostal churches (Assemblies of God).

In the meantime various Fang had migrated throughout northern Gabon and had penetrated the southern coastal regions as far as Setté-Cama. In the process there were renewed conflicts with other Gabonese peoples, European traders, and the French administration. Among the most notable examples were Fang blocking of the middle and upper Ogooué River for nearly a decade from 1865 to other traders and European explorers and the resistance led by Chief Emane Tole (q. v.) in 1901-1902 to the SHO's attempts to dominate the rubber trade around N'Djole.

French troops undertook the military penetration of the Woleu-N'Tem in the course of delimiting the frontier with the German Cameroons during the first decade of the twentieth century. In several instances the Fang resisted but were overpowered by the superior French weaponry. The installation of colonial rule on the eve of the First World War would have disastrous consequences for large parts of the population. Labor recruitment for forestry work on the Ogooué and N'Gounié rivers in the 1920s removed one third to one half of the young men. Hundreds of others were taken away to construct the Congo-Ocean Railroad between 1921 and 1934. Other administrative exactions, including the forced cultivation of cocoa, also contributed to the shortage of farm labor for food crops, which gave rise to the famines of the mid-1920s. The weakened populations succumbed by the thousands in the early 1920s to influenza (the Spanish flu) and smallpox. In these circumstances the populations of the Woleu-N'Tem and Okano circonscriptions (the administrative units of that period) fell from 142, 000 in 1911 to 65, 000 in 1933. At the same time the Fang of the Woleu-N'Tem began to accept the cultivation of cocoa, and later coffee, as cash crops. Many of them were transformed into genuine peasants working individually owned plots in family groups.

During the 1940s among the northern Fang there took place a movement to revitalize the clans by regrouping them. The alar ayong (q. v.) movement, as it was called, had its origins across the frontier among the Boulou of the French trusteeship territory. The alar ayong did a good deal to restore Fang self-esteem, particularly among those who remained in the northern rural areas. At the same time the French administration sought to address Fang problems through the Fang or Pahouin Congress held at Mitzic in February 1947. Under the leadership of the Fang deputy in the French National Assembly, Jean-Hilaire Aubame (q. v.) whose parents had come from the Woleu-N'Tem, there was an administrative regroupment of populations, as much as possible on the basis of clan ties, in order to permit increased social services (schools, dispensaries, sports facilities, meeting places). Aubame, and a leader of the Estuary Fang, Léon Mba (q. v.), became two of the three most important political figures during the era of decolonization and independence (the other being Paul Gondjout (q. v.), a Myènè). See BWITI; CHIWA; MADEMOISELLE. [261, 257, 286, 177, 178, 300]

FARA, BROTHER DOMINIQUE (1876-1922). The first African in Gabon to become a Catholic brother, in 1895. Of Congolese origin, he assisted Father Théophile Klaine (q. v.) in the school at St. Mary's near Libreville and taught the beginning class at the Ecole Montfort (q. v.). He died of sleeping sickness on June 21, 1922. [530, 555]

FELIX-ADANDE RAPONTCHOMBO, KING (1847-1911). Also

called King Félix-Denis and King Louis-Félix. First Mpongwe (q. v.) clan head who was Christian and western-educated, he headed the Asiga clan from 1876 to 1911. Louis Félix-Adandé was the son of King Denis (q. v.), who chose him as successor. Félix-Adandé was educated at the primary school and minor seminary of the Holy Ghost Fathers (q. v.) at Libreville. Thereafter he served as an accountant in the French naval administration where he had European subordinates. In 1867 he married Elisa Antchondie Bobié (1850-1883) whose father Henri Oréniga was one of the first Catholic converts in Quaben village and whose brother Rémi Remombe (q. v.) (1852-1873) became a seminarian. Elisa was a pupil of the Immaculate Conception Sisters' school at Libreville. Félix and Elisa had six children; their eldest son, Jean-Félix Rapontchombo (q. v.) (1872-1903), was the first Gabonese to earn a baccalauréat (French secondary diploma), and their second son, Jean-Rémi Onanga, was the father of Prince Félix Adandé (q. v.) head of the Mpongwe collectivity of Glass at Libreville in the 1950s. (The Prince's mother belonged to the ruling lineage of the Agekaza-Glass.)

Félix-Adandé accepted French rule and western civilization. He personally encouraged and advanced western education and Roman Catholicism among his subjects. At the same time he expected the colonial administration to respect his authority as clan head, to live up to the terms of the treaties France had made with his father, and to allow him and his subjects the protection of French law and the enjoyment of the same basic rights as Frenchmen. In an age of increasing colonialism and rising French nationalism, Félix-Adandé clashed almost immediately with the local French commandants, who were intensely concerned about their own authority in a colony where British and German traders and Anglo-American cultural influence remained preponderant. There is also some evidence that Félix-Adandé may have been involved in the clandestine slave trade between Cape Lopez and São Tomé, which the French had failed entirely to suppress. In 1878 he was imprisoned for organizing a successful boycott against the French merchant Caron whose business practices the Asiga considered to be unjust. In 1880-1881 he used his good offices at the request of Commandant Hanet-Cléry to settle a commercial dispute between French merchants and the Nkomi (q. v.) of Fernan-Vaz. Hanet-Cléry recommended him for the Legion of Honor but it was awarded only many years later, shortly before his death. Late in 1882 Félix-Adandé was unable to pay a debt to a French commercial house because Commandant Edouard Masson had halved his government pension, which embroiled him in a legal dispute with the authorities for the next decade. Then in October 1884 Commandant Cornut-Gentille accused him of enslaving some escaped slaves from São Tome and had him put in chains aboard a ship for trial in West Africa. He escaped with the aid of Mpongwe relatives and Bishop Pierre Le Berre (q. v.) and was ultimately acquitted. The French later accused him of capturing and retaining some slaves fleeing Cape Lopez. Félix-Adandé eventually won his case with the French commercial house in the court at Gorée, Senegal, but was unable to collect the damages awarded to him as a result of local officials' abuses of authority. Though protesting his continued loyalty to France, he refused to make the kind of abject submission demanded by the local authorities.

Félix-Adandé failed in his attempts to revitalize agriculture among the Asiga to replace the revenues lost through the suppression of the slave trade. He spent his last years seeing many of his subjects transferring to the north shore to engage in commerce in Glass Town (Libreville). There they became assimilated to the Agekaza clan to such an extent that after 1938 the Asiga no longer possessed their own clan head. [251, 243]

FELIX-DENIS ADANDE RAPONTCHOMBO, PRINCE or DENIS-MARIE ADANDE (1899-). The great-grandson of King Denis (q. v.) was born at Fubu in June 1899. He graduated from the Ecole Montfort and taught there. In 1921 he went to work as an accountant at Kinshasa in the Belgian Congo. After his return to Libreville perhaps a decade later, he worked in the same profession and became active in the movements among the Mpongwe (q. v.) to assert their traditional rights, especially rights to lands in the Estuary, in the face of administration and Fang encroachments. The Comité Mpongwe (q. v.) advanced his candidacy for head chief of the Mpongwe of Libreville. They succeeded in the late 1930s in having him named _chef de groupe de quartier_ for the Glass section of Libreville, from whose nineteenth-century rulers he was descended through his mother. The French also named him as one of the first Africans on the Libreville municipal commission. He remained active in Mpongwe affairs throughout the Fourth Republic and at one point headed a delegation to Paris to secure further indemnification for lands. After independence, he directed the

National Tourist Office (1962-November 1966) and served as president of the Supreme Court (November 1966 to November 1968). [682, 335]

FIDES. During the Fourth French Republic (1946-58), France promoted the economic, social, and educational development of its African territories through public programs under the Fonds d'Investissements pour le Développement Economique et Social (FIDES), the initials of which form the Latin word for faith. FIDES involved grants from the metropolitan taxpayers and long-term, low-interest loans through the Caisse Centrale de la France d'Outre-Mer. Most of these loans were ultimately cancelled at independence or thereafter. The African territories also made budgetary contributions to the various projects. What was new about FIDES was both the overall planning and the outright grants, for prior to the Second World War all development was supposed to be funded by the territories themselves. FIDES funded public projects and contributed to private ones. In French Equatorial Africa as a whole FIDES invested 59 billion francs CFA and private interests 51 billion, that is, over four hundred million U. S. dollars.

Gabon, which had one twelfth of the population of the federation, received roughly the same fraction of the investments, that is, approximately $25, 000, 000. The bulk of this amount went for development of the economic infrastructure in order to permit the expansion of production, especially timber. The largest single project, which cost eleven million dollars, was construction of the road from Libreville to Lambaréné. Other important sums modernized the ports and airfields of Libreville and Port-Gentil and built an okoumé factory at the latter town. Lesser sums went for the construction and equipment of schools, a hospital, and dispensaries. [54]

FORD, HENRY A., M. D. (1818-58). American missionary and specialist in tropical fevers. A New Yorker, Dr. Ford served under the ABCFM in Gabon from 1850 until his death on February 2, 1858. He is buried in the Baraka cemetery. Dr. Ford's study, *Observations on the Fevers of the West Coast of Africa*, was published in New York City in 1856. [517]

FOREIGN RELATIONS. Gabon achieved political independence on August 17, 1960, without possessing the technical and administrative personnel to operate its government and economy. It lacked the expertise and capital to promote further economic development. In these circumstances it turned primarily to France, in whose Community it had retained membership, for continued aid and assistance. The framework for French support was provided in the coopération agreements or accords signed at independence or shortly thereafter. These fifteen agreements included several key policy areas (foreign policy, defense and strategic materials, education and culture, monetary policy and currency); economic, financial, and technical assistance; and such matters as fishing, civil aviation, and the merchant marine.

Gabon became an associate member of the European Economic Community, to which its French mentor belonged, and thereby expanded its economic relations with these states, particularly with the Federal German Republic, and received development assistance from the EEC's Development Fund and Investment Bank. These arrangements perpetuated the association of Gabon with the EEC which had begun under the terms of Article 131 of the Treaty of Rome of 1957 while Gabon was still an overseas territory of the Fourth French Republic. Later on Gabon adhered to the first Yaoundé Convention (operational June 1964-May 1969) between the Common Market nations and their African associates. It provided for a common market and free monetary exchange as well as gradual suppression of the bilateral preferences between France and its former territories.

Under President Léon Mba (q. v.) Gabon followed a liberal economic policy. It therefore sought to secure aid and assistance from western governments to develop its infrastructure and private investments from these same nations to develop its natural resources, particularly its minerals and forests. During the 1950s France had brought in American and West German investors to participate in the development of manganese and iron while keeping uranium and forests entirely as its own preserve. The Mba government retained this policy in seeking investments from the United States, West Germany and other Common Market countries to develop its oil and natural gas. Gabon derived revenue from these activities primarily through taxation at the time of export.

It was the desire of Gabon to retain the revenues derived from its own resources that had caused it to oppose the maintenance of the federation of French Equatorial Africa (q. v.) in 1957 and after. During the period of the federation (1910-57) it had seen its customs revenues, particularly from wood exports, go to develop the other territories, especially the Congo and the federal capital at Brazzaville. Gabon thus in May 1960 refused membership in a political federation, the Union des Républiques de l'Afrique Centrale (URAC), which would have acceded to independence as a single state within the French Community. But Gabon was willing to and interested in cooperating with the other Equatorial states and Cameroon in a number of economic and financial matters. Soon after the formation of the Community, the four Equatorial states worked out the principles for a customs union, the Union Douanière Equatoriale (1959) to which Cameroon adhered a year after its independence (1961). The five states arranged to maintain the franc CFA as their common currency issued by a central bank. The Equatorial states established common agencies for transportation facilities such as ports and railroads and for posts and telecommunications. A Conférence des Chefs d'Etats d'Afrique Equatoriale organized on June 24, 1959, met at least twice a year to decide policies and to discuss other matters of mutual interest. In December 1964 the Equatorial states and Cameroon formed the Union Douanière et Economique de l'Afrique Centrale (UDEAC) (q. v.) and organized a Banque des Etats de l'Afrique Centrale (BEAC). UDEAC established a common market and sought to promote economic development, including industrialization, by harmonizing customs, fiscal, and investment policies. The arrangements for UDEAC granted a preferential status to the countries of the EEC (including France, of course) and to the members of the Organisation Africaine et Malgache pour la Coopération Economique (OAMCE); it thereby disadvantaged other industrial nations such as the United Kingdom, the United States, and Japan.

Between 1959 and 1971 under French auspices Gabon cooperated with the other three Equatorial African states in the field of higher education. With France the four countries formed the Fondation de l'Enseignement Supérieur en Afrique Centrale (FESAC) to share students and facilities. This form of cooperation, which was always uneasy because of the problem of the distribution of facilities among the four states, after August 1963 became acute as a result of the coming to power of Marxist elements in Brazzaville where the liberal arts, law, and education divisions were located. Cooperation in higher education broke down completely by the late 1960s and was officially terminated in 1971. FESAC was replaced by national institutions in Gabon and elsewhere.

During mid-September 1962 troubles broke out in Brazzaville between a visiting Gabonese football team and local Congolese, which produced brutal retaliatory attacks on the Congolese populations of Libreville and other centers on September 18-20 and their abrupt official expulsion. Congo responded by expelling the tiny numbers of Gabonese in its territories. Ultimately the heads of state, Mba and Fulbert Youlou, met in November 1962 under Cameroonian auspices, to restore peace and agreed to indemnify the victims. Gabon has since sought to maintain good relations with all of its neighbors but especially the Congo, through whose territory runs the *téléférique* and railroad that evacuate Gabon's manganese. Gabon's dependence on this route will persist until such time as the Transgabonais can be extended into the Haut-Ogooué Province, probably not until the mid-1980s.

Under President Mba Gabon established links with the other former French states that had joined the Community. Thus it joined the Union Africaine et Malgache in 1961, which was subsequently replaced by the Organisation Commune Africaine et Malgache (OCAM) in 1964. OCAM involved a good deal of consultation and functional cooperation in such enterprises as an inter-state airline, Air Afrique. Gabon joined the Organization of African Unity in June 1963 but not the African Development Bank organized in September 1964. Though it joined the United Nations in late 1960, it played a very minor role there and its delegates were often absent from the sessions prior to 1968.

The Mba government maintained only a dozen embassies abroad, including six in non-African countries (France, Spain, West Germany, USA, Israel, Taiwan). The ambassadors in these countries handled relations with a number of other states. Gabon chose to play a modest role in keeping with its size and resources at the time. It maintained very close relations amounting to a dependency upon France from whom came the bulk of its aid and assistance. It had relations with Spain, which until 1968 controlled its neighbor, the Rio Muni or Spanish Guinea, which after independence together with Fernando Po would be known as Equatorial Guinea. It received technical aid and assistance from the other four states, for forestry from Israel and for rice culture from Taiwan. From the United States beginning in 1962 it received Peace Corps Volunteers, who were active in secondary education and school construction in all nine provinces.

The military coup and French intervention of February 1964 to restore President Mba to power focussed the latter's attention upon domestic concerns for much of the remainder of his life. Serious health problems and a long illness in a Paris hospital further precluded any real changes in foreign policy during the last two years of his regime. Albert-Bernard Bongo (q. v.) as vice-president exercised day-to-day supervision of foreign relations during the last year of Mba's life. At Bongo's accession to the presidency in November 1967 he turned his attention inward to healing the wounds left by the political struggles of the previous decade. Some of those whom he released from prison or detention abandoned politics and a few of them left the country. But the majority of Mba's opponents were willing to accept Bongo's leadership in the development of the country and were thereforce incorporated into the regime. Once he had established a firmer political base, Bongo was free to proceed to economic development and to the changes in foreign relations that might facilitate it. For his accession to power had taken place simultaneously with the first important output from the country's petroleum resources. This new situation presented Gabon with vastly increased revenues to use to raise standards of living while promoting further development of its other resources. At the same time it offered possibilities for decreasing some aspects of the country's dependence upon France, particularly in the areas of policy-making and control of resources.

From 1968 Gabon gradually undertook new orientations in foreign policy, which were most clearly articulated by President Bongo only in 1973. The changes involved the abandonment of the isolation or very limited role in world affairs established by President Mba, a loosening of the kind of ties with France that amounted to a close dependency, and a search for world-wide support and cooperation to escape under-development and to promote development. In 1973 Bongo enunciated the main lines of the new orientations under the slogans "Gabon First" (*Gabon d'abord*) and "realism." He expressed the desire to establish relations with all nations which would respect Gabon's sovereignty and role as a free arbiter (*libre arbitre*) and which would cooperate in its development.

As part of the new orientations, between 1968 and 1973 Gabon established commercial and/or diplomatic relations with three groups of nations: additional western nations (Switzerland, Italy, United Kingdom, Netherlands, Canada, Japan); Eastern European Communist nations (Bulgaria, Czechoslovakia, Romania, Yugoslavia, the Soviet Union); and Arab states, particularly those of North Africa (Mauritania, Morocco, Egypt, Libya, Algeria, and Sudan). From all three groups Gabon hoped for profitable commercial exchanges plus aid and assistance for development. In the case of the Communist nations, Gabon had feared that diplomatic relations would bring the dangers of subversion through liaisons with local Marxists. In 1970 Bongo said that he did not like the countries of the East. But in 1972 he spoke of an open door for Gabon's products towards the East as well as the West. In the case of the Arab nations, Gabon was propelled in their direction by the general movement of Black African countries towards them after the 1973 Arab-Israeli war. This movement involved a loosening or abandonment of ties with Israel. Gabon acquired additional contacts and common interests with the Arab oil producers as an oil producer and OPEC member (1973).

Gabon's relations with the Arab countries entered a new phase in late 1973 and 1974 in the course of the search for funds with which to construct the Transgabonais Railroad. By the early 1970s the railroad had come to be seen as the necessary means to all further development--in order to tap the iron and woods of interior regions and to open them to world markets as well as better to exploit the manganese and uranium. Long negotiations with the World Bank, which was to be the chief supplier through loans for the first stage of $200, 000, 000 from Owendo to Booué, finally resulted in a negative decision during 1972. After this failure, President Bongo stated Gabon's readiness to look anywhere in the world for the necessary support.

Gabon had enjoyed commercial relations with Israel since 1962 and had established an embassy in Jerusalem in 1965. It received Israeli aid in forestry development. But it became obvious that Gabon could not develop close relations with the Arab nations, much less obtain development aid from their oil producers, if it maintained relations with Israel. In September 1973 Gabon, which had not attended the first summit of non-aligned nations at Cairo in September 1964, sent a delegation to the second summit at Algiers in September 1973. It is believed that there Gabonese leaders made contact with Libya, which promised aid if Gabon broke relations with Israel, an action that an important portion of the cabinet opposed.

On October 30, 1973, Gabon broke relations when Israel refused to heed the United Nations resolution on peace negotiations in the wake of the war with the Arab states earlier that month. After a visit to Libya and conferences with its president Khaddafi, Bongo, who professed no religion but had previously shown some interest in the Roman Catholicism of his wife, announced his conversion to Islam. After a pilgrimage to Mecca he took the name and title of El Hadj Omar Bongo. In April 1974 he went to the U. N. in the company of the Arab oil producers. Unfortunately for Gabon's development plans, the promised aid from Libya for the Transgabonais which was to result from their cooperation treaty was not forthcoming and the treaty itself was abrogated in June 1974.

The imperatives for building the Transgabonais caused Bongo to reestablish good relations with the United States. Relations had been tense with the U. S. since the 1964 coup, for some French residents had convinced President Mba that the Americans supported his opponents. These same Frenchmen, of course, feared that the United States wished to replace French interests in Gabon. In 1968 Bongo had sent away the Peace Corps on the grounds that he did not like large numbers of foreigners whom the government could not control working at the grass roots throughout the country. But he arranged for the return of the Peace Corps in 1972 and secured American help for the financing of the Transgabonais. American investors were encouraged to play a greater role in prospecting and marketing Gabonese oil, the bulk of which was going to France.

As for France itself, Gabon secured changes in the cooperation agreements on February 12, 1974, as the bulk of the former French states had already done or were doing. Bongo chose to call the changes an "adaptation" rather than a revision. Taken as a whole, they render Gabon more independent in policy-making areas and in the control of its resources but perpetuate its dependence upon French aid and assistance. Gabon no longer coordinates its foreign policy and monetary policy with France's though it remains within the franc zone. France no longer has the right of pre-emption of primary materials and its access to strategic materials such as uranium is no longer tied to the question of defense. The French have agreed to pay more for the uranium and must compete for other products. Frenchmen can no longer possess Gabonese nationality; the double nationality provision, which was terminated by de Gaulle's regime for

Gabonese and other Black Africans in France in the early 1960s, has now ended for the French in Gabon. Thus they can no longer vote nor play a formal role in the country's internal affairs. The one aspect of cooperation which remained unchanged was the defense agreement which permits Gabon to call upon France for both internal and external threats. The decision of the French government not to come to the rescue of the Hamani Diori government in Niger, which was threatened internally by an overthrow, and in a territory where France had an agreement to purchase strategic materials, may cause the Bongo government to wonder about the value of the accord if it should become genuinely unpopular. Gabon also signed a new agreement on civil aviation with France in 1977 following its withdrawal from Air Afrique.

France has shown a willingness to continue aid and assistance on these changed terms as it has elsewhere in its former territories, nearly all of which renegotiated their cooperation agreements in the first half of the 1970s. In 1978 there were 725 French functionaries detached for service in Gabon of which 435 were in education, almost entirely at the secondary and higher levels. Although the period of independence has seen many more Gabonese university graduates, the number of positions has also increased and few Gabonese have entered such technical fields as engineering and business administration. In 1977 France gave Gabon 226 million French francs in aid (roughly $55,000,000) and through the FED of the EEC additional assistance. France remains Gabon's single most important source of financial aid. It is also Gabon's most important trading partner, supplying 69 percent of its imports and taking 42 percent of its exports (1976). Other EEC countries supplied 13 percent of the imports and took 19 percent of the exports.

Gabon adhered to the second Yaoundé convention of the African states with the EEC in 1969. It also adhered to the Lomé Convention of February 28, 1975, and seven protocols between the EEC states and countries of Africa, the Caribbean, and the Pacific. It continues to receive aid through the EEC's FED and Investment Bank.

In June 1972 Gabon required all companies doing business in the country to turn over without compensation 10 percent of their capital to the state. In February 1976 it required that a representative of the government sit on the administrative council of each firm. In March 1977 while declaring that economic liberalism would be maintained, it decreed that all future enterprises installed in Gabon would have a minimum of 49 percent participation by the state. At present the state's participation varies from 10 to 60 percent. In 1974 Gabon had increased its participation in many enterprises, including French banks (40 percent); petroleum distribution (51 percent); 30 percent in Sogara; 60 percent in cables; 60 percent in Somifer (which previously since 1963 had been 50 percent Bethlehem Steel, 34 percent French, and 10 percent German).

Concerning Gabon's relations with other Black African states, including its neighbors, Gabon followed De Gaulle's lead in recognizing the secessionist state of Biafra. It was one of four African states to do so--Ivory Coast, Tanzania, and Zambia being the others. Gabon gave sanctuary to 4, 500 Biafran refugee children who returned home only after January 1973 when relations with the federal government of Nigeria were restored.

In 1968 Zaire attempted to destroy UDEAC by taking away some of its members into a new Central African union under its leadership, the Union des Etats de l'Afrique Centrale. Chad was lost permanently by UDEAC but the Central African Republic returned after a time and the seat of UDEAC is located in Bangui. On May 28, 1970, the Conference of Heads of Equatorial States was dissolved. Gabon has provided leadership for cooperation towards industrialization in the UDEAC states and helped to organize an oil refinery in June 1966 that would serve their needs. On May 3, 1976, UDEAC formed the Development Bank of the Central African States (BDEAC) with its headquarters at Brazzaville.

On August 23, 1972, Gabon, in an effort to establish ownership of the possible offshore oil deposits, unilaterally extended its territorial waters to 170 miles. It was immediately accused by Equatorial Guinea of invading several of its tiny islands, really sandbanks (Congo, Mbanié, and Cocotiers), which were located 18 km. offshore from Gabon but 35 km. from Equatorial Guinea. In September 1972, when Guineans fired upon Gabonese fishermen in the disputed areas, Gabon sent two ships and forty gendarmes into the zone. Congo and Zaire offered their good offices to settle the dispute. It was agreed to let a four-nation commission from the Organization of African Unity fix the maritime frontier between the two states, which was apparently done. In early 1974 there was renewed trouble over Mbanié Island, which seems also to have been settled quickly. The oppression of the Macias regime caused up to

60,000 Equatorial Guineans to take refuge within Gabon. Some of those at Libreville, where many thousands located, were causing grave problems in maintaining order. Whether they will return home since Macias's overthrow and death by firing squad in 1979 remains to be seen.

In May 1977 Gabon expelled most of the eleven thousand Béninois (Dahomeyans) from the country in the wake of Colonel Kérekou's accusations that high Gabonese officials, including President Bongo, were involved in the unsuccessful invasion plot to overthrow him. Gabon denied connection with the attempted coup but retaliated by sending home all the Béninois who were not on government contract. Some of them had been residing and working in Gabon for many decades.

In September 1976 Bongo pulled Gabon out of OCAM, which he felt no longer served its interests and was expensive. He withdrew Gabon from Air Afrique as of June 1977. As of November 1978 OCAM had only nine members left: Benin, the Central African Republic, Ivory Coast, Upper Volta, Mauritius, Niger, Senegal, Togo, and Rwanda.

While some African countries became active against the minority regimes in Rhodesia (Zimbabwe) and South Africa, Gabon did not. It has followed a wait-and-see policy (*attentisme*). Though not maintaining formal relations with these states, Gabon has nevertheless received regular flights of vegetables, fruits, and meats from them unofficially. Soon after the World Bank rejected loans for the Trans-Gabonais Railroad, Pretoria reportedly offered five billion francs CFA (roughly twenty million U.S. dollars) in loans. Though President Bongo had publicly stated that he would make a pact with the devil if necessary to get the funds to build the railroad, it appears that he did not ultimately accept the South African offer, which would have endangered his relations with other African states.

Gabon joined the OAU's Development Bank during its search for funds to build the Transgabonais. It is giving 250,000,000 francs CFA annually to the OAU's Sahel Fund.

It is difficult to secure accurate statistics concerning the amounts of foreign aid and assistance African countries have received. A French scholar, Michel Cathala, indicates that between 1959 and 1972 non-French sources gave Gabon 14,164,500,000 fr. CFA in aid, nearly all of it for economic development. *Africa South of the Sahara, 1978-1979* reported that the French Fonds d'Aide et de Coopération gave grants of 12,800,000,000 fr. CFA between 1959 and 1970; between 1971 and 1975 it gave approximately two thirds of the 95,000,000,000 fr. CFA, the rest coming from the European Development Fund, West Germany, United Nations, agencies, and the United States. Europe-France-Outre-Mer reported that annually during the late 1970s France was providing Gabon fifty to sixty million U.S. dollars in aid. Gabon was also receiving other millions from western sources, including Canada and Japan, for construction of infrastructure and development of its natural resources. See UDEAC. [343, 344, 348, 358, 379, 81]

FORESTRY. Various kinds of forests cover 225,000 sq. km. out of 267,000 sq. km., that is, over 80 percent of Gabon. Dyewood or redwood from the southern coast around Mayumba was exchanged perhaps even before the arrival of Europeans on the coast. It became an important export in the seventeenth century and after. In the 1880s okoumé (q.v.), a softwood used in the manufacture of plywood, began to be exported to Germany and Holland, and after the First World War to France. By 1903 Gabon had become the leading African producer of tropical woods, a position it ceded to the Ivory Coast only in the 1970s. Mahogany, ebony, and walnut came to be exploited by French firms during the 1920s in important quantities though they never achieved the significance of okoumé. The economy of Gabon depended heavily upon the timber industry until the start of mineral exploitation in the early 1960s. In the late 1970s timber still represented about ten percent of the exports in value and Gabon remains the chief African exporter of plywood.

Timber exploitation is carried on by mechanized French and Gabonese firms and by non-mechanized Gabonese family groups, the so-called coupes familiales. Government policy encouraging and favoring Gabonese involvement resulted by the early 1970s in reducing production by French firms to a slight majority of the total. In the wake of the depletion of forests in the coastal areas--the "first zone"--where evacuation by water routes was generally possible, exploitation has increased in the "second zone," which covers the central portions of the country from north to south. In this zone rapids and waterfalls preclude water transportation for much of the export route so that construction of a road network has been necessary. These projects are already underway as are reforestation schemes in the first zone. The portion of the Transgabonais Railroad connecting the port of Owendo on the Estuary with Booué on the middle Ogooué, which was half completed in 1978, will aid evacuation of the timber from the second zone. The eventual extension of the Transgabonais north-east to the iron industry at Mékambo and south-east to the manganese industry would further facilitate the exploitation of the considerable forest riches of both the second and the third zones.

The sawmills of the timber industry are located at Port-Gentil, Libreville, and Mayumba. The construction of the new port at Owendo, the western terminus of the Transgabonais, includes facilities for timber. Work began in 1975 on a large cellulose plant for SOGACEL (Société Gabonaise de Cellulose) at Kango on the Como River 70 km. east of Owendo. It will use one million cubic meters of timber annually to produce 250, 000 tons of pulp, which will be evacuated by barges along the Como River to Owendo. Electric power for the cellulose industry will come from the hydroelectric plant near the dam project at the Kinguélé Falls on the M'Bei River, a northern tributary of the Como. [478, 384, 415, 457]

FRANC ZONE. The franc zone is a monetary transaction association first organized by France in the aftermath of the Second World War and including its Black African territories. It was reorganized after the independence of these countries and continues to include all of them except Guinea and Mali. National and regional currencies, including the CFA franc of the four Equatorial countries and Cameroon, are pegged to the French franc. They are freely exchangeable and transferable within the franc zone under French fiscal control. [408]

FREE EMIGRANTS SCHEME or FREE LABORERS SCHEME. In March 1857 the Régis Company of Marseilles signed a contract with the French government to provide 20, 000 African workers for the French West Indies over a six-year period. The Africans were destined mainly for labor on the sugar plantations in the aftermath of the abolition of slavery in 1848, which had freed 74, 000 slaves on Martinique and 93, 000 on Guadeloupe. The Régis firm, already known for its promotion of French commerce and of French political control in West Africa, established its headquarters for this enterprise at the Congo mouth and in Angola. By 1862 Régis had signed up 15, 000 Africans from the regions between Gabon and Angola. An unknown number of them came from southern

Gabon. Of the estimated 1200 to 1500 recruited between 1857 and 1860 in the Estuary, none ever returned to Gabon at the end of their seven-year contracts.

The African "volunteers" were called "free laborers" in Britain and free emigrants (émigrants libres) or free enlistees (engagés libres) in France. Their terms of employment resembled those of indentured servants in the British North American colonies during the seventeenth and eighteenth centuries. But the conditions under which they were recruited and were kept at the coastal factories and onboard ship, closely resembled the slave trade. Growing British criticism of these aspects of the scheme resulted in an Anglo-French agreement of July 1, 1861, to end the program within one year. [170, 155]

FREE FRENCH MOVEMENT (1940-1944). On June 18, 1940, the government of the Third French Republic made an armistice with Nazi Germany. The Germans occupied the northern three fifths of France, including the Atlantic coasts, and a French state at Vichy headed by Marshall Philippe Pétain controlled the remainder. On the same day in London General Charles de Gaulle, a longtime critic of France's inadequate defenses, issued a call for formation of the Free French movement to keep Frenchmen in the war on the Allied side. De Gaulle hoped to use the resources of the vast French Empire, still in French hands, to liberate the mother country. Whereas the French communities in North Africa and West Africa rejected de Gaulle's appeals and gave allegiance to Vichy, those in the Cameroons and French Equatorial Africa rallied to his side between August 26 and 30, 1940.

But in Gabon complications immediately arose. The colonial governor, Pierre Masson, who on the 30th, after consultation with French notables, including the influential Chamber of Commerce president Henri Seignon (q. v.), had taken Gabon into the Free French camp, on September 1st reversed his decision. He was apparently influenced by the criticism of the Catholic bishop of Libreville, Monsignor Louis Tardy, and the prominent businessman René Labat, as well as by the arrival of two Vichy gunboats on the coast and high Vichy colonial appointees by air. Gabon thereafter became the scene of a civil war among the Free French, based in the Cameroons and the Middle Congo, and their French supporters in Gabon, on the one hand, and the Vichy forces and their local French supporters, on the other. Free French Colonel Parant (1897-1941) in early September took

Mayumba, rallied the N'Gounié Province, and laid siege to Lambaréné, which the Vichyites abandoned only on November 5th. On the ninth Parant's forces combined with those of Colonel Leclerc from the Cameroons, which had previously rallied the Woleu N'Tem Province, to take Libreville from the Vichyites. After Port-Gentil surrendered to the Free French on November 11, further Vichy opposition ceased. Colonel Parant briefly headed Gabon under Governor-General Félix Eboué (q. v.) at Brazzaville.

During the war years the British purchased Gabon's exports, using the okoumé (q. v.) in the construction of Royal Air Force planes. Hundreds of Gabonese served in the Free French forces in North Africa and Europe, and subsequently received pensions. These war veterans (anciens combattants) would be an important element in upholding close ties with France in the coming decades.

The Free French government sponsored the Brazzaville Conference of January-February 1944 which planned for post-war liberalization of the colonial regime within a French framework. The conference advocated greater participation by Africans in their own administration as well as public programs to promote economic and social advancement. [98, 207, 116, 333, 345]

FREEDOM VILLAGES (VILLAGES DE LIBERTE). At the beginning of the twentieth century the French Anti-Slavery Society (Société Anti-Esclavagiste de France) sponsored the organization of three villages in the Gabonese interior for slaves whose freedom it had helped to purchase. The communities were located adjacent to the mission posts of the Holy Ghost Fathers on the lower N'Gounié River (1899), at Franceville (1902), and at Lambaréné (1903). During the previous half century the Catholic missionaries had purchased the freedom of ill-treated slaves, generally orphan children whom they subsequently raised, educated, and prepared for Christian marriage. On several occasions they had also formed villages of free converts near their posts to provide continued instruction and to protect them from the pressures of their pagan relatives. But the freedom villages, which were first initiated by the colonial administration of French West Africa, contained mostly adults of both sexes whose freedom was purchased with funds from the French Anti-Slavery Society, a body organized by Cardinal Lavigerie in 1888 with the blessings and support of the papacy. The three in Gabon were among thirty organized throughout French West and Equatorial Africa. The Holy Ghost Fathers (q. v.) formed two other villages, among the Eshira (1887) and at Fernan-Vaz (1901), without outside support. Though the freedom villages did not promote evangelization to the extent the missionaries had hoped, they did secure the permanent freedom of several hundred persons in an era when the colonial administration was not yet in a position to terminate the worst forms of domestic slavery. [163]

FRENCH EQUATORIAL AFRICA. Between 1910 and 1958 Gabon was administered as part of the federation of French Equatorial Africa. The federation was created from a model developed in French West Africa to administer the lands France had acquired in Central Africa during the nineteenth and early twentieth centuries. It included four territories: Gabon, Middle Congo, Ubangui-Shari, and Chad. Each territory was headed by a lieutenant-governor (1910-46) or governor (1946-58) responsible to the governor-general in the federal capital at Brazzaville. The federation possessed a budget in addition to the four territorial budgets. Thus revenues raised in Gabon through customs duties and other taxes were transmitted to Brazzaville to help pay for the central services and federal functions. For example, Gabonese revenues aided construction of the Congo-Ocean Railroad (1921-34) from which Gabon derived no benefits at a time when it needed a railroad for its own development.

The federation was changed into a "group of territories" in April 1957 as a result of the decrees implementing the Loi-Cadre of June 23, 1956. The federation was abolished at the end of the Fourth Republic in September 1958. Attempts by the four states to replace the federation with some sort of cooperative political structure failed. Gabon saw few advantages in having a federation with states that were poorer than itself and that it might have to continue to subsidize. It wanted to use its own considerable timber and mineral resources to develop itself. Ultimately Gabon agreed to cooperation in a number of economic areas, which led to UDEAC (q. v.), and between 1959 and 1971 in higher education. See GOVERNORS. [15, 108]

- G -

GALOA (or GALWA). The Galoa are a Myènè-speaking (q. v.) people who early in the nineteenth century migrated from their homes around Lakes Onangué, Ezanga, and Oguemoue to Lambaréné Island in the Ogooué and along the river downstream. The Galoa were submitted at first to the rule of the Enenga (q. v.). At the death of the Enenga king Re-Mpole, Nkombe (d. 1874), his paternal nephew, whose mother was Galoa, declared Galoa independence and became their king. Ruling from his village at Adolinango, he procured slaves upstream for transport to Cape Lopez and Fernan Vaz. He aided various explorers to obtain canoers for their trips farther upstream. He encouraged British and German as well as French trading firms to establish in his territories in 1867 and after in order to deal directly with them and eliminate the Orungu (q. v.) and Nkomi (q. v.) middlemen on the coast. It is likely that he accepted French sovereignty in 1867 though the treaty is missing. It is in large part Nkombe's policies that resulted in Lambaréné and vicinity becoming the center for European commercial penetration and exploration of the middle and upper Ogooué system in the 1870s and 1880s. During Nkombe's reign the Fang (q. v.) began to encroach on Galoa territory. At his death he left 120 wives and several hundred slaves. The French clashed with Nkombe's successor, Magise, whom they deported to Dakar.

In 1877 American Presbyterians founded a mission at Kangwe on the north bank of the Ogooué near Lambaréné and the Holy Ghost Fathers (q. v.) located on the island itself in 1881. The Galoa flocked to the schools of both missions and there acquired the skills that permitted them to serve as the agents and auxiliaries of European firms, French exploration parties, and eventually the colonial administration. The Galoa also converted either to Protestantism (the French Protestants replaced the Presbyterians in 1893) or to Roman Catholicism.

The Rev. André Raponda Walker (q. v.) claimed that the Galoa were originally an offshoot of the Eshira (q. v.) people who adopted a Myènè language as a result of their migration to the Lambaréné area. This view has been refuted by Paul-Vincent Pounah (q. v.) on the basis of oral data he gathered from Galoa notables from the 1940s on. [251, 237, 238, 239, 309]

GEORGES, KING or RASSONDJI (d. 1847). Georges headed the Agulamba clan of the Mpongwe (q. v.) on the southern shore of the Estuary from at least the 1810s until his death. At his village of Nghaga near the lower Remboué River, he possessed 300 to 500 slaves. He and his clan were much involved in the slave trade with the Ogooué and Cape Lopez, which was at its height during his reign. Georges allowed the ABCFM missionaries to open a school in his territories in the 1840s staffed by an Afro-American so that the boys might learn English, the leading trading language. In a treaty with Lt. Mecquet of November 4, 1846, Georges ceded the Avazé River or Georges Creek to France. At his death Georges was succeeded by his brother, the best known of the Agulamba traders, called Tom Lawson, who reigned from 1847 to 1860 under the same names, Georges and Rassondji, which had led to a good deal of confusion. To compound matters, other successors also took the name of Georges without adding numbers or other names that might have distinguished them from their predecessors. [170, 232, 251, 172]

GLASS, KING or R'OGOUAROWE (d. 1848). R'Ogouarowe headed the Agekaza-Glass or Agekaza w'Olamba clan of the Mpongwe (q. v.) people on the northern shore of the Estuary from 1839 to 1848. His village of Glass was the most important trading center in the region. It was the headquarters for British and American traders and after June 1842 the site of an American Protestant mission. The territories of R'Ogouarowe were also the center of the opposition to the establishment of French rule in the 1840s. King Glass recognized French sovereignty in a treaty of March 28, 1844, which was probably obtained through deception by naval officers and their African colleagues. He thereafter sought to repudiate the agreement but could not obtain the support of the British and American governments to this end. Glass eventually served on the French commission for arbitrating trade disputes. There is confusion about the identity of the heads of the Agekaza-Glass clan because several of R'Ogouarowe's successors also used that name without further distinction. [173, 170, 232, 251]

GOLD. In 1937 Mr. Raynal, a former agent of the Compagnie de la Haute-N'Gounié, who had had experience with gold-mining in the Belgian Congo, began prospecting in the areas of the Mitsogo (q. v.) people, around the villages of Eteké, Mombo, and Punga. By 1941, his company, the Société Or-Gabon, was exporting 1,686 kg. annually. Gold was subsequently located in other portions of the interior but the sites were soon worked out. The production of gold, which is now in Gabonese hands, in the late 1960s and early 1970s averaged 400 kg. annually. Recent prospecting has located new important lodes north-east of Lastoursville in the Ogooué-Lolo Province. Purchase and sale of the gold is handled by the Société Gabonaise de Recherche et d'Exploitations Minières (SOGAREM). [478]

GONDJOUT, PAUL INDJENJET (1912-). Politician. Gondjout was born on June 4, 1912, at Lambaréné of Enenga and Orungu parents. His father was an active member of the Ligue des Droits de l'Homme and a friend of Léon Mba (q. v.). Young Paul was educated at Catholic schools at Libreville, including the Ecole Montfort (q. v.). From December 1928 through 1964 he served in the administration, at first at Port-Gentil. In 1943 he founded the Cercle Amicale Mutualiste des Evolués in response to encouragement from Governor-General Félix Eboué (q. v.) for organizations that would provide leadership by the French-educated in a liberalized French Empire. In November 1946 he won election to the Territorial Assembly from Port-Gentil. In 1949 that body elected him as a Senator in the French upper house, the Council of the Republic, to which he was re-elected in 1952 and served until 1957. In 1954, after re-election to the Assembly in March 1952, he founded the Bloc Démocratique Gabonais (q. v.) and became its secretary-general and editor of its newspaper, the Union Gabonaise. The BDG sought to organize the peoples outside the Woleu-N'Tem against Jean-Hilaire Aubame (q. v.), his UDSG (q. v.), and the northern Fang. It became the local branch of the inter-territorial RDA after Léon Mba joined and became an officer. In 1958 Gondjout became president of the Legislative Assembly, a post which he continued to hold until November 1960 when President Mba jailed him for attempting a motion of censure designed to prevent Mba from transforming the government from a parliamentary to a presidential type. After his release from prison late in 1962, Mba appointed him president of the Economic and Social Council. As a member of the provisional government established in the wake of the February 1964 coup, he was arrested and tried but exonerated. President Bongo appointed him as secretary-general of the National Council of the Office des Bois in January 1968 and then president of the Supreme Court from September 1968 to April 1975. On April 16, 1975, he became president of the National Assembly. [335, 336, 682, 364]

GOVERNORS AND GOVERNORS-GENERAL, FRENCH. [700, 701]

Lieutenant-Governors of Gabon:	1886-1889	Noël Ballay
	1889-1891	Charles de Chavannes
	1891-1904	(directly under the French Congo)
	1904-1905	Louis Ormières
	1905-1906	Alfred Fourneau
	1906-1907	Fernand Therond
	1907-1909	Alfred Martineau
	1909-1910	Léon Richaud
	1910	Joseph François
	1910-1911	Adolphe Cureau
	1911-1913	Georges Poulet
	1913-1919	Casimir Guyon
	1919-1922	Maurice Lapalud
	1922-1923	Jean Marchand
	1923	Jocelyn Robert
	1923-1924	Louis Cercus
	1924-1931	Joseph Bernard
	1931-1934	Marcel Marchessou
	1934-1935	Louis Bonvin
	1935-1936	Charles Assier de Pompignan
	1936-1937	Louis Bonvin
	1937-1938	Georges Parisot
	1938-1940	Georges Masson
	1941-1942	Victor Valentin-Smith
	1942-1943	Charles Assier de Pompignan
	1943-1944	Paul Vuillaume
	1944-1946	Numa François Sadoul
Governors of Gabon:	1946-1947	Roland Pré
	1947-1949	Numa François Sadoul
	1949-1951	Pierre Pelieu
	1951-1952	Charles Hanin
	1952-1958	Yves Digo
	1958	Louis Sanmarco
High Commissioner of Gabon:	1959-1960	Jean Risterucci
Commissioners-General of the French Congo:	1886-1898	Pierre Savorgnan de Brazza
	1898-1901	Henri de la Mothe
	1901-1904	Louis Grodet
	1904-1908	Emile Gentil
	1908-1910	Martial Merlin

Governors-General of French Equatorial Africa:	1910-1917	Martial Merlin
	1918-1919	Gabriel Angoulvant
	1920-1924	Victor Augagneur
	1924-1934	Raphaël Antonetti
	1934-1935	Edouard Renard
	1935-1939	François Joseph Reste
	1939-1940	Pierre Boisson
	1940	Louis Husson
	1940	René de Larminat
	1940-1944	Félix Eboué
	1944-1947	Charles-André Bayardelle
	1947	Charles Luizet
High Commissioners of French Equatorial Africa:	1947-1951	Bernard Cornut-Gentille
	1951-1958	Paul Chauvet
	1958	Pierre Messmer
	1958	Yvon Bourges
High Commissioner-General of French Equatorial Africa	1959-1960	Yvon Bourges

GROUPE D'ETUDES COMMUNISTES (GEC). The GEC founded at Libreville in 1944 or 1945 was modelled upon the GEC's organized throughout French West Africa in 1943 and after by European administrative employees who had received appointments during the era of the Popular Front. The GEC's sought to provide a political education for _évolués_ that would be both Marxist and anticolonialist. The European leaders encouraged and aided the African members in the formation of territorial political parties affiliated with the Rassemblement Démocratique Africain (RDA) and labor unions linked with the Communist-influenced Confédération Générale du Travail (CGT).

In Gabon the federal administration encouraged Fernand Saller, an Antillese, and two physicians, Drs. Lucien Cordier and Eggenberger, to organize a GEC in order to keep left-wing political activity under European direction and to counter conservative and mission influences. The GEC at Libreville helped to organize labor unions of European and African civil servants and private employees affiliated with the CGT. It also aided the formation of a political party, the Parti Démocratique Africain (PDA) (q. v.), to contest elections in 1945-46 for the French Constituent, French National, and Gabonese Territorial Assemblies. The most important figures in the PDA were Emile Issembé (q. v.), Léon Mba, Georges Damas (q. v.), and Paul Gondjout (q. v.).

The PDA became the Gabonese branch of the RDA in 1946 but was not allowed by the administration to send the delegates it selected to the Bamako conference of that year. In March 1947, the administration, now under different direction and acting as part of the Africa-wide repression of the French Communists' African allies, transferred the two physicians to other areas. At that moment Léon Mba became the president of the GEC and Gérard McKenzie, an Mpongwe métis (q. v.), the secretary. Other leaders were Frédéric Moreau, the secretary of the Comité Mpongwe; Paul Taty; Jean-Pierre Tchikaya, a Vili and a close friend of the RDA deputy, Jean-Félix Tchicaya (q. v.); and David Cadorelle, a young Congolese schoolteacher. Moreau, Taty, and Cadorelle were very active in the CGT unions among civil servants. Under strong pressures from the administration, the GEC was forced to stop meeting by the end of 1947. Some of the members would join Léon Mba's Comité Mixte Gabonais (q. v.), which had succeeded the PDA as the local branch of the RDA. [335]

- H -

HEALTH AND SANITATION. Historically the population was plagued by endemic parasitical diseases and malnutrition. Smallpox epidemics on the coasts in the mid-nineteenth century and in the far north in the early twentieth century decimated various peoples. Sleeping sickness and malaria were endemic in many areas. Almost all African peoples had doctors who employed natural medicine to deal with various ailments. Western medicine arrived with the Christian missionaries and French naval physicians in the 1840s and after. Under the federation of French Equatorial Africa (q. v.), health services based at Brazzaville pretty well eradicated sleeping sickness during the interwar period. In 1913 Dr. Albert Schweitzer (q. v.) established his famous hospital at Lambaréné. His use of methods of treatment adapted to local conditions brought much criticism in the West. His hospital, which had financial problems after his death in 1965, was transferred to the government in 1977. The bulk of health care and preventive medicine is conducted by the government. Two thirds of the 144 physicians in 1976 were in government service. At that time Gabon had eleven hospitals, 24 medical centers, and 116 infirmaries and dispensaries. There were four thousand hospital beds. The government operated various programs of sanitation, disease prevention and control. [471, 464, 484, 486]

HOLY GHOST FATHERS (or SPIRITANS). The most important Catholic missionary congregation in Gabon since 1844. In 1841 Rev. François Libermann (1802-1852) founded the Congregation of the Holy Heart of Mary to evangelize the black race. In 1848 his group merged with the older Holy Ghost Congregation (Spiritans) of which he became the ninth superior. Libermann and his clergy were well in advance of their time in their comparative lack of ethnocentrism. They also worked from the very start to prepare an indigenous clergy and skilled tradesmen. Spiritans held the position of bishop until gradually replaced by Gabonese diocesan clergy with the coming of independence. Among the most noted Spiritans in the nineteenth century were the co-founders of the mission, Jean-Rémy Bessieux (q. v.) and Pierre-Marie Le Berre (q. v.); Alexandre Le Roy (q. v.), who with Le Berre organized the late nineteenth century expansion outside the Estuary; an amateur botanist, Théophile Klaine (q. v.); and an ethnologist, Henri Trilles (q. v.). In 1980 there were 50 French Spiritans in Gabon. [518, 528, 498, 525]

- I -

IBEA (or IBIYA), J. IKENGA (1834-1901). The Rev. Ibea J. Ikenga was a Benga (q. v.) from Corisco who became the first convert to Presbyterianism there. He was later ordained as the first African pastor in 1865. He practiced his ministry among the Benga on the island of Corisco and on the Gabon mainland opposite it. He is notable for his plans to free the African church from dependence on outside funding by the establishment of plantations and the acquisition of skilled trades among a people at that time involved mainly in fishing. He published Customs of the Benga and Neighbors. He died on February 28, 1901. [505, 500]

IMMACULATE CONCEPTION SISTERS (or BLUE SISTERS). The Sisters of Our Lady of the Immaculate Conception of Castres, France, have carried on educational and charitable work in Gabon since 1849. The congregation was founded by the aristocratic Emilie de Villeneuve (1811-1854) to educate poor and orphaned girls and to improve the condition of women. In response to an appeal from Monsignor Jean-Rémy Bessieux (q. v.) in 1847, the founder arranged with the Holy Ghost Fathers to send sisters to Senegal and Gabon to educate girls and to care for the sick. The first four sisters arrived near Libreville in July 1849. Among them was Sr. Constance Fontaine, who held the *agrégation* and who taught school among the Benga at Cape Esterias until her death in 1851. Among the best known of the sisters have been Mother Louis Raynaud (1818-1905) who headed the IC community at Libreville from 1849 to 1889; Sr. St. Charles Villeneuve (1834-1911) who operated an open-air dispensary that treated thousands of persons between 1860 and 1909; Mother Edouard Prat (1839-1927) who initiated educational work among Fang girls at Donguila in 1893 in order to prepare them for Christian marriage and who remained there until 1919; and Sr. Dorothée Fournié (1849-1920) who cared for the sick for forty years at Lambaréné. In 1980 fifty IC sisters were involved in education, health care, and social service in close cooperation with Gabonese Sisters of St. Mary. [511, 530]

INDIGENAT. The *indigénat* refers to the civil status of the native Africans as French colonial subjects between 1910 and 1946. The indigénat was a product of French colonial thinking in the wake of the large-scale territorial expansion of the late nineteenth and early twentieth centuries. The goal of assimilation was abandoned in favor of a policy of association under which only a tiny elite would be assimilated to French culture and a French life style. This group would serve the colonial regime as auxiliaries and intermediaries with the traditionally oriented masses. While individuals from the elite group might be admitted to the status of French citizen with the accompanying rights and legal protection, most of the elite would have the same status as the *sujets indigènes* (native subjects) or masses. The latter would retain much of their traditional culture and would be administered under a special system having its historical roots in colonial Algeria. It was more authoritarian and more restrictive than the system for citizens. Thus

African subjects did not possess the same rights of free expression, association, and movement as Europeans. They were required to provide unpaid labor for public purposes (prestation) and were liable to be conscripted for paid forced labor on projects of public utility as well as for portage. In Gabon all able-bodied persons over ten years of age had to pay an annual poll tax (impôt), the rate of which varied from region to region and which could sometimes be paid in produce or labor.

The indigénat gave to French administrators the right to impose penalties on subjects for violations which in some instances they themselves had previously defined without having to justify their actions before any judicial authorities. Thus heads of regions and districts could impose sentences of up to fifteen days' imprisonment and fines up to 100 francs without appeal. In dealing with offenders the administrators served at one and the same time as policeman, examining magistrate, public prosecutor, judge, and executor of the sentence. The system in effect gave administrators a wide rein to control their African subjects and to enforce the policies and decisions of the government and its officials.

Arbitrariness was perhaps even more widespread in cases involving the African common or customary law, which was unwritten and therefore open to all kinds of interpretations. The administrators, who generally did not know indigenous languages and customs, were dependent upon the knowledge and integrity of African notables in obtaining the information necessary to decide cases. Their ignorance and incompetence often gave these assistants the opportunity to influence decisions in directions that served neither justice nor those judged.

The indigénat was a constant source of friction between the French administration and the Gabonese. It was a major factor in the elite's quest for French citizenship in the interwar period, a status only a handful achieved. The indigénat was dismantled piecemeal by various metropolitan laws and decrees in 1945 and 1946. Its continuance was incompatible with the Lamine Guèye Law of May 7, 1946, making African subjects French citizens, a provision incorporated into the constitution of October 13, 1946. [103, 73]

INTERNATIONAL BOUNDARIES. The international boundaries of Gabon were established between 1885 and 1946. A Franco-German Treaty of December 12, 1885, and a convention of March 15, 1894, established the northern frontier with the Cameroons. After joint delimitation on the actual terrain, slight adjustments were made to fix the frontier along the courses of rivers, formalized in the convention of April 18, 1908. Portions of northern Gabon assigned to Germany under the convention of November 4, 1911, were returned to France in the Versailles treaty of 1919.

The Franco-Spanish convention of June 27, 1900, established the frontiers between Gabon and Spanish Guinea (Rio Muni). Small adjustments took place at the completion of delimitation in 1924.

The boundary between Gabon and the neighboring French territory of the Middle Congo was fixed in its present form by a decree of October 16, 1946, as part of a general reorganization of the territories of French Equatorial Africa. The Kwilou Region and the Divénié District of the Niari Region, which had formed parts of Gabon prior to 1918, were permanently placed in the Middle Congo. But the Haut-Ogooué Region, which had been part of the Middle Congo from 1925 to 1946, was returned to Gabon. The Haut-Ogooué is the site of Gabon's manganese (q. v.) and the home of its president since 1967, Omar Bongo (q. v.). [14, 212, 185]

IRON. The existence of iron deposits in many parts of Gabon, particularly the southwest, far north, and northeast, has been known for centuries. The peoples of these areas made iron tools and weapons, sometimes of a high quality. Prospecting during the colonial period revealed important deposits in three different provinces: the Ogooué-Ivindo (at Mékambo, Belinga, Boka-Boka, and Batoala); the Nyanga Province (at Tchibanga, its capital); and in the Woleu N'Tem Province (at Minkébé). The deposits at Mékambo have a very high quality (65 percent iron) and the reserves are estimated at a billion tons. Exploitation was assigned in the 1950s to a consortium in which the Bethlehem Steel Company of the United States had a 50 percent share and French and German companies most of the rest. In 1974 the Gabonese state acquired 60 percent of the firm, the Société des Mines de Fer de Mékambo (SOMIFER). Production will begin on a large scale as soon as rail and port facilities can be constructed. In 1978 the Trans-Gabonais Railroad opened as far as N'Djolé on the Ogooué and construction was proceeding towards Booué in the middle Ogooué. Preparations are now underway for the portion north-east to Mékambo. Port facilities for the ore are to be constructed at Cape Santa Clara, a few miles northwest of Libreville. [478]

ISLAM. There are only a few dozen indigenous Gabonese Muslims. Islam in Gabon is represented almost entirely by non-Gabonese Africans, especially Hausas, who are involved in trade and commerce. There are mosques at Libreville, Port-Gentil, and Lambaréné, which serve approximately 3,000 Muslims there and in the other commercial centers.

In 1973 President Albert-Bernard Bongo (q. v.) announced his conversion to Islam. He took the first name of Omar. Though the president emphasized the personal nature of his decision, he thereafter made official visits to a number of Arab countries, including Libya, and Gabon broke diplomatic relations with Israel. [488]

ISSEMBE, ARISTIDE (1910-). Civil servant and diplomat. Issembé was born at Libreville on December 20, 1910. His father, Jean-Rémy Issembé, a wealthy Mpongwe lumberman, sent him and his brother Emile (q. v.) to a lycée in Nice, France, where Aristide received his baccalauréat in 1932. The Issembé brothers and André-Gustave Anguilé (q. v.) were the only Gabonese to earn the bac during the inter-war period. Aristide Issembé spent four years studying law at the University of Paris where he was the only Equatorial African to belong to Leopold Sédar Senghor's Association des Etudiants Ouest-Africains. Though a French citizen, he was refused entrance to the Colonial School which trained the top-level overseas administrators. Upon his return to Gabon, he nevertheless was admitted to the European section of the federal civil service. He served in the financial branch at Bangui, Fort Lamy, and Ati (Chad) where he ran unsuccessfully for the Territorial Assembly. In 1949 he accepted an administrative assignment in Gabon. From 1957 to 1959 he served the first Gabonese executive, vice-president of the government council, as attaché de cabinet. In 1959-1960 he represented Gabon as the Secretary-General of the French Community and in 1961-1962 became his country's first ambassador to France. In August 1964 he served as government prosecutor at the Lambaréné trials of the military rebels and provisional government members. Since 1969 he has served in ambassadorial posts, most recently in Canada. [682]

ISSEMBE, EMILE. Son of the wealthy Mpongwe lumberman, Jean-Rémy Issembé, Emile Issembé studied at the Ecole Montfort (q. v.) and earned the baccalauréat at Nice in 1932 at the same time as his younger brother Aristide

(q. v.). He thereafter served, partly as a result of his French citizenship, in the European section of the federal civil service in Chad. During the Second World War he fought with the Free French forces, including for a time in Cameroon. He became widely known throughout Equatorial Africa for his newspaper articles condemning racial discrimination. Without returning to Gabon, he ran unsuccessfully for the French National Assembly in the territory in November 1945. Then in February 1946 he assumed an important position in the political affairs division of the administration at Libreville. He joined the Groupe d'Etudes Communistes (q. v.) and the Parti Démocratique Africain (q. v.), which was affiliated with the inter-territorial Rassemblement Démocratique Africain. He was the PDA's unsuccessful candidate for the National Assembly in November 1945 and November 1946. The following month he failed to win election to the Territorial Assembly as part of a list in the N'Gounié Province. In 1949 he became president of the administration's cultural center in the capital. Between 1951 and 1959 he served at his own request in the administration of Oubangui-Chari (CAR) and Chad. [335]

- J -

JAMES, BENJAMIN VAN RENSSALAER (1814-69). First printer in Gabon, 1844-46. James was an Afro-American printer from New York who served in the ABCFM mission at Cape Palmas from 1836 to 1844 and at Baraka from 1844 to 1846. He helped to print the first works in Mpongwe. Ill health forced James's departure from Gabon. He eventually settled in the Afro-American colony at Monrovia, Liberia, where he taught English. [517]

JEUNES GABONAIS (or JEUNESSE GABONAISE). The first Gabonese political party, which was founded around 1922, mainly by young educated Mpongwe and other Myènè at Libreville and Port-Gentil, to secure _évolué_ participation in the management of public affairs. It launched the newspaper _L'Echo Gabonais_ (1922-1932), which became _La Voix coloniale_ at Nice in 1932. The paper contained articles on all Africa as well as Gabon. Its criticisms of the decisions and practices of the colonial administration led to a crackdown by the latter in 1924 and its near extinction in 1926. The group and its local committees were also plagued by personal and ethnic antagonisms. Through its brief existence, it was closely allied with the Libreville branch of the Ligue des Droits de l'Homme, to which many of its members also belonged. The program of the Jeunes Gabonais was anti-colonialist but not anti-French. The group sought assimilation of the évolués and the rights that such a status carried. It wanted the creation of secondary education in Gabon, which would facilitate further integration. It rejected both Garveyism and communism. [335]

- K -

KANIGUI (or AKANIGUI or BAKANIKE). The Kanigui are an Mbédé-speaking people who have villages northwest of Franceville and east of the Ogooué. Pushed eastward from the Middle Congo by the Mbochi, they crossed the Sébé River, where they found the Shaké (q. v.), and then went on to their present locations after fighting with the Ambamba, a sub-group of the Obamba (q. v.) people. [189]

KLAINE, THEOPHILE (1840-1911). Spiritan priest who taught school at St. Mary's near Libreville from 1865 to 1911, during much of which time he had charge of the lower primary grades. He was an amateur botanist who identified and raised several dozen species of fruits and flowers in an experimental garden with the aid of his pupils. The famous species of light wood, okoumé (q. v.), was named Aucoumeia klaineana in his honor by a Parisian botanist. [518, 528]

- L -

LABOR UNIONS. It became legally possible for both European and African workers to join unions for the first time under the French law of August 7, 1944. The French organizational model was introduced into Gabon and French Equatorial Africa with local unions (syndicats) grouped by profession, trade, and industry into municipal, regional or territorial organizations (unions locales). These organizations then combined at the territorial, federal, and inter-African levels, depending upon the size of their membership, and established ties with both French and international labor confederations.

The formation of unions among both the European and African employees of the administration, commerce, transportation, and lumbering saw the divisions between Christian and Marxist elements in the French labor movement projected into the territory. Following the split within the Marxist ranks in 1947, there would be both Communist and Socialist unions in addition to Christian and independent ones in Gabon. These divisions weakened the effectiveness of the unions in securing greater benefits and improved working conditions for their members. So also did the failure of the French Parliament to enact an Overseas Labor Code to define the legal relationship between unions and employers and to establish minimum wages until 1952. In its absence the administration refused to bargain collectively with public employees and took sanctions against civil servants involved in strikes. The first collective agreements under the labor code were negotiated throughout the federation only in 1957. By then the overseas territories had headed along a path to self-government and independence that would lead to the restructuring of the unions at the national and inter-African levels. The presence of multiple unions with different inter-African and international ties would persist until April 1969. At that time the government abolished all existing unions and created a single national confederation that would later become a special organ of the single political party.

The first union in Gabon was organized with the encouragement of the missions on August 9, 1944, by Félix Adandé (a cousin of Prince Félix Adandé (q. v.)) among the Myènè employees of the administration to press for better salaries and working conditions. Called the Syndicat des Employés de Libreville, in 1946 it formed with other unions of a Christian orientation the Union Territoriale des Syndicats CFTC affiliated with the metropolitan Confédération Française des Travailleurs Chrétiens (CFTC). Concerned about the African direction of the organization and its militancy, the administration sponsored the formation of bi-racial unions affiliated with the French Marxist Confédération Générale du Travail (CGT). Among them by the end of 1945 were the Syndicat des Employés du Gouvernement of which Frédéric Moreau served as secretary and a union of private employees headed by Georges Damas (q. v.). The Union des Syndicats Confédérés (USC) included these unions and several others of CGT affiliation with Damas as secretary-general. Damas attended the first African conference of the CGT at Dakar in 1946. The CFTC and CGT unions joined forces in 1946-1947 in order to present a united front towards the administration through the Cartel des Syndicats with Paul Taty of the CGT, a civil servant, as secretary-general. When the administration refused to negotiate with the Cartel, its members launched a strike at Libreville and Port-Gentil in June 1947. The administration broke the strike by pressuring Taty to resign and by transferring other strike leaders to remote posts. The administration persuaded Félix Adandé's employer to transfer him to Port-Gentil. Also in 1947 the French CGT split, with its Communists retaining control of the organization and the Socialists forming the rival CGT-Force Ouvrière. In Gabon the CGT-FO was mainly an organization of European civil servants. The Africans in the CGT unions either remained with the older body or followed the USC into autonomy when in December 1948 Damas at the administration's request broke its CGT ties. When Frédéric Moreau decided to remain with the CGT, he was ousted from the civil service. Though the Overseas Labor Code legalized public employee membership in unions and collective bargaining, the Marxist unions never recovered from the administration's repression.

Throughout the period 1944 to 1969 the Christian unions remained the strongest in the country. They had 3,000 members in 1953 and 13,500 in 1965. They promoted the social doctrines of the Roman Catholic Church and had considerable mission sympathy but remained under African direction. Between 1946 and 1960 they held annual congresses and study sessions to educate their membership. With the coming of self-government the CFTC unions of the federation organized the Confédération Générale Aéfienne du Travail (CGAT) at Pointe-Noire, Congo, in 1957. The Union Territoriale des Syndicats CFTC thereafter was renamed Union Nationale des Syndicats Croyants (the "Croyants" in order to attract non-Christian believers) and in 1966 it became the Union Gabonaise des Syndicats Croyants (UGSC). Internationally these bodies affiliated with the International Federation of Christian Trade Unions. In 1964, after the French military restored President Mba (q.v.) to power, the Christian unions launched a general strike to protest Mba's manner of rule. Their action resulted in no political changes but led to higher minimum salaries. The Leaders of the UNSC between 1957 and 1966 were Auguste Walker-Anguilet, secretary-general, a member of the Economic and Social Council; Bernard Ntoutoume and A. Richard N'Zoghi, both employees of the Société Pétrolifière de l'Afrique Equatoriale; and Moise N'Dong, a teacher in the private schools. At the congress of 1966, when the UNSC became the UGSC, Moise N'Dong became secretary-general. The following year, N'Zoghi, who had served as *chef de cabinet* in Aubame's ministry in 1961-1963, went into voluntary exile in Europe.

With the coming of self-government, the CGT unions linked with the inter-African Confédération Générale Africaine du Travail (CGAT) between 1957 and 1962 and retained ties with the World Federation of Trade Unions. They were strongest at Libreville and Port-Gentil. In 1953 they had 1,700 members and in 1960 3,000. Their most important leaders were Augustin Anguilet and Leon Dicky. From 1961 on some of the CGAT leaders were in jail charged with civil offenses while others entered the BDG and abandoned syndicalist activities.

A third labor organization, the Confédération Nationale des Travailleurs Gabonais (CNTG) was created in 1962 and affiliated with the International Confederation of Free Trade Unions (founded in 1949 by Socialists opposing Communist domination of the World Federation of Trade Unions). Leaders of the CNTG were Laurent Essone, an employee of the CFAO, and Pierre N'Kogho, a public school teacher. Its influence extended throughout Gabon and was strongest at Libreville, Port-Gentil, and Franceville. It had 4,500 members in 1962 and 6,800 in 1969.

After the government organized a single political party, the PDG, to work for national unity and construction, in April 1969 it summoned delegates of the CATC, CGAT, and CNTG to form a single national labor federation, the Fédération Syndicale Gabonaise (FESYGA), which in 1973 became a special organ of the party. The FESYGA leaders have been required to pursue the interests of the workers within the guidelines set forth by the party. Beginning in 1973 the government became more directly involved in the negotiations between the FESYGA and the organization representing private employers, UNIGABON. At the same time, divisions in the FESYGA's leadership led to its greater involvement in the selection of the organization's executive bureau and officers. Wildcat strikes by dissatisfied workers at various times, including 1975-1976, suggested the difficulties of the leaders effectively to represent the membership in the present framework. Secretary-General of the FESYGA in the late 1970s was Gaston Indassy-Gnambault and president Goba Wora. [372, 350, 335]

LANGUAGES. The official language of Gabon and the medium of instruction is French. Prior to the Second World War only a tiny portion of the population received instruction in French but most persons employed in the market sector of the economy or by the administration learned to speak the language. In the period after the Second World War, France sought to achieve universal primary education in Africa. While a majority of young people were eventually enrolled, the average child remained only two or three years and thus did not learn French well. The 1960-61 census revealed that only 47 percent of those over fourteen years of age spoke French, 76 percent of the males and 26 percent of the females. Only 23 percent of the males and 5 percent of the females were literate in French, that is, 13 percent of the adult population. By the early 1970s as a result of intensified efforts, including adult education, an estimated 25 percent of those over fourteen were literate.

Since independence Gabon has nearly achieved universal primary education. At the same time several thousand persons, who have obtained secondary or higher education, have learned French very well. They form part of an international Francophone elite that can communicate with the educated classes in other formerly French African states.

The indigenous languages of Gabon are Bantu, thus part of the larger group that encompasses most of central and southern Africa. They were introduced into Gabon perhaps two thousand years ago and were further developed and differentiated there. The Bantu tongues were spoken but not written. Christian missionaries from the United States and France transcribed various languages such as Mpongwe, Dikèlè, Benga, and Fang using the Latin alphabet from the 1840s on. They translated the Bible and prepared mainly religious materials in them. French colonial policy discouraged or prevented the use of African languages for anything but religious purposes, especially from the 1880s. At the same time it promoted the study and use of the French language. Thus the Bantu languages have tended to remain mainly spoken languages transmitted in the family and not studied at school. Many Africans, especially in urban areas or in regions where many peoples are in contact, learn to communicate in several Bantu languages.

During the 1970s the government of Gabon sponsored research on indigenous languages within the Ministry of Education and at the National University. It is possible that some of these languages may eventually be used in primary instruction or studied at the primary and secondary levels. It is very unlikely that the government would seek to adopt one particular language as a national language as has been done elsewhere in Africa or Asia or that it would abandon instruction in French for its educated elite.

The 1960-61 census indicated the following distribution of Bantu languages for those fourteen years of age or older. It omitted the Bakouélé, who were classified for some reason as Apindji, Bakèlè or Bakota. (For the peoples within the groups, see PEOPLES.) [587, 589]

Group	Percentage
Omyènè	5.0
Séké	1.9
Eshira	22.0
Okandé	4.0
Bakèlè	2.0
Fang	31.0
Bakota	6.0
Mbédé	25.0
Téké	0.5
Vili	0.5

LAWLIN, CAPTAIN RICHARD E. (d. 1861). Lawlin was the leading American trader on the northern coasts from 1830 to 1861. He aided the ABCFM missionaries to locate in the Estuary in June 1842 and befriended them thereafter. But he undermined their work through the sale of rum. As the representative of various Yankee firms, he purchased ivory and rubber between the Rio Muni and Fernan Vaz. In 1854 Lawlin received the island Adjanga on which he established a factory called "Brooklyn" from the Nkomi chief, King Rotimbo, While purchasing rubber, he undertook extensive plantations to try to develop a greater taste for commercial agriculture among the Nkomi (q. v.). They regarded him as a benevolent father and made his burial place a kind of sacred site. [197, 251]

LE BERRE, PIERRE-MARIE (1819-1891). Co-founder of the French Roman Catholic mission and second bishop. Born at Neuillac, Britanny, in the Vannes diocese on August 1, 1819, Monsignor Le Berre evangelized in Gabon from

May 1846 until his death on July 16, 1891. He headed the Holy Ghost Fathers (q. v.) community near Libreville from 1859 and was named bishop in September 1877. Bishop Le Berre became an expert in the Mpongwe (q. v.) language. He prepared an excellent Mpongwe grammar and gave sermons in Mpongwe in St. Mary's Church. He initiated the second period of Catholic expansion by establishing missions among the Fang (q. v.) of the upper Estuary (1878), the Galoa (q. v.) and Fang around Lambaréné on the Ogooué (1881), and at several new points on the coasts and in the interior during the following decade. [498, 528]

LE COUR, CAPTAIN A. A French trader along the West African coast from 1823 and a member of the Chamber of Commerce of Nantes, Captain Le Cour attempted to grow cotton on lands of the Asiga clan of the Mpongwe (q. v.) under terms of the commercial treaty of April 4, 1844, between France and King Denis (q. v.). Denis was to provide the necessary labor. Experiments with varieties of wild cotton found in Gabon as well as with rubber, peanuts, sugar cane, and touloucouna were successful. But Le Cour failed to obtain expected subsidies from the French government and Denis not only failed to provide labor but discouraged his people from working for the captain. Le Cour with the help of Captain J.-B. Amouroux obtained a commercial treaty with Chief Quaben or Kaka-Rapono (q. v.) in March 1846 securing land near Fort d'Aumale. He encountered some success raising coffee there but mismanagement by his local French agents caused the failure of this attempt as well. [170]

LE ROY, ALEXANDRE (1854-1938). Spiritan priest who as vicar apostolic of Gabon from 1892 to 1896 insisted upon teaching the Gabonese children to read the catechism in their own language before teaching them French, which went counter to the official government policy of the day. Le Roy continued the Catholic advance into the interior by founding several new stations and by developing the work of the catechists who resided in the villages. While superior-general of the Holy Ghost Fathers, he wrote influential works on the pygmies and primitives as well as the sections on Gabon and the Congo in Piolet's history of the missions (1902). [635, 525]

LIBREVILLE. The capital of Gabon, located on the northern

shore of the Estuary, had a population in 1970-1971 of 167,394 compared to 44,598 in 1960-1961. These totals include several thousand Europeans, mostly French. This population growth has occurred since independence, for in the mid-1950s the city had a population of only 18,000 of whom 1,500 were Europeans.

Libreville (which means free town or city in French) takes it name from the settlement organized by the French navy in August 1849 for fifty freed adult slaves and two children of Vili (q. v.) origin from the Congo who had been rescued several years before from the slaving ship Elizia. The slaves had been taken in May 1846 to Gorée, Senegal. In Gabon they were given plots of land and huts between the lands of the Mpongwe (q. v.) clans, the Agekaza-Glass and Agekaza-Quaben. The French post, which was moved in 1850 to higher ground nearby (the so-called Plateau), the residence of the Sisters of the Immaculate Conception (q. v.), and St. Peter's Church also came to be known under the name Libreville, and ultimately the name was applied to all the settlements on the right bank of the Estuary above Owendo. Libreville at first served as the capital of the French Congo until it was moved to Brazzaville in 1904. Libreville remained the administrative capital of Gabon and an important commercial center, the roles it still plays today. [473, 168, 195, 425, 440, 468]

LIGUE DES DROITS DE L'HOMME, LIBREVILLE BRANCH. Civil servants from Guadeloupe and Martinique were instrumental in founding branches of a French civil liberties organization, the League of Human Rights, in various African colonies, including Gabon, in 1918. The presidency was vested in an educated Séké, Jean-Baptiste N'Dendé (q. v.), and most of its members were young educated Mpongwe (q. v.). Among the most active members were Mpongwe who had served as non-commissioned officers at Libreville or in the French campaigns against the Germans in northern Gabon and Cameroon, 1914-1916. Among them were Louis Bigmann (q. v.) and his cousin Laurent Antchouey (q. v.). Antchouey articulated Ligue issues in the monthly paper l'Echo Gabonais from Dakar and Nice, France, between 1922 and 1926. The most important figure in the Ligue between 1926 and 1930 was François-de-Paul Vané (q. v.), a Benga whose family was long settled in Libreville. In 1930 the Ligue presidency was transferred through trickery to a Frenchman who put an end to its anti-colonialist agitation. Among the issues in which the Libreville branch was active were: an appeal for the return of the Brothers of Saint Gabriel (q. v.), who had provided the highest level and quality of education before their departure in 1918 (they returned in 1924); demand for autonomy of Gabon within the federation of French Equatorial Africa (q. v.) in view of the situation where taxes on okoumé were being used to support the other territories instead of to develop Gabon; defense of traditional land rights in the courts in face of administrative encroachment and failure to provide just compensation (the decree of March 28, 1899, establishing the concessionary system had denied the existence of African property rights and had given the administration the power to control all land); demand for the end of the indigénat (q. v.), which had been extended to Gabon in 1910.

Among the early members of the Ligue were Antoine M'Ba, Ignace Békalé, N'Tutume Ossame, Maurice N'Gôme Obiang, Victor Obame Otsague, Paulin N'Dinga, Martin Tambané, Jean-Remy Issembé, and Léon Mba (q. v.). After 1930 the former Ligue members split between métis (q. v.) and full-blooded Africans in their pursuit of elite interests throughout separate organizations. [335]

LOANGO. A centralized kingdom of the Vili (q. v.) people dating from the late fourteenth or early fifteenth centuries. Its core was located in the coastal areas of today's Congo Republic but its sway extended south into the Cabinda enclave (today part of Angola) and north into present-day Gabon. Loango's sway encompassed the Ngowe (q. v.) people at Lake Iguéla, the Loumbou (q. v.) at Setté-Cama and around Mayumba, as well as some Vili along the Banio Lagoon. Though Loango's political control of the Gabon coast was only nominal, trading networks centered at Loango Bay persisted into the twentieth century. Under French colonial rule economic activity on the Loango coast was transferred to Pointe-Noire where a modern harbor was built. Pointe-Noire became the terminus of the Congo-Ocean Railroad, completed in 1934, and the point for the penetration of French Equatorial Africa. [214, 247, 147, 291]

LOUIS, KING or ANGUILE DOWE or RE-DOWE (ca. 1800-1867). Louis, the Mpongwe village headman of the Agekaza-Quaben or Agekaza w'Anwondo clan, through the treaty of March 18, 1842, ceded sovereignty over his territories on the northern shore of the Estuary to the

French. He also gave them the lands on which they built their post, Fort d'Aumale, in June 1843, and the Holy Ghost Fathers (q. v.) constructed St. Mary's Church and other buildings at the village of Okolo. Louis was the nephew of King Quaben or Kaka-Rapono (q. v.) (d. 1863), head of the clan. Though a relatively weak underling of King Quaben before 1842, Louis's openness to France increased his influence immensely in the next two decades. He served on the French commission for arbitrating trade disputes. It was composed of two African traders and a French merchant who served as its president. [170, 251, 232, 172]

LOUIS BERRE MONGUITIGANA, PRINCE (1906-ca. 1974). Prince Louis Berre was a direct descendant of King Louis Dowe (q. v.) who made the treaty of 1842 with the French which gave them the land on which they built their first fort. Louis Berre worked as an artisan. During the 1930s he became active in the movements to assert traditional Mpongwe rights, including to lands in the Estuary. With the support of the Comité Mpongwe (q. v.) he was named chef de groupe de quartier of the Louis section of Libreville and later sat on the governor's administrative council. In August 1958 he became active in the Parti d'Union Nationale Gabonaise (PUNGA) (q. v.), which advocated a negative vote in the referendum of September 1958 on membership in the French Community. At that time he asked for strict application of the treaties which the Mpongwe had made with the French between 1939 and 1848. He was subsequently removed from his chiefship by the government. [335, 371, 364]

LOUMBOU or BALOUMBOU. A people of the southwest (Nyanga Province) whose territories were under the sway of the Vili kingdom of Loango (q. v.) through the nineteenth century. According to tradition the Lombou came from Mongo near present-day Pointe-Noire in the Congo Republic via the savanna (grasslands) many centuries ago. They settled as far north as the marshy coastal areas of the Ndugu Lagoon (Setté-Cama); in the coastal savannas from Banio Lagoon north to a point beyond the Nyanga River; inland in the forested Mayombe mountain chain (300-600 meters above sea-level), and in the savannas beyond this range, south of the Nyanga. The coastal Loumbou evaporated seawater to obtain salt for trade with the interior. The coming of the Europeans in the 1480s saw the inhabitants of Setté-Cama selling ivory and beeswax and those of Mayumba ivory and a redwood that was much sought after by both Europeans and Africans for its valuable red dye. In the sixteenth and seventeenth centuries Setté-Cama and Mayumba sent the small numbers of slaves they obtained from interior peoples to Loango. Neither place became very important in the greatly expanded slave trade centered on Loango during the eighteenth century.

The Loango kingdom, whose core lay north of the Congo River, held sway over the Gabon coast as far north as Cape St. Catherine. The various clans of the Loumbou apparently acknowledged the nominal overlordship of its Vili (q. v.) rulers and until the late eighteenth century paid them tribute. The Loumbou themselves had only territorial chiefs, called "kings" by European traders, whose main function was to settle disputes among the clans. According to tradition, during the 1760s a Vili princess called Nsoami fled from her home at Loango and established an independent kingdom among the Vili and Loumbou at Mayumba, until that time a northern province of Loango. Despite its origins, the kingdom in the late nineteenth century seems to have had a Loumbou king called Mayombo Ignondrou. His authority extended over the areas of Setté-Cama, the Mayombe mountains, and Mayumba, which had a population of one thousand at that time, a good-sized town.

Between the 1840s and 1870s Anglo-French suppression of the slave trade in the Gabon Estuary and around Cape Lopez helped to make the Mayumba area the scene of increased slave trading under the auspices of Portuguese, Spanish, and Brazilian merchants. But by 1873 rubber had become the most important export from Mayumba, an activity from which both Loumbou and Vili traders profited. [189, 214, 247]

- M -

MADEMOISELLE. Mademoiselle is an anti-witchcraft movement which apparently was introduced into several regions of Gabon from the Middle Congo in the 1940s and acquired some importance in the 1950s. It achieved its greatest following among the Fang in the Woleu N'Tem Province but encountered strong opposition from the colonial administration and the missions. Mademoiselle, like Bwiti, can be viewed as an attempt by Gabonese to deal with the rapidly changing conditions resulting from a deterioration of traditional ethnic structures and the acculturation resulting from colonial rule. [381]

MAHONGWE. The Mahongwé people belong to the Bakota linguistic group. They inhabit the southern part of the Mékambo Prefecture, Ogooué-Ivindo Province. The Mahongwé originally occupied the junction of the Ivindo and the Mouniangui Rivers. Poupou's War in the nineteenth century caused them to flee to the northeast, some towards Okondja, others towards the Louaï and Liboumba Rivers. [235, 189]

MAKOUAKA, FELICIEN-PATRICE (1922-). Monsignor Makouaka is the first Catholic bishop of the new diocese of Franceville, which was created on October 5, 1974. He was born in 1922 at Ngomo-Boulongo in the diocese of Mouila and was ordained a priest on October 10, 1954. [488]

MANGANESE. Exploitation of manganese began in 1962 around Moanda in the Haut-Ogooué Province under the auspices of the Compagnie Minière de l'Ogooué (COMILOG). United States Steel originally owned 49 percent of the company and French interests the rest. In 1974 the Gabonese state acquired a share. Since the 1960s Gabon has been the fourth largest producer of manganese in the world. The reserves would last for 150 years at the present rate of production. Expansion is currently hindered by limited transportation. The ore is presently evacuated via an aerial cable line (téléférique) that carries buckets of the metal. It was constructed for this purpose over a distance of 76 km. to M'Binda in the Congo Republic. At M'Binda the Congo-Ocean Railroad carries the ore 85 km. farther west to its Atlantic terminus at Pointe-Noire. These arrangements, which were planned when Gabon was part of the federation of French Equatorial Africa, have made its government dependent upon the People's Republic of the Congo. Thus for the moment production remains something over two million tons annually. Plans for the extension of the Trans-Gabonais Railroad from Booué south-east to Moanda would permit at least a 25 percent increase as well as putting transportation entirely under Gabonese control. The ore is exported chiefly to the United States, France, West Germany, and Japan. [478, 437]

MAPAKO-GNALI, HERVE. Ponty School graduate and teacher.

Mapako-Gnali belonged to a Vili (q. v.) family from Diosso on the Loango coast, some of whom were settled at Libreville in the period when their homeland formed part of Gabon. As one of the two most promising graduates of the public school in 1914, he was sent, along with Jean-Félix Tchicaya (q. v.), on government scholarship to the William Ponty School at Dakar to prepare to be an upper-primary teacher. At Ponty he was in the same class as Félix Houphouet-Boigny and Mambo Sano, and one year behind Mamadou Konaté, all future deputies in the French National Assembly. Mapako-Gnali in 1921 on his return to Libreville was appointed to the teaching staff of the public primary school. [335]

MASSANGO (or SANGOU). The Massango people who are linguistically related to the Eshira (q. v.), inhabit a forested mountainous area of the south-central interior between the Ogoulou and Offoué Rivers. Their traditions assert a common origin with the Eshira. While the Eshira migrated towards the coast, they stayed in the interior but later transferred a bit westward to seek warmer temperatures. In the nineteenth century the Bakèlè (q. v.) made war upon them. The Massango exchanged slaves, palm cloth, iron utensils and weapons for salt from the Bapounou.

In September 1917 a Massango called Mabiale Mabioko died in a French prison, having been jailed for what the administration judged to be the slave trade. This sparked a revolt by men who considered themselves protected from the French guns by a supernatural power. The Massango leaders organized thirty-six villages to fight the French and gained support among the Mitsogo (q. v.), Bakèlè, and smaller groups. The French were able to suppress the revolt only in 1918-1919 after the death of its main leader, Mayambo. [189, 134]

MBA, GERMAIN (1932-). Diplomat. Mba was born at Libreville on December 15, 1932. He graduated from the Institut d'Etudes Politiques of the University of Paris and the Ecole Nationale des Douanes et de Législation Financière de Paris at Neuilly. Between 1962 and 1964 he served as Assistant Secretary-General of the Union Africaine et Malgache at Cotonou, Benin. He resigned this position in protest against the de Gaulle government's intervention to restore Léon Mba (q. v.) to power in February 1964. He went to Brazzaville where he helped to organize an opposition movement, first called the Mouvement Gabonais d'Action Populaire and then converted into the Mouvement de Libération Nationale du Gabon. Along with Mba-Ndong he protested the amendment of the constitution creating the post of Vice-President of the Republic in November 1966. But after the death of Léon Mba he rallied to the regime and in September 1968 was named economic and commercial counsellor to President Bongo. Between 1969 and 1971 he held a number of diplomatic posts in Europe. During a visit to Libreville he was kidnapped and probably murdered by unidentified assailants believed to be Frenchmen. His body has never been found. [682, 372]

MBA, LEON (1902-1967). Fang (q. v.) leader, first prime minister and first president of the republic (1961-67). Mba was born at Libreville on February 9, 1902, the son of a Fang village chief. His older brother, the Abbé Jean Obame, was the first Fang to be ordained a Roman Catholic priest. The numerous Fang immigrant population of the Estuary were both held in low esteem and feared by the native Mpongwe (q. v.) and by the colonial administration in this period. At the same time they were being actively evangelized by both Catholic and Protestant missions. Léon Mba was educated in Catholic primary schools, including the Ecole Montfort (q. v.) at Libreville. Thereafter he entered the service of the colonial administration in various humble positions, including interpreter.

In the early 1920s Mba became active in the Libreville branch of the Ligue des Droits de l'Homme. He joined the Jeunes Gabonais or Jeunesse Gabonaise (q. v.) and contributed articles to its newspaper, L'Echo Gabonais. He showed determination to improve both the status of the évolués and the Fang in relation to the Myènè (q. v.) populations with whom they frequently were disputing land rights. Mba often wrote letters for illiterate Fang who wished to protest against various administrative practices or to make requests and thereby incurred the suspicion of the administration.

In 1922 he was condemned for an offense on apparently slim evidence and fined. In December of the same year he was imprisoned arbitrarily under the indigénat (q. v.) for fifteen days, where someone reportedly tried to poison him. But Governor-General Victor Augagneur attributed his troubles to the dislike of the governor of Gabon and came to his defense in 1922.

In the meantime Mba was becoming a specialist in

Fang customary law and was frequently being called to adjudicate disputes and to give expert advice in proceedings before the customary tribunal. In 1924 the administration named Mba the Fang canton chief (chef de canton) at Libreville instead of Ndongo-Edzo, the son of his predecessor. But he thereafter became unpopular with elements of the administration for denouncing, in the name of the Ligue, the murder of a Gabonese by the French administrator heading the post at Akok. Mba's rigorous execution of the administration's orders made him unpopular with some of the Fang, who held him responsible for recruiting forced labor. Mba reportedly joined the Free Masons with the aid of administrators from the Antilles working in Gabon. He also encouraged the spread of Bwiti as a means of revitalizing shattered Fang society and of gaining increased authority among the Fang. He thus incurred the hostility of the mission authorities. In 1931 Mba was charged with having a role in the ritual murder of two young Fang women and the sale of their flesh in the Libreville market, human flesh being required in certain Bwiti (q. v.) ceremonies. His conviction in 1933 resulted at least as much from the hostility of the various groups he had antagonized, some of whom may have given false testimony against him, as from the evidence presented by the prosecution.

Mba was sentenced to three years in prison, spent at Birao in the Oubangui-Chari, and ten years at Bambari in the same colony, where he remained until 1946. There he became the trusted financial agent of the administration and in August 1940 rallied to Free France. He wrote an authoritative study on Fang customs. Upon his return to Libreville in 1946 he worked for the John Holt Company and later for SEPEMIAG. Though not a Communist, he joined the local Groupe d'Etudes Communistes (q. v.), an agency for political education that was both anti-colonialist and comparatively radical. The candidate which the GEC supported in the November 1946 elections for the French National Assembly was defeated by Jean-Hilaire Aubame (q. v.), a young Fang évolué who had been the protégé of Mba's priest brother and whom Mba had aided in securing employment in the colonial administration. Aubame had the support of the administration and missions as well as the northern Fang and non-Fang notables throughout the interior regions. Aubame thereafter organized the Union Démocratique et Sociale Gabonaise (q. v.) for purposes of presenting candidates for the Territorial Assembly. In early 1947

Mba and other Estuary Fang, most of whom belonged to the GEC, had formed the Comité Mixte Gabonais (q. v.), a more militant and radical anti-colonialist party, which affiliated with the inter-territorial Rassemblement Démocratique Africain. The RDA in this period was Communist-advised and linked in the French Parliament with the French Communist Party, which until March 1947 had ministers in the government. The colonial administration severely weakened the Comité Mixte Gabonais by transferring most of its members, who were civil servants, to distant points in the interior. In the meantime at the Pahouin or Fang Congress, which the administration organized at Mitzic in February 1947 to discuss Fang problems, Mba played an important role. Though the Congress was largely composed of officially-appointed chiefs and local Assembly members, Mba convinced them to take some positions at odds with official wishes. He emerged from the Congress as a progressive, authoritative leader with influence among both traditionalist and modernist elements. In 1951 he went along with the RDA majority in its break with French Communism and thereafter moderated his militant stances. He rebaptized his Comité Mixte Gabonais as the Comité Mixte Franco-Gabonais to point out that his orientation was not anti-French. He failed, however, in his bid to replace Aubame as deputy in the French National Assembly during the elections of June 1951. Later in 1951 Mba joined forces with Senator Paul Gondjout (q. v.), a Myènè in the Territorial Assembly, and various southerners to oppose Aubame and his party (the UDSG), which they accused of representing only the interests of the northern Fang. Mba, Gondjout, and Aubame all won seats in the Territorial Assembly in the elections of March 1952. In 1954 Gondjout organized a new party, the Bloc Démocratique Gabonais (q. v.), to which Mba later adhered and of which he became the secretary.

The BDG, which was avowedly anti-tribalist, failed to prevent Aubame's re-election to the National Assembly in January 1956 in which he again defeated Mba. But it helped to secure the election of Mba as mayor of Libreville in November 1956 following a reform which increased the powers of the elected representatives. The mayor's position enabled Mba to place his allies and supporters in key positions in the city government.

In the wake of the Loi-Cadre of June 23, 1956, Gabon acquired a Territorial Assembly with some real legislative powers and a Government Council in which Africans held executive posts for the first time. While the elections of March 1957 gave the UDSG a majority of the popular votes, it gave the BDG and Independents a majority of seats in the Territorial Assembly. It enabled them to name Mba as the Vice-President of the twelve-member Government Council (the Governor was the President). Later in July 1958 Mba replaced the governor as president of the council. The BDG's control of eight out of the twelve ministries presented the opportunity for placing its supporters throughout the administration. Prior to the 1957 elections important French lumbering firms had shifted their support from the UDSG to the BDG whose attitudes about their interests seemed to be more advantageous.

In the aftermath of the May 1958 revolution in Algiers, which led to the demise of the Fourth Republic and the return to power of de Gaulle, both the UDSG and the BDG supported Gabon's membership in the general's Community in the referendum of September 1958. Both parties also favored the establishment of a republic within the Community in November of that year. Thus Mba became the first prime minister under the new constitution of February 19, 1959, leading a government that contained ministers of both parties. During the eighteen months of the operation of that constitution, friction developed between the executive and the legislative, with Gondjout and a majority of both the BDG and the UDSG supporting a strong parliament and a weak executive. Mba and his ministers were forced to accept an essentially parliamentary constitution for the independent republic on November 3, 1960. But ultimately these arrangements proved unworkable and after further conflicts, in which Mba utilized emergency powers against the Gondjout faction and ordered new Assembly elections, he secured the new constitution of February 17, 1961, establishing a strong presidency.

For the next two years Mba pursued a policy of national unity aimed at bringing all elements into cooperation with the government. Aubame and Gondjout and their followers were brought into the government or given responsible positions in the civil service. René-Paul Sousatte (q. v.), who in 1958 had organized a third party to oppose the Community, was awarded a ministerial post. Early in 1963 Mba sought to institute a single party regime by forcing all of these elements to join the BDG and to accept his dominant role in that party and in the government. His actions provoked resistance and in their turn repression and new conflicts, which culminated in the coup of February 17-20, 1964 (q. v.). The coup, which toppled Mba, led to French intervention to restore him. Mba's determination to punish those opponents whom he held responsible, rightly or wrongly, even in the face of much popular discontent, led to an increasingly authoritarian regime, the violation of civil liberties, and ultimately to the end of the democratic experiment in Gabon. Holding close to absolute power and backed by French forces, a terminally ill Mba chose a talented and loyal young administrator, Albert-Bernard Bongo (q. v.), to be his successor. In November 1966 he replaced Vice-President Paul-Marie Yembit (q. v.) with Bongo and then advanced the date of the presidential elections to March 1967 so that Bongo was elected as vice-president and successor at the time of his own re-election as president. During the last year of his life, Mba remained in Paris for medical treatment and died there on November 27, 1967. See COUP OF FEBRUARY 17-20, 1964; DECOLONIZATION; FOREIGN RELATIONS; POLITICS. [335, 336, 381, 347, 364, 382]

MEBIAME, LEON (1934-). Prime Minister. Mébiame was born at Libreville on September 1, 1934. He studied at the Ecole Montfort (q. v.) and Collège Moderne there. He later graduated from the Centre de Préparation aux Carrières Administratives and the Ecole Fédérale de Police at Brazzaville. He has been a civil servant since 1959. He was named to the cabinet in January 1967 and became prime minister on November 12, 1975. He served as mayor of Libreville from 1969 to 1975. [682, 642]

MEDIA. Since 1977 Gabon has had a private daily newspaper, L'Union, published at Libreville by Sonapresse. The official Agence Gabonaise de Presse (AGP) publishes the daily Gabon Matin. Other newspapers, mainly in French, from France and neighboring countries, also circulate throughout the country. Representatives of the Agence France Presse (AFP) and Reuters of London are based in Libreville to send news out of the country.

Radio Télévision Gabonaise (RTG), the official agency, operates radio and television stations in Libreville, Port-Gentil, and Franceville, and a radio station in Oyem, as well as smaller radio stations in the other provinces. Gabon has had black and white television since the late 1960s and color since 1975. A second network in color was inaugurated in August 1977. The television employs French exclusively. There are only a few local programs, mainly news. France provides several hours of programs daily, of which over half are films made in the United States. A majority of the radio programs are in French, but the various stations also employ local languages. [710]

METIS. Persons of mixed race, mainly French-Mpongwe. The presence after the mid-nineteenth century of scores of European traders, administrators, and military men, who were either unmarried or without their wives, gave rise to concubinage with Gabonese women and frequently to marriage according to local customs (_mariage à la mode du pays_). The women, in the case of the traders, were often the sisters, daughters or slaves of trading partners or chiefs. These unions led to the creation of a class of mixed race, generally called _métis_ in French, _mestiço_ in Portuguese, and mulatto in English. In the latter part of the nineteenth century, the British trader and explorer R. B. N. Walker (1830-1900), fathered at least a dozen children by Mpongwe wives, the most prominent of his offspring being the Rev. André Raponda Walker (1871-1968) (q. v.). Others among R. B. N.'s descendants have played important roles in the economic and political life of the country. Like Walker, many French fathers recognized and continued to support their métis offspring. They sought preferment for them in education and employment so that by the 1920s the several hundred métis in the Estuary formed an important part of the educated elite and the civil service. Socially they were closely linked to the Mpongwe (q. v.). In late 1933 educated métis at Libreville founded the Association Amicale des Métis mainly to aid the growing number of métis orphans who had been abandoned by their fathers and rejected by the families of their mothers. Under the leadership of Joseph-Gaston Walker-Deemin, one of the few successful non-European lumbermen, the Association gained a subsidy and an _okoumé_ (q. v.) concession from the administration for this purpose.

Given the interest which Governor-General François-Joseph Reste (1935-1939) showed in their problems, the Association thereafter petitioned for privileges for the métis in French Equatorial Africa (q. v.) similar to those already held by métis in other French colonies, including easy access to French citizenship. On September 15, 1936, Governor-General Reste decreed a special métis status, which allowed four hundred of them to acquire French citizenship in the following years. In keeping with the special status, the Association won admission for métis to the previously all-European school at Libreville which taught the metropolitan programs necessary for secondary and higher education and, in turn, entrance to the European cadres of the civil service. The group secured creation of a special orphanage (internat) for métis children near the school where those aged five to seventeen received maintenance and a free education. The group also petitioned for special privileges in the civil service, military service, allotments of lands, and okoumé-cutting permits. In 1938 the Association became the Libreville branch of the Amicale des Métis de l'AEF with other branches at Pointe-Noire, Brazzaville, and Bangui. In 1943 the administration built the Cercle des Métis in the Glass section of Libreville with a library and meeting-room.

In the meantime the activities of the Association provoked the formation of the rival Mutuelle Gabonaise (q. v.) in October 1934 by leading Mpongwe, Benga, and Séké, as well as a few métis opposed to the special status. Métis activities also created bitter resentment among the Fang of Libreville, who were excluded from events at the Cercle des Métis until after independence at a time when Myènè were welcomed there. [473, 335]

MEYE, FRANCOIS (1922-1970). Teacher, author, and politician. Meye was born on February 22, 1922, near Oyem in the Woleu-N'Tem Province. He received his early education at Samkita in the N'Djolé Prefecture where his father served as a teacher and preacher for the French Protestant mission. From 1933 to 1940 Meye attended the Ecole des Cadres Supérieurs in Brazzaville to prepare for a career in primary teaching. He thereafter served as a teacher and school administrator in the Middle Congo and Gabon. In 1947 he joined the Comité Mixte Gabonais (q. v.) and contributed articles to the RDA newspaper, AEF Nouvelle, at Brazzaville. He later belonged to the Bloc Démocratique Gabonais (q. v.) but was elected to the Legislative Assembly in March 1957 from N'Djolé under the banner of the Défense des Intérêts Gabonais, which thereafter allied with the Union Démocratique et Sociale Gabonaise (q. v.). He was re-elected to the National Assembly in 1961 and during the period 1959-64 held ministerials posts. In 1965 and after he served in the education and information ministries where he gathered documentation for the history of Gabon. His autobiography, Souvenirs de Saison Sèche, contains valuable material on his career in education, politics, and lay leadership of the Evangelical Church. [580, 335, 569]

MIGOLET, JEAN-STANISLAS (1920-). Politician. Migolet was born at Koula-Moutou in the Ogooué-Lolo Province on August 1, 1920, and was educated at Catholic mission schools. He entered the colonial administration in 1941. In 1947 he was elected to the Territorial Assembly and later to the National Assembly in which he continued to serve until 1975. Migolet was a member of the first Gabonese executive from March 1957 and continued to hold various ministerial and BDG (q. v.) party posts under Presidents Mba (q. v.) and Bongo (q. v.). He represented Gabon in the Senate of the French Community from 1959 to 1961. In November 1975 he became Vice Prime-Minister, a position which he held until dropped from the cabinet in late February 1980. [682, 642]

MITSOGO (or MITSHOGO or TSHOGO). The Mitsogo belong to the Okandé linguistic group. Their traditions indicate a migration from the Ivindo River southwestward into the mountainous areas between the Offoué and N'Gounié Rivers as a result of wars and slave raids by the Bakèlè. When the explorer Paul de Chaillu (q. v.) visited them in 1857 they numbered several thousand and were occupying a strip of mountainous territory 150 miles long northeast to southeast and parallel to the N'Gounié. They were skilled cloth weavers and iron workers. They sold slaves to the Bapounou (q. v.) and Eshira (q. v.) for salt and European merchandise. As late as 1899 the Bakèlè (q. v.) were still attacking Mitsogo settlements and taking away women as slaves. With the establishment of the French administrative post at Sindara in 1899 and of the Catholic mission not far away, the Mitsogo came under regular European influences. In December 1904 some Mitsogo rose against the exactions of the Compagnie de la Haute-Ngounié, a concessionary company to which the French had given exploitation of the region, and killed two of its most abusive European agents. French forces suppressed the revolt and the following year instituted a tax on all able-bodied persons over ten years of age. Gold was discovered in the Mitsogo areas in 1937-38. [189, 200, 287, 317]

MPONGWE. Oldest known people to inhabit the Estuary, including the area on the northern shore that is today Libreville. Recent linguistic studies of the Bantu expansion have placed Myènè speakers (the group to which Mpongwe belongs) in the region encompassing Libreville, Port-Gentil, and Lambaréné as long as two thousand years ago. But it is likely that Mpongwe clans began arriving or coalescing on the shores and islands of the Estuary only in the sixteenth century, quite possibly in response to the new trading opportunities offered by the coming of the Europeans. This process seems to have continued into the late seventeenth and even the early eighteenth centuries. While the Mpongwe continued to fish, hunt, and farm, they gradually became the middlemen traders between the Europeans and peoples farther inland such as the Bakèlè (q. v.) and Séké (q. v.). During the last third of the eighteenth century the Mpongwe clans of the southern shore, in particular, became increasingly involved in the slave trade; these trading networks extended overland into the Ogooué and Congo river systems and south along the Atlantic coast to Cape Lopez. In the 1830s the Mpongwe traders were transmitting slaves, dyewood, redwood, ebony, ivory, rubber, beeswax, and gum copal to European merchants in exchange for cloth strips, iron bars, firearms, powder, knives, rum and other strong alcoholic beverages.

On the eve of the arrival of American Protestant missionaries (June 1842) and the establishment of a French naval post (June 1843), the Mpongwe communities contained 6-7,000 freemen and 6000 domestic slaves Four clans (a clan was formed by several patrilineages) among the two dozen identifiable clans had risen to prominence as a result of their leadership in trade, which was based in part on their geographical location. These were the Asiga and Agulamba clans on the southern shore and the Agekaza-Glass and Agekaza-Quaben clans on the northern shore of the Estuary. The Asiga, situated on the Atlantic peninsula called Point Pongara, and the Agulamba, found farther east along the Remboué River, dominated the slave trade. The two Agekaza clans, located between Owendo and Point Santa Clara, were involved in non-human commodities as well as slaves. Though by the 1840s the Mpongwe clans possessed a common language and culture, they regarded one another as rivals, especially in trade. Each clan was presided over by a head (oga) called a king by the European traders, but was ruled by an oligarchy of clan patriarchs that included lineage heads and the leading traders.

Weak government, inter-clan rivalries, and the absence of central political institutions hindered Mpongwe resistance to French pressures for treaties ceding sovereignty and land for installations between 1839 and 1844. The strongest resistance to French penetration was offered by King Denis or Antchouwé King Rapontchombo (q. v.) of the Asiga clan, who by diplomacy prevented the French from establishing a post on his territory, and by King Glass or R'Ogouarowé (q. v.) of the Agekaza-Glass clan, who submitted in 1845 only as a result of a French bombardment to enforce a treaty that was probably obtained by deception. The French incorrectly attributed much of Glass's resistance to the activities of the American missionaries who had been headquartered in his territories since June 1842. As a result of British and some American trade, Glass Town continued to grow in size and prestige after 1845 and remained the most important village in the Estuary in the mid- and late-nineteenth-century.

In contrast to Denis and Glass, King Louis or Anguilé-Dowe (q. v.), a village headman of the Agekaza-Quaben clan, in 1842 freely ceded his village of Okolo to the French and established a new one. Okolo became the site of the French naval station, Fort d'Aumale, in June 1843 and the French Catholic mission in September 1844.

Under British pressure the French intermittently sought to suppress the slave trade in the Estuary from which the Mpongwe had so greatly profited. It was largely eliminated there by the 1860s. By that time the French were using their authority to protect European trading houses in their quest for direct contact with the interior peoples, thus eliminating the middleman role of the Mpongwe traders. In the same period mission education was providing young Mpongwe with literacy skills, thus equipping them to play new roles as the employees and agents of the companies and administration under the expanding colonial regime. From the Mpongwe people would come as well the first Gabonese schoolteachers and Christian clergy.

During the period 1845-1870 the Mpongwe declined in numbers by a third to a half as a result of smallpox epidemics and a diminishing birthrate. In 1884 the total Mpongwe population was estimated at only 3000. This decline, accompanied by their diminished status and the pressures of Fang (q. v.) migration, promoted a regrouping of the remaining Mpongwe around Libreville, particularly at Glass Town. Their ownership of much of the land of the capital, their long experience in commerce, and their continued benefits from western education enabled them to occupy a place in twentieth-century Gabonese life well out of proportion to their dwindling numbers. During the 1920s and 1930s educated Mpongwe organized to defend their traditional land rights against both French and Fang encroachments, to secure a larger role in the management of public affairs, and to gain access to quality education. At independence in 1960 1200 of the estimated 1800 Mpongwe inhabited the Libreville area, where their members continued to play important roles in the civil service, the professions, education, religion, and business. Prince Félix Adandé (q. v.), a descendant of King Denis on the paternal side and the Agekaza rulers on the maternal, was serving as the head of the Mpongwe collectivity of Glass. The rebuilding of the Agekaza clan foyer or council house in 1974 at Nomba, the historic home of the Agekaza-Glass, was the most obvious sign of the persistence of Mpongwe vitality and of determination to play an active role in public affairs. [170, 172, 232, 251, 199, 216, 188]

MUSIC. The traditional music of the Bantu peoples of Gabon resembles that of the other Bantu populations of the southern half of Africa in its forms and genres. Vocal music is frequently accompanied by stringed instruments, wooden flutes, xylophones, and drums. Among the most notable instruments is the Fang *mvet*, in which a calabash provides the sounding chamber for the strings, which are plucked to accompany recitation of the epic of the same name. The Bantu peoples possess songs and chants in fixed form as well as traditional themes for instrumental improvisations, which are used to accompany religious rituals and social events of various kinds. [700, 604, 609, 615, 623, 628]

MUTUELLE GABONAISE. A political group formed at Libreville in October 1934 by educated Mpongwe, Benga, and Séké (qq. v.) to oppose the special privileges being sought by the *métis* (q. v.). A branch formed among the Gabonese working at Brazzaville served to establish a group which was subsequently to dominate the beginnings of postwar politics. Among the latter was a young Mpongwe, George Damas (q. v.), who attacked métis privileges in the columns of the *Etoile de l'Afrique Equatoriale Française*. [335]

MYENE (or OMYENE). A subdivision of the Bantu linguistic group that takes its name from the words "myè nè," "I say that." There are six Myènè languages, which are spoken by the peoples of the same name: Mpongwe, Orungu, Nkomi, Galoa, Adyumba, and Enenga (qq. v.). These peoples are located within a circle whose circumference includes the three largest cities: Libreville in the Estuary; Port-Gentil at Cape Lopez; and Lambaréné in the Ogooué River.

From the seventeenth to the nineteenth centuries, Myènè languages served as linguae francae on the coasts between southern Cameroon and Cabinda. Myènè speakers were among the first Gabonese to have contact with Europeans and to experience the cultural and economic impact of the West. In 1960 Myènè speakers formed 5 percent out of an estimated population of 450,000 in Gabon.

The Myènè speakers were non-literate peoples. Myènè languages were first transcribed by Christian missionaries using the Latin alphabet beginning with Mpongwe in the 1840s. John Leighton Wilson (q. v.) of the ABCFM mission employed the transcription system developed by John Pickering for American Indian languages. American Protestant and French Catholic missionaries prepared religious tracts and school booklets in Mpongwe, and the Protestants translated the entire Bible. French Protestants prepared materials in Galoa. French policy, which after 1883 required the use of French in all academic instruction and restricted the use of local languages to religious instruction, discouraged the growth of a written literature in African languages. Though the government of Gabon has encouraged research on indigenous languages at the university level and within the pedagogical bureau of the Education Ministry, so far it has retained French as the language of instruction at all levels. Consequently, the Myènè languages remain predominantly spoken rather than written languages. They nevertheless possess an extensive oral literature. [170, 251]

- N -

NASSAU, ROBERT HAMILL, M.D. (1835-1921). American Presbyterian missionary among the Benga, Galoa, Bakèlè, and Fang (qq. v.), 1861-98. Nassau was born at Lawrenceville, New Jersey, on October 11, 1835. He graduated from Princeton University, its Theological Seminary, and the University of Pennsylvania Medical School in 1861. He became an expert in the Benga language while working on Corisco Island and the mainland nearby between 1861 and 1871. He helped the Rev. Ibea (q. v.) prepare a history of the Benga people. He established the first Christian mission up the Ogooué River in 1874, above Lambaréné (moved there in 1876) among the Galoa and Bakèlè, and another farther upstream at Talaguga (near modern N'Djolé) among the Bakèlè and Fang in 1881. A gifted linguist and talented observer, Nassau was comparatively free of the ethnocentric bias that characterized the attitudes of his peers. His many published volumes and manuscripts form a rich source for the history of these four peoples in the last part of the nineteenth century. His works also contribute to tropical medicine and natural science. Nassau and his sister Isabella (1829-1906) also pioneered in the formation of African teachers, catechists, and pastors. They struggled to secure a meaningful role for these agents in the face of missionary paternalism and conservatism. Dr. Nassau died on May 6, 1921. [144, 551, 505, 500]

N'DENDE, JEAN-BAPTISTE. N'Dendé was a Séké who studied at the Ecole Monfort (q. v.) in Libreville and taught there while a novice of the Brothers of Saint-Gabriel (q. v.). In 1918 he became the president of the Libreville branch of the Ligue des Droits de l'Homme (q. v.), which agitated a number of issues of concern to the educated elite of the Estuary. N'Dendé served in this capacity until 1930 when tricked into transferring the presidency to a Frenchman who refused to seek redress of African grievances. In 1935, at a moment when he was at odds with elite Mpongwe, Benga, and <u>métis</u> (q. v.), N'Dendé helped Fang elders of Libreville to organize <u>La Voix du Pays</u> (q. v.) for purposes of cooperative agriculture and fishing. He also intended that <u>La Voix du Pays</u> should unite the Fang community, the largest in the capital by this time, in defense of its interests vis à vis the other peoples. [335]

NDIWA. The Ndiwa are either the first of the Mpongwe (q. v.) clans to arrive in the Estuary or a separate people who preceded the Mpongwe on the southern shore (left bank) as far west as Point Pongara. Under a leader called Rogombe some Ndiwa went to live on Dambe or Coniquet Island where they were residing in 1698 when tradition holds that the Dutch attacked in reprisal for Mpongwe attacks on Dutch shipping. The Mpongwe assimilated the survivors as well as other Ndiwa who came directly from the southern shore to Owendo on the northern shore in the sixteenth or seventeenth century. In turn Rogombe is regarded as the creator of the Mpongwe language and laws, an "African Confucius" according to the description of Rev. William Walker, an American missionary, in 1847. [251]

NDONG, FRANCOIS (1906-). Monsignor Ndong was born at the Fang village of Nzamaligé in 1906 and was ordained a Catholic priest on April 17, 1938. He was named auxiliary bishop of Libreville on November 15, 1960, the first Gabonese to be appointed a bishop. In May 1969 he was named bishop of the diocese of Oyem. [487, 488]

NDONG, MENDAME. Son of a Fang (q. v.) clan head in a part of the Woleu-N'Tem Province that was transferred to Germany in 1911, he was sent to the school for chiefs in Berlin from 1912 to 1919. In 1947 Ndong played an important role in the Fang Congress at Mitzic as an advocate of the preservation of Fang culture. Between 1947 and 1961 he sat in the Territorial Assembly (later called Legislative and then National Assembly) as a member of the Union Démocratique et Sociale Gabonaise (q. v.). [381]

NDONG, PHILIPPE. Editor and politician. Ndong was elected to the Legislative Assembly in March 1957. In 1959 while serving in the Ministry of Education, he founded the review _Réalités Gabonaises_ to succeed the defunct cultural review _Liaison_ of Brazzaville, which had served all of French Equatorial Africa. Through _Réalités Gabonaises_ he sought to promote knowledge and understanding of Gabonese history and culture, particularly among teachers. Ndong held a position in the short-lived Provisional Government of February 1964, which led to his internment for several years. He was later released by President Bongo. [347, 344, 371]

NDOUMOU (or MINDOUMOU). An Mbédé-speaking people who live along the M'Passa River in the area of Franceville. Chief Nguimi from this people gave Brazza the land on which he founded the French post of Franceville in 1880. [189]

NGOWE (or NGOVE). The Ngowe people are probably a branch of the Eshira (q. v.) who migrated from the interior plains to the coast around Cape Sainte Catherine and the Iguéla Lagoon possibly as early as the fifteenth century. They dispersed southward some of the Vili who were sparsely settled along the coasts north of Loango. The Ngowe in turn ceded place at Cape Sainte Catherine to the Nkomi (q. v.), who arrived in the fifteenth or sixteenth centuries. The territory of the Ngowe was known in the seventeenth and eighteenth centuries to Europeans as the province or kingdom of Gobby. Gobby paid at least a nominal allegiance at that time to the kingdom of Loango (q. v.). The Ngowe, who probably never numbered more than a few thousands, were middlemen traders with the interior peoples, especially the Eshira. Today the remnants of the Ngowe at Iguéla speak Nkomi, the language of their northern neighbors. Many others have resettled at Port-Gentil (q. v.) and at Omboué near Fernan-Vaz among the Orungu and Nkomi respectively. At the same time Fang and Loumbou have settled around Iguéla Lagoon, which during the twentieth century became the scene of the lumbering industry. [251]

NGUEMA, FRANCOIS OWONO (d. 1978). Scientist and educator. Nguema held a doctorate in nuclear physics. After directing a technical lycée from June 1969 to September 1971, he was named vice-rector of the university and then rector. From April 1975 until his assassination in 1978 he served as Minister of Scientific Research, responsible for the environment and the protection of nature. [682]

NKOMI. The Nkomi people form part of the Omyènè linguistic group. When the Portuguese first arrived along the coast in 1482, the Nkomi were already inhabiting the lagoon they called Eliwa Nkomi or lake of the Nkomi, which became Fernan Vaz for the Portuguese, and the river which flowed into the lagoon, the Rembo Nkomi. Nkomi traditions state that they had earlier supplanted the Vili (q. v.) at Cape Sainte Catherine and chased them beyond Lake Iguéla southwards towards Loango. With the arrival of the Dutch in 1595, the Nkomi became middlemen in relation to the peoples farther inland up the Rembo Nkomi in the exchange of iron goods for ivory, polychrome fabrics, and slaves. The Nkomi also sent slaves northward to the Orungu of Cape Lopez. As a result of a war with the Orungu over the marketing of slaves, most of the Nkomi fell under the rule of King Ogoul Issogué (q. v.) (1802 or 1804 to 1840). But they thereafter regained their independence. In 1857 Chief Quinguéza, who controlled the Rembo Nkomi, facilitated Paul du Chaillu's (q. v.) access towards the N'Gounié River and Mitsogo country. Between 1854 and 1861 the American trader, Captain Richard Lawlin (q. v.), maintained a factory at the entrance of the lagoon on land given him by King Rotimbo, where he purchased rubber. On January 18, 1868, France, which already controlled the Estuary and Cape Lopez, signed a protectorate treaty with several Nkomi chiefs or clan heads. With the decline of the slave trade and the establishment of several European trading factories on the lagoon in the 1870s and 1880s under the protection of the French navy, rubber became the most important export.

In 1864-1868 the ABCFM of Boston had maintained an African schoolteacher among the Nkomi but lacked staff to found a mission. In 1887 the French Holy Ghost Fathers (q. v.) established a mission, including a school. One of their priests, Rev. Marie-Georges Bichet (d. 1900) was elected as a kind of chief (renima) of the Nkomi in 1897, which reflected his great influence as well as the transformation of traditional institutions. During the period between the two world wars numbers of Fang, Eshira, Bapounou, and Varama began to settle on traditional Nkomi lands. Hundreds of Nkomi, in turn, migrated to Port-Gentil, the port which the people at Fernan Vaz supplied with fish and other foodstuffs. [197, 251, 198, 255]

NTAKA (or TOKO) TRUMAN (1832-1894). The Rev. Ntâkâ Truman was the first Mpongwe (q. v.) to be ordained as a Presbyterian minister on January 7, 1880. He was the son of the leading trader of Glass (near Libreville), Toko (q. v.), who had helped the ABCFM missionaries to locate at Baraka on the northern shore of the Estuary in 1842 and who had given them a plot of ground. Ntâkâ was educated at the American Protestant school at Baraka. He thereafter spent a lifetime in church service as teacher, assistant pastor, and pastor in the Estuary region. He died on November 19, 1894. [505]

N'TCHORERE, CHARLES. A Gabonese captain in the French army shot to death by a German officer in the battle of the Somme on June 7, 1940. He commanded the Seventh

Company of the 53rd RUCMS, which after three days of valiant resistance against German bombardment, contained only ten African and five European survivors. He was a graduate of the Ecole Montfort. [221]

NYONDA, VINCENT-DE-PAUL (1918-). Politician. Nyonda was born in 1918 at N'Tchenguipaga among the Eshira (q. v.) people. He entered the Catholic school at Mouila only in 1937 and from there went on to the seminary at Brazzaville. By 1957 he had qualified as a teacher in the Catholic schools. Elected to the Legislative Assembly from the N'Gounié Province in March 1957, he entered the first Gabonese executive as Minister of Posts, Telecommunications, Transport, and Mines, a post which he held until 1963 when given other ministerial responsibilities. Nyonda represented Gabon in the Grand Council of French Equatorial Africa from 1957 to 1959. He served in the National Assembly after independence and from December 1960 headed the executive bureau of the BDG. [335]

NZABI (or BANDJABI). The Nzabi are one of the most numerous peoples in Gabon and the Congo. In the early 1970s they were spread out over a vast area of 32,000 sq. mi. about equally between the two countries. Not much is known about the Nzabi prior to the mid-nineteenth century. It is believed that at that time they had already for two centuries inhabited the heart of the forested Massif du Chaillu where they lived from hunting with nets and shifting cultivation of food crops. They formed the eastern end of trading networks that extended into the Ogooué and Nyanga rivers and into which they sent rubber, tobacco, groundnuts, red dye, and a few slaves. One branch of the Nzabi produced iron tools and weapons of good quality, which were also sold to neighboring peoples. In the late 1860s, in response to Fang (the Osyéba clan) closure of the Ogooué River near the juncture of the Ivindo River, which persisted for a decade, thousands of Nzabi began a southward and southwestward migration into a nearly uninhabited region between the Louesse River, a tributary of the Niari-Kwilou, and the Nyanga River. Through their migration they sought to move closer to the route that led to Mayumba and the Loango coast. Though predominantly peaceful, this migration brought them into conflict with the Massango (q. v.) and Ngomo. Other Nzabi remained in their older territories between the upper Ogooué and upper N'Gounié.

Between 1914 and 1918 the Nzabi interrupted commerce in the course of their refusal to accept the installation of the French colonial administration. In the mid-1930s missionaries of the Christian & Missionary Alliance began evangelistic work among the Nzabi and today 85 percent of their 7,000 adult church members come from the Nzabi people. [190, 203, 289, 290, 296, 316]

- O -

OBAMBA (or MBAMBA). The Obamba are an Mbédé-speaking people who inhabit the northern part of the Franceville Prefecture and nearly all of the Okondja Prefecture in the Haut-Ogooué Province. As a result of conflicts with the Mbochi of north-western Middle Congo, they migrated down the Sébé River to the vicinity of Okondja. There they encountered the Kanigui (q. v.) people, who shared the area with pygmies, fought against them, and forced them to flee westward towards the Ogooué. [189]

OBAMBA, CYRIAQUE SIMEON (1918-). Monsignor Obamba is the first Gabonese to serve as Catholic bishop of the diocese of Mouila. Born on February 28, 1918, at Oghéwa near Lambaréné, Monsignor Obamba was ordained a priest on May 12, 1946. Pope Paul VI named him to his present post as second bishop of Mouila on November 30, 1976. [488]

OGOUL' ISSOGOUE, KING (or ROGOMBE or PASSOL). Orungu (q. v.) monarch from ca. 1802-1804 to 1840 at the height of the kingdom's power and involvement in the slave trade. During this period the Orungu were occupying Apomande and Mandji Islands and controlling the two most important mouths of the Ogooué River delta, the Nazareth and the (San) Mexias mouths as well as the course of the river for eighty miles inland, that is, halfway to Lambaréné. Ogoul' Issogoué fought a successful war with the Nkomi to the south, who were receiving slaves from the Galoa at Lambaréné, and who wished to sell them directly to Europeans, not through Orungu middlemen. The Nkomi (q. v.) remained under Orungu control until after his death, when a disputed succession gave them the opportunity to regain their independence. Ogoul' Issogoué maintained his father's capital at Point Apomande but centered the slave trade at Sangatanga to avoid surveillance by European anti-slavery patrols. The dispute over the succession among his sons at his death saw one of them abandon Orungu territory and with his followers move closer towards the Estuary. [232, 251]

OGOOUE (OGOWE in English). Gabon's most important river, it is 1200 km. long. Its basin extends over 220,000 of the 267,667 sq. km. of the country. In this volume the Ogooué is subdivided into Lower Ogooué, from its mouths to the confluence of the N'Gounié, which enters it from the south just above Lambaréné Island; Middle Ogooué, from the N'Gounié River to the confluence of the Ivindo River, which enters from the north; Upper Ogooué, from the Ivindo to the source. [478]

OKANDE. The Okandé people inhabited both banks of the middle Ogooué east of the Okano River junction and west of Booué. During the age of European expansion and exploration, they provided expert boatmen for many of the expeditions. In the process they came into conflict with the Chiwa or Osyéba, now considered a branch of the Fang.

Okandé traditions relate origins along the Ivindo River which they travelled down to reach their mid- and late-nineteenth-century locations. They apparently advanced down the Ogooué past Lambaréné and towards Lake Zilé before returning upstream to these locations. The Okandé developed a flat-bottomed canoe, decorated fore and aft, which was well-suited for maneuvering the rocky passages of the middle Ogooué. Unlike practically all the rest of the peoples of Gabon, the Okandé did not hold slaves. But they bought slaves from the Shaké, Bakota, Adouma, and Nzabi (qq.v.) to exchange with the Galoa (q.v.) and Enenga (q.v.) for salt, palm cloth, matches, and tobacco. Okandé canoes travelled the Ogooué from Lastoursville to Lambaréné and later, after the establishment of French rule, from Franceville to Port-Gentil. [189]

OKOUME. Okoumé is a softwood used in the production of plywood. It comes from a tree that is usually 30 to 40 meters in height and has a trunk with a diameter of 1.5 meters. Gabon is the world's leading producer. The wood was identified by Rev. Théophile Klaine (q.v.), a Holy Ghost priest from France and an amateur botanist and later named Aucoumea Klaineana in his honor. Okoumé had been traditionally used by the Gabonese to make canoes and its resin was burned in torches. Fang canoers brought the first logs to Glass, then near Libreville, in July 1889. On the initiative of the Lieutenant-Governor of Gabon, Charles de Chavannes, the local director of the SHO (q. v.), M. Sajoux, sent seven to eight tons to France where it sold well. But the merchants of Le Havre preferred to stick with the older woods of northern Europe and Canada and combined to prevent further sales at good prices. They thus delayed the use of okoumé in France for twenty years. Okoumé was sent to Hamburg in 1892 by the Woermann firm where it soon replaced Cuban cedar in the making of cigar boxes. A Dutch firm, Picus, in 1898 and various German firms thereafter began to use okoumé for plywood. During the First World War the French military began to employ okoumé for construction, including airplanes. The inter-war period saw French companies become much more involved in the production of okoumé, which could be floated down streams to ships. Okoumé production, which reached 381,000 tons in 1930 before the impact of the world depression was felt, had risen to 737,000 tons in 1960, the year of independence, and in the 1970s has generally exceeded one million tons annually. [410, 434]

OMBAMBO-ROGOMBE, KING (or PASSOL or PASCAL). Orungu (q. v.) monarch ca. 1840 to ca. 1860. As a result of Orungu contacts with Brazilian and Portuguese traders, he stayed at Maranhão, Brazil, in 1805 and thereafter spent two years in Lisbon. He spoke Portuguese, Spanish, and French. Ombambo-Rogombe gained victory over his brothers in a succession dispute at the death of their father, Ogoul' Issogoué, in part as a result of the backing of the Spanish traders who operated the slave barracoons at Cape Lopez. Ombambo-Rogombe presided over the Orungu kingdom during a period of Anglo-French pressure to terminate the slave trade. To avoid surveillance, he moved his capital from Apomande Island to Sangatanga, two miles inland from the coast. He refused to permit the Holy Ghost Fathers (q. v.) to evangelize in his lands and was in part responsible for ousting them in 1850 from another clan that had invited them to establish a post. He refused to make a treaty recognizing French sovereignty over his territories. [232, 251]

ORSTOM. The Office de la Recherche Scientifique et Technique Outre-Mer (ORSTOM) is a French government research bureau that was organized under the Fourth Republic to undertake studies in the social and physical sciences, and to a lesser extent in the humanities, in the overseas territories. Since the independence of the African countries ORSTOM has continued its work in cooperation with their governments. In Gabon ORSTOM has undertaken systematic studies of the country's hydrology and pedology. It has sponsored the research of several social scientists, including the Gabonese sociologist, Laurent Biffot (q. v.) and the French anthropologist of the Libreville Museum, Louis Perrois.

ORUNGU. A Myènè-speaking (q. v.) people who inhabited the delta of the Ogooué River from the seventeenth century and who developed a centralized kingdom during the era of the slave trade (1760s to 1870s). The Orungu were originally called the Ombéké. They were probably an offshot of the Eshira who moved down the lower Ogooué River early in the seventeenth century and located behind the coastal creeks, especially the upper Gange, next to several Mpongwe clans along the coast. From these locations the Orungu supplied wood and ivory to the Adyumba (q. v.) clan of the Mpongwe from whom they learned boatbuilding and ironworking, and whose language they adopted. During the seventeenth century the Orungu gradually settled along the Nazareth River, an important mouth of the Ogooué River north of Cape Lopez, and on the Atlantic coast northward. Around 1700 they made a successful bid for control of the coast and direct access to trade with Europeans. They killed many Adyumba and chased the remnants of their clan towards Lake Azingo. They drove the Adoni and Angwengila clans of the Mpongwe northwards towards Point Pongara. Thereafter, an assembly of the heads of the twenty or so Orungu clans decided that the head of the Aboulia clan should henceforth be their king. They gave him control over maritime commerce and relations with Europeans. Another clan, the Awandji, was assigned control of inland commerce.

At first the Orungu traded ivory, beeswax, honey, gum copal, dyewood, and ebony with merchants from Portugal and Britain. During the 1760s the Orungu became involved in the slave trade in which slaves drawn from the Ogooué River system were often sent to São Tomé and Príncipe for transporting to the New World. We lack precise figures for the Orungu areas alone. But we know that by 1788 the Estuary and Cape Lopez together were exporting 500 slaves annually and between 1809 and 1815 1,500 each year. Between the late 1700s and 1860 the Orungu monarchs controlled the two most important mouths of the Ogooué, the Nazareth and the (San) Mexias, and navigation up the river for eighty miles. They grew rich and powerful from taxing and regulating the slave trade. King Ogoul 'Issogoué or Rogombe (q. v.) (ca. 1802-1804 to 1840) and his son King Ombango-Rogombe or Passol (q. v.) (1840-1860) could even be described as despots, for they no longer submitted to either advice or control from the traditional council of clans.

A reduction in Brazilian slave imports in 1850 and increasing British anti-slavery patrols influenced Ombango-Rogombe to move his capital from Olibatta on the Nazareth River northward and inland to Sangatanga, where shallow waters and winding channels prevented surprise patrol raids. On February 2, 1853, Ombango-Rogombe signed a treaty with Britain agreeing to end the slave trade and to trade in various other commodites but he did not live up to its terms. His brother and successor, Ndebulia-Rogombe (1860-1865) made a treaty on June 1, 1862, recognizing the sovereignty of the French, who were actively extending their at least nominal control along the coasts southward from the Estuary. Ndebulia-Rogombe thereafter moved his capital to the Ogooué delta, where he and another brother Ntchengué (1865-1882?) saw their power shrink rapidly as the slave trade sputtered to its deserved end in the late 1860s and 1870s. In this period European merchants under French protection established houses at Cape Lopez (1867) and then up the Ogooué in order to bypass the Orungu middlemen. Protests by the Orungu chiefs and a blockade of the Nazareth River failed to halt this commercial penetration. The Orungu at this time probably numbered no more than 5,000 persons. On August 6, 1873, King Ntchengué signed a second treaty with France. Under its terms the French in 1880 established posts on Mandji Island; one of them at Cape Lopez on the north-west tip of the island became the site of Port-Gentil, an important commercial center.

The Holy Ghost Fathers, whose efforts to found a mission among the Orungu in 1850 encountered the hostility of the slave trading elements and ended in withdrawal, returned only in 1927. Thus the Orungu did not benefit, as did the Mpongwe to the north, from the western education that might have permitted them to play new roles under the colonial system. Independence in 1960 found some Orungu traditional chiefs remaining on their ancestral lands in which the Orungu people had become a tiny minority. [232, 251, 151]

- P -

PARTI DEMOCRATIQUE AFRICAIN (PDA). Organized by progressive elements at Libreville and Port-Gentil in late 1945 to contest the elections for the French Constituent and National Assemblies. It twice unsuccessfully supported a well-educated career civil servant, Emile Issembé (q. v.), for African representative in these bodies. But it was plagued by personal rivalries and experienced the hostility of the administration when it became the local branch of the inter-territorial RDA. For the RDA at this time had ties with the French Communist Party and the Communist-dominated labor confederation, the CGT. Quite a number of the PDA members also belonged to the Libreville GEC (q. v.). In the face of internal tensions and external pressures the PDA ceased to function by the end of 1946 and much of the membership joined the CMG. [335]

PARTI DEMOCRATIQUE GABONAIS (PDG). The PDG is the only legal political party in Gabon and the one to which the members of the government belong. It was founded by President Bongo (q. v.) in March 1968 shortly after he dissolved all existing parties. Bongo has served as the PDG's Secretary-General. The PDG has held several annual congresses and two extraordinary ones (1973 and 1979). See POLITICS. [344, 374, 330, 337, 349]

PARTI D'UNION NATIONALE GABONAISE (PUNGA). Punga by coincidence also means "tempest" in Eshira. PUNGA was a political party formed in August 1958 by René-Paul Sousatte (q. v.) and Jean-Jacques Boucavel (q. v.) to express dissatisfaction among such southern peoples as the Eshira (q. v.) and Bapounou (q. v.) with the political leadership of the Fang (q. v.) and Myènè (q. v.) of northern Gabon. It opposed Gabon's membership in the French Community in the referendum of September 28, 1958. It was able to secure a majority against membership in only the Nyanga Region where the Bapounou and Eshira populations were numerous. Gabon as a whole voted 190, 334 to 15, 244 for entry into the Community. In September 1959 Sousatte demanded immediate independence for Gabon only a few months after the country had become an autonomous republic. His declaration was apparently motivated by the Mba government's refusal to sanction new elections to the Legislative Assembly. PUNGA at this time also had a small electoral clientele from a miscellaneous group of progressives and critics of the regime (the Conseil de la Jeunesse, students, labor leaders). After independence, the Mba regime refused to include PUNGA in the negotiations for a government of national union. Sousatte and Boucavel took posts as individuals and the party itself ceased to function. [381, 364, 372, 335]

PEOPLES. Gabon, like other African states that were brought into being as a result of European expansion and competition during the nineteenth century, contains many different peoples. A people may be defined in the sense of the Greek term "ethnos" or the Latin "natio" as a group related by biology, culture (including language), and history. While these factors serve to differentiate over three dozen distinct peoples, various ones among them possess similarities that permit some grouping or classification. All of the peoples except the pygmies speak Bantu languages. The pygmies (q. v.), who are believed to be the descendants of the earliest inhabitants of Gabon, retain their own languages in some cases while frequently employing the languages of their Bantu neighbors. The basically linguistic classification of eight groups developed by the French ethnographer Marcel Soret in the 1950s, to which are added the Vili group (a majority of whom live in the neighboring Congo) and the pygmies is as follows:

Group	Peoples
Omyène (Myènè)	Mpongwe, Adyumba, Enenga, Galoa, Orungu, Nkomi
Séké	Séké, Benga, Bakouélé
Eshira	Eshira, Ngowe, Varama, Voungou, Bapounou, Loumbou, Babuissi, Massango
Okandé	Apindji, Mitsogo, Pove, Shimba, Okandé, Evéia
Bakèlè	
Fang	
Bakota	Bakota, Mahongwé, Shaké, Dambomo, Shamai, Mindassa, Woumbou
Mbédé	Obamba, Mbamba, Ndoumou, Kanigui, Nzabi, Batsangui, Awandji, Adouma

Téké
Vili
Pygmies

National boundaries divide several of these peoples. The Vili, Bapounou, Nzabi, Téké, Bakota, and Bakouélé are also found in the Congo. The Fang are also located in Equatorial Guinea and Cameroon. The present frontiers were arbitrarily drawn, often in ignorance of the precise locations of the various peoples. Many of the peoples were fixed in their present locations only in the nineteenth century and in some cases only as result of the installation of colonial rule. Throughout the previous centuries relocations and migrations, most often from an eastern or northeastern direction, were a regular feature of Gabon's history. The basic unit of social organization for all these peoples was the extended family or lineage, whose members shared a common ancestry. Related lineages formed clans and related clans composed peoples (formerly called tribes). At the same time, as a result of the constant movement of populations in search of fresh lands or in flight from warlike neighbors, some clans became divided and over the decades regrouped as parts of different peoples. In the process they gradually adopted the language of the people to which they henceforth belonged.

Economic factors in the colonial period and since independence have contributed to the relocation of numerous individuals within the various groups of peoples. The introduction of the French language and culture, and its large-scale generalization since the late 1940s, have helped to create a Gabonese people. Civic education since independence has further promoted this identity. At the same time the average person still derives a very important part of his identity from belonging to a particular extended family and people. [251, 189]

PETROLEUM. The existence of petroleum from Cape Lopez south to Mayumba, both onshore and offshore, has been known since 1929. But the exploitation dates only from 1956. Spectacular growth has occurred since 1967 with the coming into production of the Gamba-Ivinga deposits, onshore south of the Ndogo Lagoon and Setté-Cama, and offshore Anguillé deposits just south of Port-Gentil. Port-Gentil became the site of the refinery of the Société Gabonaise de Raffinage (SOGARAF). Prospecting and exploitation have been handled by Elf-Gabon, Shell-Gabon, Mobil, and the Gulf Oil Company. In 1976 a second refinery opened at Pointe Clairette to the east of Port-Gentil. Petroleum production increased from 1,400,000 tons in 1966 to 11,300,000 a decade later, with off-shore accounting for 80 percent of this production. Eighty-five percent of the production is exported overseas, the rest being used in Gabon and neighboring countries. At the present rate of extraction, known reserves will be exhausted by the end of the 1980s. The Third Five-Year Plan (1976-80) has therefore involved important investments in prospecting for new deposits.

A by-product of petroleum is natural gas production at Port-Gentil, the production of which increased from 25,000,000 cubic meters in 1968 to 239,000,000 in 1976.

Since the late 1960s crude petroleum has formed three quarters of Gabon's export earnings. [478, 387, 394]

POLITICS. Modern politics in Gabon fall into several periods of unequal length. In a sense they begin in the aftermath of the First World War in the form of activity by the western-educated elite in the larger towns through a number of organizations that were anti-colonialist and liberal in outlook but not anti-French. From the 1840s American and French missionaries had provided a western education to handfuls of Gabonese. But the organization of Catholic boys' schools at Libreville and Lambaréné in 1900 staffed by a congregation of professional teachers, and the creation of a public day school at Libreville in 1911 staffed by professionals, greatly increased the numbers of the elite and their academic level. For the first time there were dozens of persons whose competence in French reached the upper primary levels. Members of this elite were among those who became non-commissioned officers in the French army in the Cameroons campaign against the Germans and thereby enlarged their horizons. Some of these young men received further experience in the outside world as employees in such colonies as Senegal, the Ivory Coast, and the Belgian Congo before returning to Gabon to work for European commerce or the administration.

The first political organization in the modern sense in Gabon was the Libreville branch of the French Ligue des Droits de l'Homme, which functionaries from Martinique and Guadeloupe organized in 1918. The Ligue in Europe tended to be republican, liberal, and anti-clerical, and thus had the sympathy of many of the European functionaries, who were almost entirely freemasons or socialists in this era. The Gabonese members of the Libreville branch, however, were not anti-clerical but anti-colonialist. Under the leadership of Jean-Baptiste N'Dendé (q. v.), its Séké secretary, the Libreville branch became a vehicle for the expression of the interests of the Gabonese elite. The members were gravely concerned about the departure of the Brothers of Saint-Gabriel (q. v.) from Lambaréné in 1911 and Libreville in 1918 for lack of funds (the administration having cut off subsidies in 1907 in the wake of separation of Church and State in France) and staff, which meant that the quality and level of instruction reverted to their pre-1900 status under priests and African monitors. Education for the elite was a means to full equality with Frenchmen in public employment and the enjoyment of basic rights. For the elite wished to cease being subjects and to become French citizens. Their aspirations extended to their own class and not to the traditionally-oriented masses. They were also concerned about various aspects of colonial rule such as the impôt (head tax), prestation, forced labor, and the indigénat (q. v.), which had been applied in Gabon really only at the end of the nineteenth and the beginning of the twentieth century, as well as the violation of customary land rights. In the latter matter the Mpongwe (q. v.) long implanted on the northern shores of the Estuary were also in conflict with later arrivals, particularly the thousands of Fang (q. v.) who by now formed a majority of the population. The French legislation establishing the concessionary system in 1898 had not respected indigenous land rights and the practices of the local administration trampled upon those in the urban areas. Though the French had made treaties with various clan heads and chiefs in the process of securing recognition of their sovereignty, they failed to respect them or to live up to their terms. They had a tendency to choose the chiefs with whom they subsequently would deal rather than allow the local peoples to select their own. But they did not seek to dispense with chiefs entirely for with such a very limited number of administrators, only one thousand for all of French Equatorial Africa in 1910, they depended upon chiefly intermediaries to assist in carrying out their orders and transmitting them to the peoples. As far as the elite were concerned, they tried to have the administration select chiefs from among the educated and in the interwar period were increasingly successful when such persons were available. So that the young Léon Mba (q. v.), a graduate of the Catholic schools, became

Fang canton chief at Libreville in the early 1920s and educated Mpongwe became the chefs de quartier there in the 1930s. The decision of the federal administration to allow election of African representatives to the governor-general's administrative council in 1937 presented the first opportunity for the various elements to compete in an electoral process. Those of Gabon elected François-de-Paul Vané (q. v.), a Libreville resident from a Benga chiefly family and one-time seminarian, who had played a leading role in various anti-colonialist organizations since the mid-1920s. The decision to name Africans to the municipal commission of Libreville also opened the way for African representation though of course the choices lay with the administration. But the French were not likely to select those without education or some backing. The conviction of Léon Mba in 1931 for involvement in ritual murders and his exile to Oubangui-Chari deprived the Estuary Fang of their most capable leader for the next fifteen years. Mba improved his standing by rallying to Free France in 1940 and was allowed to return to Gabon in 1946.

During his absence the political situation had evolved considerably. The Second World War had arrived and the Free French had taken control of the country. In 1944 they had organized the Brazzaville Conference to plan the reform of the colonial empire in a liberal direction. Late in the war and right after the most hateful aspects of the colonial regime were abolished--prestation, forced labor, the indigénat, and travel controls. The educated Gabonese, like their counterparts in other territories, were given representation in the two Constituent Assemblies of 1945-46 which charted the new relationship between France and overseas. Gabon at first shared a representative with the Middle Congo. The two territories elected Félix Tchicaya (q. v.), a schoolteacher and war veteran of Vili parentage, who was born at Libreville and had family connections in the Loango area. In November 1946, when Gabon and Congo each acquired a deputy, Tchicaya was elected to the French National Assembly from the Middle Congo and Jean-Hilaire Aubame (q. v.), a Fang linked to the Woleu N'Tem, was elected from Gabon. A one-time seminarian, as a young civil servant at Brazzaville in the early 1940s Aubame had received a political education within Free French circles at the side of Félix Eboué (q. v.), the federation's black governor-general. Solid support from the missions, both Catholic and Protestant, and also from elements in the administration and European commerce, aided Aubame to win re-election to the National Assembly in June 1951 and January 1956. There he became a prominent member of several important committees to the point that he focussed his attention upon politics in the metropole while rivals were devoting their entire energies at the territorial level. While Aubame was also elected to the Territorial Assembly and two other leading politicians, Paul Gondjout (q. v.) and René Sousatte (q. v.), acquired seats in the French Senate and Assembly of the French Union, respectively, Léon Mba failed to gain a seat in the metropole. He ran unsuccessfully against Aubame for deputy in 1951 and 1956. At the territorial level he organized the Comité Mixte Gabonais (q. v.) in 1947 to counter the Union Démocratique et Sociale Gabonaise (q. v.) (UDSG) of Aubame but there were few issues of importance that really divided them. Their differences were personal and became rooted in a division between the Estuary Fang and the northern and hinterland Fang with other ethnic groups attaching themselves to the two elements. Mba affiliated his group with the progressive inter-territorial movement, the Rassemblement Démocratique Africain (RDA), which until 1949 was affiliated in the French Parliament with the Communist Party (which belonged to the government until March 1947). Aubame belonged to the parliamentary group called the Indépendants d'Outre-Mer (IOM), which included Leopold Sédar Senghor and Dr. Louis-Paul Aujoulat and altogether had a Catholic but anti-colonialist complexion. The IOM affiliated with François Mitterand's tiny Union Démocratique et Sociale de la Résistance (UDSR) in the parliament. Back in Gabon, Senator Gondjout, a Myènè from Port-Gentil, organized the Bloc Démocratique Gabonais (BDG) (q. v.) in 1954, to rival the UDSG, and persuaded Léon Mba to drop his Comité and join it. They thus combined forces to oppose the influence of Aubame and the northern Fang and sought to group all other ethnic groups around them. Their first real victory came in November 1956 when they were able to win control of the new popularly elected municipal commission of Libreville, which chose Mba as mayor. In that position he was able to fill the city hall with his supporters. Then in the territorial assembly elections of March 1957, the BDG and independents won a bare majority of the seats, though the UDSG received a majority of the popular votes, and were able to choose a majority of the members of the first government council, that is, an embryonic cabinet instituted under the _loi-cadre_ reforms, of which Mba became the vice president with the French governor as the president.

Before the cabinet could function for very long, the Fourth Republic came to an end in the wake of the May 1958 revolution in Algiers. This situation allowed for the establishment of a new relationship between France and its overseas territories. Within Gabon, while both the UDSG and the BDG favored membership in the new French Community, probably as an overseas department or an autonomous republic, a new party called PUNGA (q. v.) composed of peoples of the south-west who felt left out of the regime dominated by Fang and Myènè and centered upon René Sousatte, who had not been re-elected by the Territorial Assembly to the Assembly of the French Union, campaigned for a negative vote, which would have meant complete independence. While the PUNGA obtained a majority against the Community in the Nyanga Province, Gabon as a whole voted overwhelmingly in its favor. Thereafter Gabon became an autonomous republic and Léon Mba became the prime minister in a coalition government of BDG and UDSG ministers. PUNGA became reconciled to the situation and most of its members joined the BDG. Both major parties opposed the membership of Gabon in a revived federation of Equatorial African states and therefore as the Community rapidly evolved, Gabon found itself an independent republic on August 13, 1960. Léon Mba became president.

The next three and a half years would be characterized by a general conflict between Mba, who wished to be a strong authoritarian leader, and the other leading politicians--Aubame, Gondjout, Sousatte--sometimes cooperating with him and sometimes in opposition. Mba's determination and the determined opposition of the others ultimately led to the coup of February 1964 overthrowing him. But the French military intervention which restored him to power provided him with the basis for virtual one-man rule of the country for the rest of his life. It allowed him to hand over his power intact to his chosen successor, President Albert-Bernard Bongo (q. v.).

Bongo, without relinquishing that power, took steps to conciliate the opponents of Mba's regime without depriving himself of the supporters. Sousatte was already in retirement. Bongo gave Gondjout and other critics of Mba positions of importance within the government and administration. He finally released Aubame in 1972, who was allowed to go and live in Paris. In March 1968

Bongo dissolved all the parties and founded a single new one, the Parti Démocratique Gabonais (PDG) (q. v.) whose role in governance is legally defined. The political system since 1968 thus has centered upon a powerful president who is also the secretary-general, that is, the top official of the PDG. He governs in consultation with a political elite of around two hundred holders of the top positions in the government, administration, parliament, and party. The members of this elite have received a secondary education in Gabon or France and many of them a higher education in France. They have advanced into their present positions through competence, loyalty to the president, and willingness to work within a single-party system. All discussion, dialogue, and criticism can legitimately take place only within the party. Political activities outside the party are regarded as disloyal if not subversive. Since the holders of high government office (40 cabinet members, 89 members of Parliament, 9 provincial governors and 37 prefects) also hold a preponderance in the 30-member Political Bureau and the 82-member Central Committee of the PDG, initiatives for policy changes or reforms have come primarily from within the government and not from the party. The party tended, at least until 1979, to remain an organization whose central organs sent out orders and information to its provincial and local committees rather than receiving recommendations and suggestions from them. There are indications, however, that at the Second Extraordinary Congress in early 1979 delegates from the local branches transmitted their constituents' discontent with the economic policies and administrative practices of the government. But the exception throughout the 1970s was the women's organization, the Union des Femmes-PDG, in which local units forwarded their concerns to higher levels, which responded positively and which acted to increase the number of women in the cabinet and parliament. In contrast, the youth organization, the Union des Jeunes-PDG, has remained moribund as the most talented young people seek to prepare themselves for jobs in the bureaucracy rather than risk activities that might lead to tensions with their elders.

The hub of the political system is the president, who as in the American system, heads both the state and the government. It has been his ability and willingness to consult and dialogue with the political elite and their cooperation, to a lesser extent, that makes the present political system function. The system has been able to incorporate the bulk of the educated elite. Most of those unwilling to work within the system have remained outside the country (in France and in other Francophone countries). A few, whose vision of the state and society is based upon Marxism-Leninism, sought to promote their goals clandestinely. Some of them were apprehended in the so-called professors' plot of 1972.

An important group that has been uneasily incorporated into the present system is the leadership of the trade unions, who represent the skilled and semi-skilled workers in forestry, mining, transportation, communications, and commerce. Organized by the Bongo regime in 1969 into a single Fédération Syndicale Gabonaise, and later affiliated with the PDG, their participation is not fully effective or responsive to their membership. But the presence of thousands of Europeans in top- and middle-level technical and managerial positions in the economy and other thousands of non-Gabonese African wage-laborers has diminished the relative strength of the Gabonese labor force and the potential power of its leaders. See CONSTITUTION; DECOLONIZATION. [335, 336, 381, 108, 372]

PORT-GENTIL. Gabon's second largest city, population 88,146 in 1970-1971, compared to 30,908 in 1960-1961, and center of the petroleum and wood industries. Port-Gentil was named in 1900 for Emile Gentil, French explorer and later governor-general of French Equatorial Africa (q.v.). In 1873 the French made a treaty with the Orungu (q.v.) people which allowed them to establish at Cape Lopez on sandy Mandji Island, which is separated from the mainland by rivers that are mouths of the Ogooué River. These are the deepwater mouths of the Ogooué, in comparison to the (San) Mexias and Fernan Vaz mouths. The French built hangars on Mandji for use by Savorgnan de Brazza's exploratory expeditions into the interior of the Ogooué River valley. In 1894 they established a customs post around which grew up commercial houses, including the British Hatton & Cookson and John Holt; the German Woermann; and the French Société du Haut-Ogooué and Compagnie d'Exploitations Forestières Africaines. Through Port-Gentil passed rubber, ivory, and especially after 1900 various woods, from the Ogooué and N'Gounié rivers and Fernan Vaz. Port-Gentil became the center for the export of okoumé (q.v.), which was used for plywood in Europe. During the 1960s Port-Gentil became the location for the petroleum refinery of the Société Gabonaise de Raffinage (SOGARAF), which processes most of the country's petroleum. In 1968 it became the site for the production of natural gas as well. A deep-water port, begun in early 1977, is presently under construction for commerce and fishing. The presence of the various industries has led to a resident European population of several thousand persons. [251, 388, 428]

POUNAH, PAUL-VINCENT (1914-). Author. Born at Lambaréné in 1914, Pounah entered the administration in 1937 as clerk in the governor's cabinet. After independence he served in diplomatic and high administrative posts. Pounah is a specialist in the history and folklore of the Galoa people and the Moyen-Ogooué Province about which he has written several books. [580]

POVE (or PUBI). A people of the Okandé linguistic group who inhabit the forest between the Lolo and Offoué Rivers. Among them live small groups of Bakèlè (q. v.). Their traditions relate that they crossed the Ogooué from the north at about the same time in the late nineteenth century as the French were arriving. The Pove refused to participate in the Awandji revolt of 1928-1929 even though they too had suffered from administrative and concessionary exactions. Men were even recruited among them to fight against the Awandji (q. v.). [189]

PRE-HISTORY. Pre-history refers to the periods for which neither written records nor oral traditions exist. The evidence about human life comes from archaeological remains, very few of which have been uncovered so far, and those few mainly in the savannas and not in the forests. Professional archaeologists have undertaken limited inquiries in the middle and upper Ogooué, between N'Djolé and Franceville, and in the Nyanga River valley. Various tools and weapons from the Paleolithic, Neolithic, and Iron Ages have been located, which taken together suggest the existence of human life in these areas many thousands of years ago. The possible relationship of these ancient peoples to the later pygmies and Bantu speakers remains a matter of speculation. [193, 236, 162, 156, 161, 179]

PRESTON, IRA (1818-86). American missionary (1848-67) and specialist in Dikèlè and Fang. Born at Danvers, Massachusetts, on April 21, 1818, Rev. Ira Preston was educated at Marietta College in Ohio and at Lane Seminary in Cincinnati. After ordination as a Presbyterian minister, he accepted service with the ABCFM mission in Gabon. In 1854 with the Rev. William Walker (q. v.) he made a pioneering exploration up the Nazareth mouth of the Ogooué River half way to the site of present-day Lambaréné. They were the first whites to make this voyage. Standard French works on Gabon, which did not know of their trip, credit this achievement to French naval officers in 1862 and 1867. Preston reduced Dikèlè (the language of the Bakèlè people) to writing and translated portions of the Scriptures into that language. Preston studied the Fang language and left a manuscript that served the Rev. Arthur Marling as the basis for further work after 1870 and ultimately the translation of the Scriptures into Fang. Preston's wife, Jane Sophia Woodruff (1817-90), taught school in Gabon from 1848 to 1866 and authored Gaboon Stories about her experiences. Ill health forced Preston's return in 1867 to the States where he taught at Marietta College. [230]

PROFESSORS' PLOT. In 1972 the government announced it had discovered a "professors' plot" at the National University. It had uncovered Marxist-Leninist cells, together with pamphlets violently hostile to state authorities. It held three professors, an attorney, and a dozen students in the central jail at Libreville on charges of plotting against the security of the state. On July 7, 1975, a court in the capital sentenced the professors (Patrice Ondo Mba, Bernard Ondo Nze, Joseph Rendjambe) and the attorney (Pierre Agondo Okawe) to terms of eight years and three of the students to lesser terms. Nine students were acquitted. [639]

PROTESTANTISM. Protestantism in Gabon is represented by three churches which were organized around the time of independence from missions established by American and French Protestants in the nineteenth and twentieth centuries. The churches are 1) the Evangelical Church of Gabon; 2) the Evangelical Church of South Gabon; and 3) The Pentecostal Evangelical Church. In Gabon, as elsewhere in Francophone Africa, the term "evangelical" is synonomous with "Protestant" and serves to differentiate the Protestant churches from the Roman Catholic.

Protestantism was first introduced into the Estuary region in June 1842 by Congregational and Presbyterian missionaries sponsored by the American Board of Commissioners for Foreign Missions of Boston. The ABCFM field was transferred to the Presbyterian Board of Foreign Missions of New York in 1870. The PBFM had already been maintaining missionaries since 1850 on Corisco Island and the mainland opposite in what is today Equatorial Guinea. As a result of the French government's requirement of April 1883 that the schools teach only in French, the Presbyterians in 1892-93 and 1913 transferred their work to the Société des Missions Evangéliques of Paris. The SME turned over direction of its work to the independent Evangelical Church of Gabon in 1961.

The Protestantism of these three consecutive missionary societies had its theological roots in the Reformation theologian, John Calvin, and reflects the subsequent experience of the churches of the Calvinist or Reformed tradition in Europe and America. The church organization in Gabon follows the Presbyterian and French Reformed model in which authority is vested in a synod of clergy and laymen.

Between 1842 and 1870 the ABCFM sent 35 missionaries to Gabon, the most important of whom were the Revs. John Leighton Wilson (q. v.), William Walker (q. v.), and Albert Bushnell (q. v.). Nearly half of these missionaries became victims of tropical diseases. The PBFM sent 66 missionaries between 1870 and 1913 and the SME 138 between 1887 and 1961, among whom there were also some deaths, especially before 1900.

The ABCFM initiated evangelization among the Mpongwe, Bakèlè, and Séké peoples and made contact with the Fang of the upper Estuary region. The Presbyterians extended their work among the Benga to the mainland around Cape Esterias after 1870. The Rev. Robert Nassau (q. v.), M. D. , founded posts up the Ogooué River in 1874 and after, near Lambaréné Island, and on Talaguga Island (N'Djolé), among the Galoa, Fang, and Bakèlè. French pastors Elie Allégret and Urbain Teisserès took over the work on the Ogooué in 1892-93 but the Americans retained Baraka (Libreville) until 1913. The SME extended its work in 1922 to the Fang of the Woleu N'Tem Province, which became their most fruitful field numerically, and south to Port-Gentil. The American missionaries reduced Mpongwe, Benga, Dikèlè, and Fang to writing and translated the Bible into them, as well as preparing grammars, dictionaries, and other instructional materials. Rev. William Walker completed translation of the entire Bible into Mpongwe. Rev. Samuel

Galley, a French Swiss pastor, building on the work of the Presbyterian, Rev. Arthur Marling, finished the Fang translation in the 1940s.

American Protestant insistence on monogamy, abstinence from alcoholic beverages, and a strict New England Sabbath hindered conversion and retention among the Mpongwe trading communities as did their opposition to the slave trade. Most of their converts were pupils in their schools, particularly their boarding schools. When the French Protestants arrived in 1887, they found only 300 Gabonese Protestants. By 1914 they had increased this number to 2,300 church members and 2,200 catechumens. The American Protestants had prepared African teachers, Bible readers, and catechists. The Presbyterians ordained the first indigenous pastors, Rev. Ibea Ikenga (q.v.), a Benga from Corisco in 1870, and Rev. Ntâkâ Truman (q.v.), an Mpongwe from the Libreville area, in 1880. The SME ordained 21 pastors between 1923 and 1960, seven of whom were Myènè and fourteen Fang. Fourteen of these pastors were serving in 1960 along with 53 other Gabonese catechists and preachers. In 1961 the Evangelical Church of Gabon had 45,000 adherents, including 20,000 baptized adult members, that is, roughly ten percent of Gabon's population. The church was governed by a National Council of seven members elected by the synod and headed from 1959 to 1969 by Pastor Ndong Amvane Basile. At the general synod of 1969 Pastor Ndong failed to obtain re-election to the council and therefore the presidency of the church. He was succeeded as president by Pastor Nang Essono. Out of the rivalries between the supporters and opponents of Pastor Ndong grew a split that was formalized when the supporters selected their own national council in 1971 in opposition to the regularly constituted one headed by Pastor Nang Essono. The division is not rooted in theology but in a complex of generational, personal, regional, and ethnic factors that has proved difficult to resolve despite the good offices of various African and European churches and the intervention of President Bongo (1971). Delegations from the two national councils meeting at Yaoundé in 1978 failed to resolve their differences. They both continue to exist within a church that is still formally a single body. In 1973, the Evangelical Church had 25 Gabonese and two European pastors plus nine evangelists working in 25 parishes throughout northern Gabon. It has approximately 60,000 members and adherents. It operates both primary and secondary schools with some government support.

The Evangelical Church of South Gabon grew out of the work of the Christian and Missionary Alliance since the 1930s. The CMA, which was founded in the United States in 1897 and has headquarters at Nyack, New York, is both a missionary society and a sect in the evangelical Protestant tradition. Its conservative theology includes a literal interpretation of the Bible and emphasizes the imminence of Christ's Second Coming. Its practices include anointing with oil for bodily healing. CMA missionaries began evangelization in the N'Gounié river valley of southern Gabon in 1933 among peoples not previously reached by Protestants. These include the Nzabi (Bandjabi) (1934); Bapounou (1942); Eshira (1946); Massango (1947) and Mitsogo (1948). The CMA has employed indigenous languages and has translated portions of the Bible into Nzabi and Ipounou. Since the early 1950s it has operated dispensaries, primary schools, and a secondary school at Bongola. In 1975 it opened the Bethel Bible College to train pastors, evangelists, and catechists for the Evangelical Church of South Gabon, which had achieved independence in 1959. Though founded by missionaries and still assisted by them, the church is directed by Gabonese. Membership doubled between 1960 and 1970 to 7,000 adults, 84 percent of them Nzabi and 11 percent Bapounou. Its membership and influence have since continued to grow through both natural increase and conversion.

The Pentecostal Evangelical Church is a product of the Great Revival of the mid-1930s. In 1935 a Swiss pastor of the French Protestant mission, Rev. Gaston Vernaud, initiated a revival involving possession by the Holy Spirit. After first affecting two Gabonese evangelists travelling in the Monts de Cristal in mid-August 1935, the revival spread to the Libreville area, to the Fang of the Woleu N'Tem Province, the Boulou of southern Cameroon, and by February 1936 to Ngômô on the lower Ogooué River. The experience has since been known as the Great Revival. Vernaud's preaching aroused much concern among his church's authorities in Paris, who were especially troubled about the miraculous cures said to be taking place. The French administration feared the creation of an independent African movement that might become anticolonialist as Kimbanguism had done fifteen years previously in the Belgian Congo. Rather than abandon the kind of work he was doing, Pastor Vernaud withdrew from the SME and founded the

Pentecostal Mission, which drew most of its followers from the Fang and Myènè. The mission affiliated with the Assemblies of God (Pentecostals) in France and the United States. Today the main churches of the Pentecostal Evangelical Church are those in Owendo, southeast of Libreville, and at Médouneu in the Woleu N'Tem. The Pentecostal church has a thousand members and African personnel, including pastors. [149, 517, 522, 513, 495, 505]

PYGMIES. Pygmies numbered 3, 320 in the last census. They are located in many parts of the country and are divided into several different groups such as the Bekwui, Bobinga, Babango, Okowa, Bakola, and Baka. The pygmies of southern Gabon are quite widely dispersed throughout the forests whereas in the area of Mékambo in the northeast one thousand Bakola pygmies are grouped in ten adjacent villages. The pygmies still live as their ancestors did, at least two thousand years ago, primarily from hunting and gathering but they also raise food crops and livestock. They often have symbiotic relationships with the adjacent peoples, such as the Bakola of Mékambo.

The pygmies are believed to be the descendants of the oldest known inhabitants of the forests. Their traditions indicate that some of them arrived in the forests from the south or east and others (such as the Baka around Minvoul in the Woleu-N'Tem Province) from the north. The traditions of most of the Bantu peoples declare that the pygmies preceded them or guided them through the forests. All of the various pygmy groups share common physical characteristics with the pygmies of Cameroon and Zaire, but some among them, such as the Babango south of Lastoursville, reflect racial mixing with Negroid people. At the same time the Babango of Dibandi near Mimongo in the N'Gounié Province bear some resemblances to the Bushmen of southern Africa, another of the aboriginal peoples of the continent. While some pygmies, such as the Baka of Minvoul who live among the Fang (q. v.), have retained their own languages, others, such as the Babango of Dibango, who live among the Massango (q. v.), have adopted the Bantu languages of their neighbors.

A few pygmies around Mékambo have become day laborers for the new mining enterprises. But in general the pygmies live outside the modern sector of the economy and reject formal education. [189, 292, 293, 321, 322]

- Q -

QUABEN, KING (or KAKA-RAPONO) (d. 1863). Head of the Agekaza-Quaben or Agekaza w'Anwando clan of the Mpongwe of the northern shore of the Estuary. He signed the treaty of April 27, 1843, with France which allowed them to construct their post, Fort d'Aumale, on the lands of his nephew King Louis/Anguilé Dowe (q. v.). He encouraged the French political, commercial, and religious presence in the hope of rivalling the hegemony of the Agekaza-Glass clan, which rested on collaboration with British, American, and German traders. [170, 172, 251]

- R -

RAPONTCHOMBO, JEAN-FELIX (1872-1903). The first Gabonese to earn the baccalauréat or French secondary diploma. He was the grandson of King Denis (q. v.) and the eldest son of King Félix-Adandé (q. v.). After primary studies with the Holy Ghost Fathers at Libreville, he was sent in February 1892 on government scholarship to the secondary school at St. Louis, Senegal, and thereafter to Sainte-Marie Lycée at Vitré, Brittany, in 1894. He was awarded the baccalauréat at Rennes in November of that year, coming in first out of thirty candidates. He was employed in the customs service in Africa until his death. [251]

REMOMBE, REMI (1852-1873). A graduate of the Holy Ghost Fathers (q. v.) school near Libreville, Rémi Remombe continued his studies for the priesthood at the Abbey of Notre Dame de Langonnet, Morbihan Department, Brittany, between 1865 and 1873. He died at Gorée enroute to Gabon to restore his health. Rémi was the son of Henri Oréniga, one of the first Catholic converts at Quaben and sister of Elisa, the first wife of King Félix-Adandé (q. v.). [517, 251]

REOMBI-MPOLO, KING. Orungu (q. v.) monarch from 1790 to ca. 1802-1804. Reombi-Mpolo was the first really strong Orungu ruler, who grew rich and powerful through controlling and taxing the slave trade. He came to power with the aid of Spanish slavers, who kidnapped his brother Ndombe, his most serious rival for the throne. Reombi-Mpolo made his headquarters on Apomande Island and later on Mandji Island where he established a virtual trading monopoly at the entrances of the Ogooué River delta. [232]

ROMAN CATHOLIC BISHOPS. The following bishops have had jurisdiction in Gabon. [487, 488]

Vicars Apostolic or Prefect Apostolic of the Two Guineas:

Edward Barron (v. a.)	1842-1844
Eugène Tisserand (p. a.)	1844-1846
Benoît Truffet (v. a.)	1846-1847

Vicars Apostolic of Gabon:

Jean-Rémy Bessieux	1848-1876
Pierre-Marie Le Berre	1877-1891
Alexandre Le Roy	1892-1896
Jean Martin Adam	1897-1914
Louis Martrou	1914-1925
Louis Tardy	1925-1947

Vicar Apostolic, Bishops, Archbishops of Libreville:

Jean Jérôme Adam (v. a. 1947-1955; bishop 1955-1958; archbishop 1958-1969)	1947-1969
André-Ferdinand Anguilé	1969-

Auxiliary Bishop of Libreville:

François Ndong	1960-1969

Bishop of Mouila:

Raymond de la Moureyre	1959-1977
Cyriac Siméon Obamba	1977-

Bishop of Oyem:

François Ndong	1969-

Bishop of Franceville:

Félicien-Patrice Makouaka	1974-

Notes: Edward Barron was an American from Philadelphia. Eugène Tisserand and Benoît Truffet were members of the Congregation of the Holy Heart of Mary, which in 1848 merged with the older Holy Ghost Fathers (Spiritans) (q. v.) and retained their name. All of the French bishops from 1848 to 1977 belonged to that congregation while the Gabonese bishops are members of the diocesan clergy. [487, 488]

- S -

SCHWEITZER, ALBERT (1875-1965). Medical missionary, religious philosopher, and musician. Schweitzer founded and maintained an independent medical mission at Lambaréné from 1924 until his death in 1965. He was born at Kayserburg, Alsace, on January 14, 1875, the son of a pastor of the Reformed Church. After brilliant studies in philosophy and theology at the University of Strasbourg and in organ at Paris, he became pastor of St. Nicholas Church, Strasbourg, and organist of the Bach Society of Paris. While retaining these positions, he undertook medical studies and received his M. D. in 1911. After marriage to Hélène Bresslau (1878-1957), a one-time music and art student who thereafter took courses in social work and medicine, the couple went in 1912 under the sponsorship of the Société des Missions Evangéliques of Paris as medical missionaries to Gabon. The Schweitzers worked at Lambaréné from 1913 to September 1917, when as Alsatians of questionable loyalty to France, they were interned in France for the remainder of the First World War. Back in Gabon in 1924, Schweitzer built his own hospital away from mission property and earned the operating expenses through lectures and organ concerts in Europe and the New World, and through recordings, especially of Bach's works in which he was considered an expert. He also won support from individuals and groups in Europe and America, including Unitarian-Universalists, who found his philosophical and theological views especially attractive.

Dr. Schweitzer felt that a western-style hospital had little chance of inducing suffering Gabonese to abandon fetishers and sorcerers. Therefore, he allowed them to bring members of their families and even small animals to the medical center. The families prepared the patients' food and gave them moral support for getting well. Schweitzer relaxed the standards of hygiene to this end. Schweitzer's medical methods generated controversy, mainly outside Gabon, as did his views on the capacities of the Africans, which some thought bordered on racism. In Gabon itself Schweitzer was much appreciated and beloved by many whom he aided. Some of them were aware of his views but chose to overlook them. Schweitzer died at Lambaréné in 1965 and was buried there, twelve years after receiving the Nobel Peace Prize. While Schweitzer had an impact upon Gabon for several decades, Gabon also had an impact upon him. His experiences at Lambaréné contributed to the shaping of his ethical humanism, which though still rooted in Christian traditions, now rested as well on broader and older ones, including some that were African.

After Dr. Schweitzer's death, his daughter Rhéna (1919-) and other associates continued his medical mission and modernized the facilities. But they could not attract sufficient private support to maintain the operations. In 1977 the Gabon government prevented the closing of the hospital by agreeing to grant regular aid. [521, 226, 52, 508, 519, 539]

SEIGNON, HENRI. Settler, lumberman and Free French (q. v.) leader. Henri Seignon as president of the Chamber of Commerce at Libreville played an important role in convincing Governor Pierre Masson to rally the colony to Free France in August 1940. Though subsequently captured by Vichy elements and sent to France, he eventually was able to return to Gabon. In September 1943 he was named to represent French Equatorial Africa in the consultative assembly at Algiers. The Gaullist regime in 1944 named him director of the Office des Bois de l'Afrique Equatoriale Française, a body that controlled the exploitation and marketing of all woods in the federation. Seignon incurred great hostility from the European lumbering interests, which saw the Office as a step towards permanent government control or even nationalization. Seignon was defeated by Gabriel d'Arboussier (q. v.) in the contest for European deputy for Gabon and Middle Congo in October 1945 but elected to the Second Constituent Assembly in June 1946. In November 1946 Maurice Bayrou defeated him in the contest for European deputy from Gabon to the French National Assembly. But he gained election to the Territorial Assembly in December 1946 where he sat for the next decade and wielded great influence. Hostility to his Office des Bois lessened in the 1950s when the drop in timber prices in world markets proved its value. [335]

SEKE. The Séké people were called Shékiani by the Mpongwe (q. v.) and Boulou by the French in the early nineteenth century. The Séké are today found on the northern coast at Cocobeach, just south of the Rio Muni, as well as in adjacent Equatorial Guinea. Some have settled at Libreville and Lambaréné. These few hundreds of Séké are all that remain of a once numerous people that played an important commercial role in many parts of northern Gabon prior to the twentieth century. Séké traditions suggest origins in the upper Ivindo River, within present-day Cameroon, from which they were driven south- and westward by pressure from Bakèlè (q. v.) hunters. Some of them arrived along the northern coasts on the Rio Muni and its tributaries (the Noya and the upper Temboni rivers) and on the estuary of Mondah Bay before the coming of the Portuguese in the 1470s and possibly as early as the fourteenth century. From these locations they traded ivory, redwood, ebony, balls of rubber, gum copal, and a few slaves with the Portuguese and later with other western traders. Other Séké, who were settled behind the Orungu (q. v.) near the lower Ogooué River and on the upper Rembоué River became involved in the Remboué-Ogooué network of the slave trade in the 1760s and after. In addition to transmitting slaves from other peoples, they sold into slavery unsatisfactory wives, unhealthy or delinquent children, and orphans from their own populations. In the 1840s American and French missionaries and traders encountered the Séké living on both sides of the Estuary behind and among the Mpongwe and the Bakèlè. These Séké collected beeswax and gum copal, and hunted elephants in the forests for ivory, which they sold to the Mpongwe. Those on the northern shore also received ivory from the Bakèlè, who both gathered it and secured it from the Fang (q. v.). By the late 1840s Fang migrations were pushing both the Séké and the Bakèlè ahead of them down the Como and Remboué rivers into the Estuary. Twenty years later Fang moving towards the Ogooué would displace the southern Séké. In the late 1850s the Franco-American explorer, Paul du Chaillu (q. v.), encountered Séké living behind the far northern coasts and as far east as the Monts de Cristal, 150 miles inland, where they too were experiencing the pressure of Fang migrations westward.

Séké and Bakèlè chiefs on the Como and Remboué rivers signed treaties recognizing French sovereignty on December 2, 1846. The Séké leader, King Kianlinwin of the Mondah, accepted French protection through a treaty of February 14, 1848.

The Holy Ghost Fathers (q. v.) in 1851-1852 attempted unsuccessfully to evangelize among the Séké, Bakèlè, and Mpongwe at Chinchoua (Ntché-Ntchuwa) on the lower Remboué. Their attempt in 1877 to establish a mission among the Séké of the Mondah River also failed. Only in 1890 did their mission on the Rio Muni, first at Kogo on the northern shore in territory eventually awarded to Spain, and then at Boutika on the southern shore, gain a modest Séké audience. By that time the trading factories of several European firms, particularly British ones, were well-established among the Séké. [251, 178]

SHAKE. The Shaké people belong to the Bakota linguistic

group. Together with a closely related people, the Dambomo, they inhabit the upper Ogooué above Booué and along the road from Booué to Lalara. Other Shaké live north of Lastoursville. A third closely related people, the Shamai, live north of Okondja in the Haut-Ogooué Province. The traditions of these three peoples relate their departure from the upper Ivindo River because of Poupou's War and their passage to Mt. Ngouadi in the Okondja District where they formed three peoples. From there in the late nineteenth century they passed into the Ogooué east of Booué where they encountered a people called the Chiwa (q. v.) whom they forced towards the junction of the Ivindo River. The Chiwa had previously fought the pygmies near Booué. The Bakèlè (q. v.) who had accompanied them towards Booué fled during the war with the Chiwa and mounted the Lolo River as far as Koulamoutou.

The three peoples made objects both of iron and of copper. The copper came from an open pit near Minc on the upper Djidji (Dilo) River. They hunted elephants, buffaloes, and sanglies, the meat of which they sold, after the arrival of the French, to the factories of the SHO (q. v.) and to the posts at Booué and Lastoursville. Earlier they had sold slaves to the Okandé (q. v.), sometimes through Chiwa intermediaries, for transmission to the coast. [235, 189]

SHIMBA (or SIMBA). A not very numerous people of the Okandé linguistic group living in the forested lower Offoué and the upper Ikoyi River. [189]

SHO see SOCIETE COMMERCIALE, INDUSTRIELLE ET AGRICOLE DU HAUT-OGOOUE

SLAVE TRADE. Gabon was never a major site of the Atlantic slave trade as were the Niger River Delta, the Congo, and Angola, but the slave trade carried on there, above all from the 1760s to the 1860s, affected a majority of its peoples. Practically all of the peoples of Gabon engaged in the slave trade at one time or another. The most notable exception was the Fang people, who possessed few slaves and refused to become involved in the slave trade despite the opportunities that the warfare connected with their frequent migrations offered to them. While some slaves were obtained in warfare and in slave raids, most of them were exchanged by members of their own societies who were interested in securing European goods and/or getting rid of "undesirables," both slave and free.

Geography helped to postpone and limit the impact of the slave trade in Gabon. Nearly 75 percent of the country is covered with tropical rainforest; slightly under 20 percent is grasslands and the remainder is coastal marshlands. The soils of the forests are generally mediocre and some of the most important food staples were introduced by the Portuguese from the New World only late in the sixteenth century and after. Thus the population tended to be sparse and scattered. Though Gabon has numerous rivers and streams, many of them contain sandbars and/or rapids which prevent the passage of vessels. The absence of very many beasts of burden because of tropical diseases, such as that spread by the tsetse fly, meant that much of the passage inland had to be on foot.

When European traders arrived in the Estuary and along the Atlantic coasts in the sixteenth century, they found few slaves available, few especially in relation to the much larger numbers available both to the north (the Niger Delta) and to the south (the Congo and Angola). Only during the last third of the eighteenth century, in response to the increased demand from the New World, did the Mpongwe (q. v.) of the Estuary and the Orungu (q. v.) at Cape Lopez become more actively involved. Because the upper reaches of the Remboué River, which flowed northward into the Estuary, lay only a few miles north of Lambaréné Island in the Ogooué, a network was able to develop linking the Mpongwe of the southern Estuary shore with the Galoa (q. v.) suppliers around Lambaréné and other peoples beyond. The Galoa were also linked with the Orungu 160 miles downstream at the mouth of the Ogooué and peoples upstream. Trade on the Ogooué was conducted under a system in which each group along the river dominated a section and acted as middlemen for goods and slaves passing up- or downstream. The inland peoples who provided the largest numbers of slaves for these two networks had the most numerous populations: the Apindji, Adouma, Eshira, and Mitsogo (qq. v.). Slaves were also drawn from the Nzabi, Massango, Shaké (qq. v.), and other peoples.

The increased demand of the New World for slaves coincided with the Industrial Revolution in Europe, which gradually lowered the price of the now mass-produced British manufactures and thus made them even more competitive with African goods. The apparently increased supply of slaves by the 1760s may have resulted from the westward migrations of various peoples into the Ogooué River system and towards the coasts during the eighteenth and nineteenth centuries, some of them seeking increased trade with the Europeans.

Complete statistics for the slave trade are lacking but reliable estimates for some periods are available. It is likely that 500 slaves were being exported annually from the Estuary and Cape Lopez in the 1780s and 1790s and 1, 500 annually between 1800 and 1815. Total slave exports from these two areas likely averaged several thousands a year between 1815 and 1830.

Beginning in 1815, Britain sought to terminate the slave trade, first north of the Equator, and to gain the cooperation of other nations such as France for this purpose. French cooperation was half-hearted and grudging, for the French resented British commercial supremacy on most of the western and equatorial coasts from the Gambia to Angola. They were suspicious, with some justification, of British motives. Though the French officially listed a desire to end the slave trade as one of the reasons for establishing a post in the Estuary in 1843, they wished even more to promote French commerce and thereby gain supremacy over the British. Between the 1840s and the 1860s the French showed much more zeal in seeking cessions of sovereignty from the Gabonese peoples and in trying to restrict the activities and influence of English-speaking traders and missionaries than in combatting the nefarious slave trade. Between 1857 and 1862 the government permitted the Régis Company of Marseilles to recruit indentured servants for the West Indies using methods that frequently resembled the discredited slave trade. It would appear that French antislaving activities became important and regular only in the 1860s, that is, after they had gained formal control of the Estuary and northern coasts. In the 1840s and 1850s they made only irregular and unsystematic efforts, and then only after prodding by the British.

After the Anglo-French convention of May 29, 1845, which provided for the involvement of French squadrons along with British and American ones in policing the coasts, the French commander in Gabon ordered the Estuary leaders to end all traffic in slaves immediately and the European slavers to leave the southern shore. Fear of British navy patrols, in particular, from the mid-1840s caused the slavers to convert a heretofore open trade into a clandestine one. Most of this was conducted by Portuguese, Spanish, and Brazilians, often using ships owned or financed by Americans. The slavers made increasing use of São Tomé and Príncipe as trans-shipment points on the way to Brazil and Cuba. The virtual closure of the Brazilian market after 1850 was only partially compensated by the agricultural boom on the Portuguese islands in 1860 and after. At that time São Tomé and Príncipe acquired cocoa plantations worked largely by slave labor. While one can cite the arrest of a Portuguese slaver in Orungu territory by the French in 1887, it appears that the slave trade had largely ended in the Estuary during the 1860s and at Cape Lopez in the 1870s.

A small slave trade was carried on along the southern mouth of the Ogooué (the Fernan Vaz mouth) among the Nkomi (q. v.) people. It drew slaves from the Ogooué River system. It appears that the Nkomi trade was never extensive, except perhaps in the 1830s. A more extensive trade was carried on farther south in the Gabon provinces of the Loango (q. v.) kingdom through the trade had a shorter duration than that in northern Gabon.

Loango, whose main provinces are today located in the Congo Republic, became an important center of the slave trade in the eighteenth century with French traders predominating. The northern provinces, now in Gabon, were at first involved in a minor way. The provinces of Mayumba, Setté-Cama, and Gobby from the seventeenth century exchanged salt, guns, and cloth mainly for ivory with the interior peoples of the upper Nyanga, N'Gounié, and Ogooué Rivers. In the course of this trade they received a few slaves whom they took south to Loango Bay for dispatch to the New World. These slaves came from the Bapounou (q. v.) and Voungou (q. v.) peoples and to a lesser extent from the Mitsogo, Massango, and Pove, in other words from some of the same populations who supplied northern Gabon. But in the late 1840s, as a result of British and French efforts to suppress the slave trade in the Estuary and at Cape Lopez, a much increased effort arose at Mayumba and Banda on the Banio Lagoon to secure slaves from these various interior peoples. Brazilian, Spanish, and Portuguese traders, as in northern Gabon, were the most active in search of the high profits of the Brazilian and Cuban markets. Many of the ships were American-built and owned since the United States refused until 1862 to allow other nations to search American ships. The new slave trade involved an increased number of points from which slaves were embarked and the establishment of more permanent white trading posts ashore. Through these tactics the slave traders sought to circumvent the growing threat from patrolling cruisers. Between the 1840s and 1870s most slaves from the Iguéla Lagoon and Setté-Cama were marched south to Mayumba, a town of one thousand inhabitants. The same traders who were already operating at Loango Bay or Cabinda maintained barracoons there, which usually held 500-600 captives awaiting a ship. At Banda, on the coast near the southern end of Banio Lagoon, 700-800 captives customarily could be found. Many of the slaves were transported to São Tomé for transfer to other slaving vessels headed for the West Indies and South America. It thus appeared that several thousand slaves annually left the southern Gabon coast in the mid-nineteenth century. Taking Gabon as a whole, the bulk of the slaves went to South America, particularly to Brazil, and to the West Indies, especially to Cuba. Some were taken to São Tomé and Príncipe but only a few reached North America.

It is difficult to evaluate the consequences of the slave trade in Gabon. Given the absence of reliable population figures, it is impossible to know the exact percentage annually captured or sold. Estimates range from one to five percent of populations numbered at 150,000 to 250,000. It should be recalled that only the young and able-bodied were generally recruited for the slave trade. A portion of those taken in the interior did not survive the trip to the coast or the stay in the barracoons. Others perished under the horrible conditions of the long voyage to the New World and of the plantations there. The past two decades have seen a number of scholars argue that this loss of manpower was not serious and was more than compensated by the economic stimulus of the European goods thus obtained. Even if one agrees with their economic conclusions, one must not forget the terrible sufferings of the victims and their families as well as the many deaths arising from the slave trade and plantation slavery. Though blacks were involved in selling other blacks to whites, the slave trade contributed to the racial attitudes and practices that have plagued black-white relations in the western world during the past four centuries. See FREE EMIGRANTS SCHEME. [232, 214, 170, 40, 48, 102]

SOCIETE COMMERCIALE, INDUSTRIELLE ET AGRICOLE DU HAUT-OGOOUE (SHO). Most important concessionary company in Gabon. The SHO held a commercial monopoly over 104,000 sq. km. out of 257,000 sq. km. in all Gabon between 1893 and 1930. The establishment of this chartered company in eastern and southeastern Gabon predated the general French policy of developing French Equatorial Africa through some forty concessionary companies in 1899. The SHO possessed even more extensive powers with fewer responsibilities than the later enterprises and its sway lasted two decades longer than most of them, in part because it was better funded and directed. The SHO was founded at the urgings of Savorgnan de Brazza (q.v.) by Marius-Célestin Daumas (d. 1894), a one-time agent of the Régis firm of Marseilles who was long involved in commerce in Gabon and was the most successful French businessman there. The SHO had its own police force and administered justice in its territories. Though it eventually had to pay customs duties, it did not have to establish native reserves as the later companies were required to do, pay rent, or make plantations. It held a monopoly of trade in its vast territories, including the sale of European imports and the purchase of local products such as rubber. It took exorbitant profits from both processes. For a kilogram of rubber, which usually took an African gatherer four work days and which brought fifteen francs in Europe (three dollars at the time), it exchanged a kilogram of salt or two needles. Because the Ogooué River above N'Djolé and most of its tributaries were blocked by waterfalls and rapids, and because steamboat transport was impossible and portage necessary, the SHO forcibly recruited porters and demanded the sale of foodstuffs from the area's peoples. Its activities frequently involved injustice and brutality. They contributed to African resistance, including opposition led by the Fang chief Emane Tole (q.v.) near N'Djolé in 1901-1902, on the N'Gounié among the Mitsogo and Apindji 1903-1909, and by Awandji (q.v.) chiefs near Lastoursville in 1928-1929. The SHO built 100 km. of roads at an expense of one and a half million francs to try to reduce portage but was unable to secure the labor to maintain them. Through a subsidiary, the SHO became active in lumbering in the 1920s, especially in the okoumé whose value Daumas had perspicaciously recognized in the early 1890s. In 1930 the SHO relinquished its concession in exchange for outright title to 35,000 hectares (70,000 acres) of choice timberland. [182]

SOCIETY. The various peoples of Gabon traditionally possessed a social organization based on kinship. Members of an extended family or lineage shared a common ancestry. Related lineages formed clans and related clans composed peoples (often called tribes in older usage). Originally a clan was governed by its elders, heads of families or lineages, and clan heads were spokesmen for their decisions and arbitrators of disputes. Some peoples had clan councils which handled disputes and regulated matters of common concern. Only the Orungu of Cape Lopez and the Vili of the Loango coast developed centralized monarchies, in both cases in response to external trade. (The Nkomi at Fernan-Vaz also had a monarchy in the 1830s at the height of the slave trade.) But changes in the patterns of this trade later helped to destroy these institutions. Succession to the monarchy and clan headship was generally confined to the members of a particular lineage. Within that lineage succession was either patrilineal or matrilineal but without primogeniture. Thus the succession ordinarily went to the oldest nephew of the previous ruler or head, that is, to the son of his brother (patrilineal) or of his sister (matrilineal). There are a few cases of female heads (e.g. the princess who founded the Vili-Loumbou kingdom at Mayumba and Enenga "queens" in the mid-nineteenth century.)

Custom and tradition governed social behavior and secret societies of both men and women enforced the decisions of the elders when necessary. The elders and clan heads exerted influence over the younger men through their control of the wealth of the society--use of the land, goods, and women.

Most peoples practiced domestic slavery, the slaves coming from other peoples by purchase, exchange, or warfare. Slaves did the agricultural work along with the free women, who ordinarily raised the group's foodstuffs. Peoples sold freemen into slavery as a means of social control and to obtain merchandise. Ordinarily they did not sell the domestic slaves, whose labor was necessary to ensure their food supply. Freemen often married slave women and their offspring became freemen. Children born to parents both of whom were slaves remained slaves.

Traders in these societies often achieved great influence because of their wealth, sometimes advancing ahead of others in succession for headships of villages and clans. Trade with Europeans on the coasts enriched some younger men, who gained more freedom from the control of their elders. During the colonial period the French transformed the role of the clan heads by forcing them to become the agents of the administration. The French also created canton or territorial chiefs who had no bases in traditional society. After the Second World War, the western educated, which included some persons who belonged to the lineages of clan heads, acquired positions in the new representative institutions and administration, which further weakened the traditional organization. The extended family or lineage nevertheless remains primary in the social relations and loyalties of most persons, even many with a western education.

Gabon today possesses social classes based upon economic and educational factors. In 1978 there were 267,000 persons involved in agriculture; 60,000 in forestry, mining, and construction; 8,200 in commerce and industry; 8,000 in the civil service; 38,200 in other activities (military, clergy, independent professionals, students in higher education, and others). Those in agriculture are largely subsistence farmers who own their own land, livestock, and tools. Commercial farmers, organized in cooperatives which utilize some machinery, are found mainly in the Woleu N'Tem Province (cocoa, coffee) and around Lambaréné in the Moyen-Ogooué Province (palm products). While Gabonese provide the unskilled and some skilled labor for forestry, mining, and construction, top-level technical and management personnel are Europeans. In the civil service French experts continue to fill a majority of the key technical and administrative positions but under the direction of Gabonese executives. The well-educated Gabonese tend to form a bureaucratic class that lives through government employment. The long-time domination of the economy by Europeans prevented the development of a Gabonese bourgeoisie during the colonial period. An economically independent class has emerged mainly since independence and primarily in the area of urban real estate investments. The economic expansion of the past decade, in particular, has greatly increased the numbers of non-Gabonese African wage laborers, which were always a feature of the labor-short society during the colonial period. [170, 197, 261, 268]

SOUSATTE, RENE-PAUL (1912-1971). Politician. Sousatte came from the Eshira area of the N'Gounié Province. He studied at the Catholic seminaries in Libreville and Brazzaville, leaving the latter shortly before ordination.

He joined the civil service at Brazzaville in 1937 where he was a colleague of Jean-Hilaire Aubame (q. v.) and Jean-Rémy Ayouné (q. v.). Sousatte supported the Free French (q. v.) movement in 1940 and under Governor-General Félix Eboué (q. v.) became head of an organization of civil servants, the Union Educative et Mutuelle de la Jeunesse de Brazzaville, which published a pro-Gaullist newspaper, L'Education de la Jeunesse Africaine. He also advised Eboué on African matters. In 1947 the Territorial Assembly elected Sousatte to represent Gabon in the Assembly of the French Union. Thereafter he founded the Comité Gabonais d'Etudes Sociales et Economiques (COGES) (q. v.) to foster cooperation among Gabon's peoples in order to promote modernization of society and to develop a political base for himself. COGES had sections in the main towns and found members mainly among the Eshira and Myènè. Paul Gondjout (q. v.) headed the Libreville section. Sousatte became active in various Franco-African groups as well as the African section of the Gaullist party, the Rassemblement du Peuple Français. He published a book, L'Afrique Equatoriale Française, Berceau de l'Union Française (1952), which discussed the Free French movement and Gabon's importance to France. He wrote articles for the RPF paper, L'Etincelle de l'AEF. His Gaullist politics contributed to his failure to be renamed to his post in 1952 as well as to the refusal of the administration to readmit him to the civil service upon his return to Gabon. For the next five years he worked in Madagascar, returning to Gabon after the collapse of the Fourth Republic to reenter politics. Several weeks before the September 1958 referendum on the French Community, with J.-J. Boucavel (q. v.) he organized a party of southern peoples, especially the Eshira and Bapounou, who were dissatisfied with the Fang and Myènè leadership of the UDSG and BDG, and urged a negative vote. The Parti d'Union Nationale Gabonaise (q. v.) or PUNGA (a name which happens to mean "tempest" in Eshira) succeeded in mobilizing a majority in the Nyanga Province, a Bapounou area, against the Community. PUNGA also had a small national following among trade unionists and students. After independence, Sousatte was arrested for his opposition to some of Mba's policies but in 1962-1963 served as Minister of Agriculture until the breakup of the coalition government. Sousatte thereafter returned to Port-Gentil where he spent his remaining years in private business. [381, 335]

SPIRITANS see HOLY GHOST FATHERS

- T -

TCHICAYA, JEAN-FELIX (1903-1961). Ponty School graduate and deputy from Gabon & Middle Congo to the French National Assembly. Tchicaya was born on November 9, 1903, at Libreville into a prominent Vili family from Diosso (Buali) on the Loango (q. v.) coast in a period when the Kouilou Region formed part of Gabon. His grandfather, André Portella, was one of the wealthiest Vili merchants at Diosso. As one of the two brightest graduates of the public school of Libreville, Tchicaya was sent in 1918 on government scholarship to the William Ponty School at Dakar where he was a classmate of Houphouet-Boigny and Mamba Sano and one year behind Mamadou Konaté, like him all future deputies. In 1921, upon his return to Gabon, he was appointed an upper-primary teacher at the Libreville school. In 1923-24, after quarreling with the French principal of the school, he was dismissed. His grandfather summoned him in 1925 to Pointe-Noire to work with the administration in the construction of the port and the Congo-Ocean Railraod. There he organized the educated young Vili and others into a club and band, L'Harmonie de Pointe-Noire, and at the same time he formed among the Vili an informal protest committee, which succeeded through Portella's influence with the administration in winning a number of local reforms. When the Ma-Loango was imprisoned on minor charges, this committee mobilized the Vili to secure his release. When a French _chef de région_ became too arbitrary and severe in his relations with the Vili, Tchicaya's committee passed letters through Portella to Governor-General Raphaël Antonetti, which won his removal. Tchicaya was instrumental in winning election to the federal council of administration in 1937 and 1939 of Louis Oliveira, a Vili _métis_ educated at Libreville.

During the Second World War Tchicaya joined the armed forces of the Free French movement. In 1945 the voters of the second college of Gabon and Middle Congo elected Tchicaya as their deputy to the First Constituent Assembly. Later when the Gabonese secured their own deputy, he was elected as Middle Congo's deputy to the French National Assembly, serving from 1946 to 1958. Tchicaya became a vice-president of the territorial RDA. He died on January 15, 1961.

He was the father of the noted poet Tchicaya U'Tamsi. [378, 335, 80]

TEKE (or BATEKE). The Téké people inhabit the grassy plateaux east of Franceville in the Haut-Ogooué Province. They are related to the Téké or Tyo of the Congo Republic but had no political ties with the Makoko of the Pool area who made a treaty with Brazza on September 10, 1880, recognizing French sovereignty. The Téké are also related to the Mbamba, Ndoumou, and Kanigui. According to their traditions they were living near Ewo and Okoyo on the Alima River (a tributary of the Congo) when pressures from the Mbochi forced their transfer into the plateaux between the Alima and the Leconi Rivers (an Ogooué tributary) where they planted palm trees. As they retreated, they divided into three groups in uninhabited territories on the upper M'Passa, Leconi, and Lelani Rivers, probably in the mid-nineteenth century. At the arrival of Brazza the Téké had two important chiefs: Ngoshama on the Leconi and Lelani and Mbani-Lekivi on the upper M'Passa. The Téké sold slaves and raphia fabrics to the peoples of the Congo and Niari River systems (Congo Téké, Balali, Bapounou) in exchange for salt, fabrics, and goats. [189, 247, 228, 280, 303, 312]

TOKO (or NTOKO) RAVONYA (d. 1858). The leading trader of the Mpongwe village of Glass from 1840 until his death who allied with British and American merchants. His opposition to the recognition of French sovereignty helped to delay the French occupation of the lands of the Agekaza-Glass or Agekaza w'Olamba clan for several years between 1842 and 1845. Toko had given the land on which the ABCFM missionaries located their Baraka station in 1842 and was their protector and friend. His son, the Rev. Ntâkâ Truman (q. v.), was the first Mpongwe to be ordained a Presbyterian minister. Toko himself headed the Agwesono clan which lived among the Glass people. [173, 170, 232]

TRANSPORTATION. In pre-colonial times the main means of transporting men and goods was canoes on waterways. Gabon has many rivers but only 3300 km. of them are navigable in all seasons. The presence of rapids and waterfalls, especially where they drop from plateaux to plains, made human portage a necessity. In a country that is both heavily forested and sparsely populated, neither the manpower nor the funds were available to build roads, even if the projects had been viable.

Trade and commerce remained water-borne in the colonial period even after the arrival of the steamboat and other power-driven vessels. The exploitation of woods that could be floated down streams became the chief industry. The colonial administration helped to develop the ports of Port-Gentil and Libreville to aid this industry and commerce in general, but the costs of constructing and maintaining very many all-season roads remained prohibitive. Most of the 6,848 km. of roads today are laterite and are cut by numerous creeks. A great number of them are usable only in the dry season. 221 km. of roads are bituminous, including the national highways from Libreville to Lambaréné built under FIDES (q.v.) in the 1950s. At present one can travel by motor vehicle in the dry season on a north-south axis from Cameroon to the Congo via N'Djolé and Lambaréné (870 km.) and on a west-east axis from Libreville to Franceville via N'Djolé and Lastoursville (774 km.)

The difficulties of road travel have led since the Second World War to the construction of a rather dense air network. Libreville, Port-Gentil, and Franceville have international airports and there are 121 smaller airports and landing fields distributed throughout the country. As of June 1977 Gabon withdrew from the inter-state Air Afrique and replaced its services with Air-Gabon, a government company that heretofore was operating only within the country. Gabon is served internationally by such lines as Air France, UTA, Sabena, and Swiss Air.

The construction of the Transgabonais Railroad has been undertaken by the Bongo regime to reach the forest and mineral riches of the interior where the rivers are not navigable for long stretches or where road-building and maintenance are not viable or would be more expensive. There are plans to vitalize the entire economic life of the regions served. The first stage of 332 km. from Owendo in the Estuary to Booué in the middle Ogooué was begun in late 1974. By 1978 the railroad was in operation as far as N'Djolé, that is, for about half the distance. The 363 km. stage from Booué to Franceville has been concurrently under construction. Definitive studies for the final stage of 240 km. from Booué to Belinga have been completed. A short section of 30 km. will link Owendo with the new mineral port at Santa Clara. The facilities for receiving the increased volume of wood at the port of Owendo 15 km. south-east of Libreville were scheduled for completion in 1979. Facilities for manganese and iron will be built later. [478, 390, 392]

TRILLES, HENRI (1866-1949). A Spiritan priest from Clermont-Ferrand who served in Gabon from 1893 to 1907. He became an expert on the Fang (q. v.) and their language as well as the Pygmies (q. v.) of the northeast, peoples about whom he wrote many volumes. He was also an amateur botanist. [635]

TRUMAN see NTAKA TRUMAN

- U -

UNION DEMOCRATIQUE ET SOCIALE GABONAISE (UDSG). The political party that formed around Jean-Hilaire Aubame (q. v.) in 1947 following his election as deputy to the French National Assembly in November 1946. It supported his re-election in 1951 and 1956 and presented lists of candidates in the elections for the Territorial Assembly in 1952 and 1957. The UDSG relied upon local influentials and regional groups to organize its electoral support. It had the support of the missions and between 1947 and 1956 the sympathy of the French administration. Though the UDSG won a majority of the popular votes in the Territorial Assembly elections in 1957, its opponents among the BDG and Independents were able to organize the first executive council and make Léon Mba its chief African member. BDG control of the government thereafter inhibited its actions and in the 1964 elections it refused to present candidates. The UDSG's legal existence was terminated in March 1968 by President Bongo's decree dissolving all parties as a prelude to formation of a single party, the PDG. [335, 364]

UNION DOUANIERE ET ECONOMIQUE DE L'AFRIQUE CENTRALE (UDEAC). A customs and economic union of Gabon, Congo, the Central African Republic, and Cameroon. During the colonial period Gabon had economic links with the other territories of French Equatorial Africa and with Cameroon, which was a French mandate and later a trusteeship territory. After the dissolution of the federation of French Equatorial Africa, Gabon and the other three states decided to remain linked in a customs union. On June 23, 1959, they signed a treaty establishing the Union Douanière Equatoriale (UDE) whose main features were 1) the free movement of goods and capital among the member countries; 2) the introduction of common import taxes; 3) the creation of a solidarity fund; and 4) the introduction of a single tax system (taxe unique). The solidarity tax sought to compensate the inland states (Central African Republic and Chad) for the advantages the coastal states derived from the transit trade. The single tax applied to products of the five states with a view to protecting and encouraging domestic industry. On June 22, 1961, Cameroon became an associate member of the UDE under terms which permitted retention of its separate import duties and taxes. But from July 1, 1962, the five countries established a common external tariff limited to customs duties.

Then on December 8, 1964, the five signed a treaty creating UDEAC whereby they undertook to strengthen the customs union and transform it into a broader economic union. To this end they took steps to harmonize customs, fiscal, and investment policies. By the time UDEAC took effect on January 1, 1966, unification of import taxation had largely been achieved while taxation of exports remained the prerogative of the individual states subject to mutual consultation. One important feature concerning import taxation retained from the UDE was exemption from customs duties of goods from the countries of the European Common Market and from the other states in the former Organization of African and Malagasy States for Economic Cooperation (Benin, Ivory Coast, Madagascar, Mauritania, Niger, Senegal, and Upper Volta). This provision had the effect of disfavoring products from non-EEC industrial nations such as the United States, Japan, and until its entrance into the EEC, the United Kingdom.

Dissatisfaction with the results of UDEAC by the inland states led to their withdrawal on April 25, 1968. On the previous February 1, the Central African Republic and Chad had joined Zaire in forming the Union des Etats d'Afrique du Centre or UEAC from which they hoped to achieve greater benefits. But on December 10, the CAR returned to UDEAC. Chad did not, but subsequently it made its own arrangements with Cameroon through which most of its transit trade passes.

The policies of UDEAC are determined by agreement of the heads of state meeting periodically and are implemented by a committee of their ministers of finances and economic affairs. The secretariat of UDEAC is located at Bangui, Central African Republic.

The UDEAC members on May 3, 1976, organized the Banque de Développement des Etats de l'Afrique Centrale with its seat at Brazzaville. A decade earlier they had established an oil refinery at Port-Gentil for common use. [383, 398, 406, 409, 418, 120]

URANIUM. The exploitation of uranium began in 1961 at Mounana 25 km. north of Moanda, that is, in the same part of the Haut-Ogooué Province where manganese was being exploited. The ore is concentrated before export by a French consortium, the Compagnie des Mines d'Uranium de Franceville (COMULF), which offers it on world markets through the French Atomic Energy Commission. Production of uranium concentrates has averaged 1, 500 metric tons annually. The reserves at Mounana are estimated at 2, 500, 000 tons. In September 1972 a huge new reserve was located at Oklo between Mounana and Franceville. Expansion depends in large part upon the capacity of France and other nations to develop atomic-energy based power. At present the uranium is transferred by truck to M'Binda in the Congo Republic and from there by the Congo-Ocean Railroad to the port of Pointe-Noire. [478]

- V -

VANE, FRANCOIS-DE-PAUL (ca. 1890-1957). Estuary political leader during interwar period. Vané was descended from a chiefly Benga family that was among the first to convert to Roman Catholicism in the 1850s. He was raised by the Holy Ghost Fathers at Libreville and educated at their seminary. Though he left in 1911 in the middle of his theological studies, he was nevertheless one of the best educated Gabonese of his day. From 1912 to 1925 Vané worked in the Ivory Coast. After his return to Libreville he became chief accountant for a Senegalese merchant and in 1926 the Secretary-General and moving spirit of the local chapter of the Ligue des Droits de l'Homme. In this capacity he sought reforms that would benefit the Estuary elite and defended their traditional land rights upon which the colonial authorities and other peoples were encroaching. After the administration succeeded in dividing the elite through its support for métis interests, Vané with various leading Mpongwe organized the Mutuelle Gabonaise (q. v.) to oppose a special favored status for just the métis. The Mutuelle, though primarily a cultural and educational organization, brought together the older generation which had supported the Ligue and the younger men who had studied at the Ecole Montfort and the Catholic seminary during the 1920s and early 1930s. Under the auspices of the Catholic mission Vané in 1933 had previously organized the Cercle Catholique, which served to educate and to heighten elite awareness. In October 1937 Vané won election as Gabon's delegate to the new federal council of administration at Brazzaville, defeating the candidate appointed temporarily the previous year, Pierre-Marie Akanda, an Mpongwe lumberman. He was re-elected in June 1939 and used his office to speak out in defense of elite and African interests. He thus successfully opposed measures initiated by French officials which would have had the effect of restricting Christian mission schools to catechismal instruction and therefore of lessening educational opportunities. He helped to secure the decree of February 10, 1938, recognizing limited traditional land rights and providing a new basis for claims for compensation for land taken by the administration. In 1938 Vané was among the first two Africans named to the Libreville municipal commission.

When French Equatorial Africa rallied to Free France in August 1940, Vané and the Mpongwe elite followed the bishop of Libreville, Monsignor Louis Tardy, in support of Vichy. The Free French replaced Vané as Gabon's delegate at Brazzaville with Akanda and later Georges Damas. Though still influential, Vané was not permitted to participate in politics until 1946. In December 1946 he ran unsuccessfully for the Territorial Assembly. For the remainder of his life he worked in private business and supervised his plantations at Cape Esterias. [335]

VARAMA. The Varama are a people of the southwestern interior linguistically related to the Eshira group. They live inland from the Loumbou along the Rembo Ndogo, which flows southwest into the Ndogo Lagoon and north of the Rembo Nkomi, as well as both north and south of the Eshira proper. [189]

VILI. A people of southwestern Gabon and the adjacent coasts of the Congo Republic. The Vili language is a branch of the large Kongo family of the West Central Bantu. It is a dialect of the language spoken in Mbanza Kingo (San Salvador), the capital of the Kongo Kingdom, which is now located within Angola. Oral traditions suggest common origins for the Vili, Kongo, Téké (Tio), and Woyo peoples in an inland kingdom called Nguunu, north of the Stanley Pool, from which a dispersion occurred, perhaps as early as the eleventh century. After proceeding to the lower Congo River, the populations that became the Vili transferred by the thirteenth or fourteenth centuries to the Loango coast, where Portuguese navigators encountered them in the 1480s. By that time Vili were found along the Gabon coast as far north as Cape Saint Catherine, including the shores of the Iguéla Lagoon, Ndugu Lagoon (Setté-Cama), and the Banio Lagoon (at Mayumba and Banda). Nineteenth-century European explorers also encountered small groups of Vili on the upper N'Gounié and Ogooué rivers where they engaged as middlemen in the salt and ivory trade. These Vili may have been remnants from a period during which the power of Loango (q. v.) extended over the whole region. If this be the case, then incoming groups such as the Eshira, Bakèlè, and Fang had pushed them south. Alternately, they may have been emigrants from Loango in the eighteenth century who moved away from the coast following a disagreement with their ruler.

The Vili of the coastal regions were traditionally involved in agriculture, hunting, and fishing. They made salt and palm cloth for trade as well as domestic purposes. Vili miners and coppersmiths lived part of each year at the mines inland beyond the Mayombe mountain range and Vili porters carried the smelted ore and manufactures to the coasts. During the seventeenth century the Vili traded in ivory and in the eighteenth century in slaves with the interior peoples. Until the nineteenth century the Vili rulers controlled the terms of trade with the European merchants.

Attempts by French Catholic missionaries to evangelize the Vili and Kongo between 1766 and 1776 met with failure. The Holy Ghost Fathers (q. v.) conducted a ministry among the Vili who composed the core of Libreville, a settlement of freed slaves, in 1849 and after. From the 1870s the Holy Ghost Fathers undertook missions on the Loango and Congo coasts, including at the town of Loango in 1883. Catholic mission work on the southern Gabon coast was based on Loango and a seminary was located at Mayumba.

With the onset of French colonial rule, the Vili became porters and agents of European firms. At the submission of the Loango monarch to French rule in 1883, the French attached the entire Loango coast as far south as the Portuguese territory of Cabinda to Gabon. It remained part of Gabon until 1918 when it was transferred to the colony of the Middle Congo. The link during several decades between Loango and the Gabon colony led to the establishment of Vili populations at both Libreville and Port-Gentil which at independence numbered 600 persons. Gabon's first deputy to the French Constituent Assembly in 1945 was a Vili, Jean-Félix Tchicaya, a native of Libreville with family ties in Loango. [214, 247, 291, 251]

VOIX DU PAYS, LA. In 1935 the Séké leader of the Libreville branch of the Ligue des Droits de l'Homme, Jean-Baptiste N'Dendé (q. v.), helped a number of Fang (q. v.) elders to organize La Voix du Pays to unite the Fang populations vis à vis the Mpongwe and the French administration. This move was a reaction to the formation of the Association Amicale des Métis and the Comité Mpongwe by métis on the one hand, and full-blooded Mpongwe on the other, to defend and assert their traditional rights to property and influence in the Estuary. By this time the Fang were the most numerous people at Libreville and had been left without effective leadership since the conviction and exile of Léon Mba (q. v.) in 1933. According to its statutes, which were drawn to secure legal recognition, the primary aim was to encourage cooperative agriculture and fishing among the Libreville Fang, and to this end a shop was established to market Fang produce. Though the group did not become involved in the elections for a delegate to the governor-general's council of administration in 1937 and 1939, behind the scenes it worked successfully to promote the careers of several Fang civil servants, to the end that these men soon controlled key posts in the office of the French administrator-mayor of Libreville. [335]

VOUNGOU. The Voungou people of the southwestern interior are linguistically part of the Eshira group. According to their traditions they originally lived on the left bank of the upper N'Gounié River at a time when the Mitsogo (q. v.) inhabited the right bank. Warlike Bapounou (q. v.) invaders pushed them a bit to the west into the forested mountainous areas west of the Moukabala River, a tributary of the Nyanga River, where they still live. Among them habitual offenders and debtors could be reduced to slavery. The Voungou also enslaved defenseless foreigners whom they transmitted to the Eshira (q. v.) for sale to the Nkomi (q. v.) of Fernan Vaz and to the Loumbou (q. v.) of Setté-Cama. In return they received salt and fabrics from Portuguese and British traders. In the nineteenth century they gathered and sold rubber to American traders based at Mayumba. [189, 247]

- W -

WALKER, ANDRE RAPONDA- (1871-1968). First Gabonese priest and the nation's most noted scholar to date. Monsignor Walker was the son of Robert Bruce Napoleon Walker (1830-1900), British agent for the Hatton & Cookson firm in Gabon between 1859 and 1875 and explorer of the middle Ogooué, and an aristocratic Mpongwe, Agñorogoulé Ikoutu (1852-1912). She was the niece of King Georges (q. v.) and a relative of King Louis (q. v.). André Walker was educated by the Holy Ghost Fathers entirely in Gabon and was ordained a Roman Catholic priest on July 23, 1899. While serving as a pastor and teacher in many parts of Gabon during the next five decades, he became an expert on the peoples, languages, history, and botany of his country. Among the most important of his extensive publications are _Notes d'Histoire du Gabon_ (1960), _Plantes utiles du Gabon_ (1959), and _Rites et Croyances des Peuples du Gabon_ (1962), the latter two volumes in collaboration with the French scholar, Roger Sillans. Walker's unpublished autobiography is a valuable source for Gabonese history. In May 1963 he was made a domestic prelate by Pope John XXIII with the title of monsignor.

In early December 1964 Monsignor Walker clashed with President Mba (q. v.) as a result of a tract he had sent to Parisian newspapers denouncing the exactions and acts of violence committed by the president's Fang supporters during October. Mba expelled the elderly prelate from St. Peter's rectory near the presidential palace and 40 to 50 Fang from the president's Essoké clan beat him unconscious and sacked his library. [189, 347]

WALKER, WILLIAM (1808-96). American missionary in Gabon, 1842-70, 1879-83, and translator of the Scriptures into Mpongwe. Rev. William Walker was born at Vershire, Vermont, on October 3, 1808, and worked as a young man as a blacksmith, a trade he continued to practice for the ABCFM mission in Gabon. Educated at Amherst College and at Andover Seminary in Massachusetts, Walker went out to Cape Palmas (now in Liberia) in February 1842 and later that year to Gabon. Over the next forty years he served as pastor of the church at Baraka, head of the boys' boarding school, and translator of large portions of the Old and New Testaments into Mpongwe. In 1854 Walker and the Rev. Ira Preston (q. v.) made a pioneering exploration up the Nazareth mouth of the Ogooué River half way to the site of present-day Lambaréné, the first whites so to venture. His diaries are an important source for the history of Gabon. Walker served as a Congregationalist minister in Milton, Wisconsin, after his final return to the States until his death on December 8, 1896. [230, 517]

WALKER-DEEMIN, HENRI (1930-). Civil servant. Walker-Deemin was born at Libreville on November 30, 1930, into a prominent métis (q. v.) family. Between 1936 and 1948 he did his primary and secondary studies in France. Back in Gabon he prepared to be a primary teacher and school inspector. Since 1956 he has held a variety of positions in education, culture, and information. He was the president of the national commission for Unesco (1970-1973) and since then has served as director of the Official Journal. Walker-Deemin is a gifted poet who writes in French. [682]

WILSON, JOHN LEIGHTON (1809-86). Founder of the American Protestant mission in the Estuary and specialist in Mpongwe (q. v.). The Rev. J. L. Wilson was born in Mount Clio, South Carolina, on March 25, 1809, into a family of prosperous Scotch-Irish landowners and prominent Presbyterians. He was educated at Union College, Schenectady, New York, and the Columbia (South Carolina) Seminary. He married Jane Bayard of Savannah, Georgia, (1809-85), a member of a well-known aristocratic family of Huguenot origins. After ordination in 1833, he was commissioned by the American Board of Commissioners for Foreign Missions of Boston, the largest Protestant missionary society in the U. S. A., which represented churches of the Calvinist or Reformed traditions, to found a mission at Cape Palmas in the colony of the Maryland State Colonization Society in 1834. Disagreements between the mission and the officials of the colony led to the transfer of the ABCFM mission to Gabon in June 1842. For the next decade, until health problems forced his definitive return to the

States, Wilson was the animating spirit of the Protestant mission. Using the orthography developed by John Pickering for American Indian languages, he transcribed Mpongwe into Latin characters, prepared an Mpongwe grammar, an Mpongwe-English dictionary, and translated a portion of the Gospels into Mpongwe. He had these works and religious instructional materials that he prepared printed at Cape Palmas and Gabon on the mission press. He founded the Baraka church east of Libreville and served as its first pastor. He opened schools staffed in part by English-speaking black Americans and West Africans. As part of his campaign against the slave trade, he wrote a pamphlet which was distributed throughout England and influenced members of Parliament. He befriended the young Paul du Chaillu (q. v.) whose interest in the fauna of Gabon and exploration he helped to cultivate. Wilson located the skeletal remains of a gorilla which he brought back to the Peabody Museum in Boston, the first to reach America. After his return to the States, he published Western Africa: Its History, Condition, & Prospects (New York, 1856), a work influential in the anti-slavery movement and in making western Equatorial Africa known to the American public. Its information on peoples remains useful today. From 1853 Wilson served as secretary of the Presbyterian Board for Foreign Missions and, with the outbreak of the American Civil War, of the Southern Presbyterian Board until a year before his death on July 13, 1886. [169, 170, 173, 149]

WOUMBOU (or BAVUMBU). The Woumbou are a Bakota-speaking group who inhabit villages west of Franceville and south of that town on the upper Ogooué around Lebagni. Their traditions relate their arrival down the Sébé River with the Mindassa (Ndasa) and the Mbahouis into an empty territory. They were pushed further west by the Ambamba. They intermarried with the Ndoumou and the Babongo Pygmies. [235]

- Y -

YEMBIT, PAUL-MARIE (1917-). Vice-President under Mba. Yembit was born on December 22, 1917, at Ndende among the Bapounou (q. v.) people. He was educated at local Catholic schools and at the public secondary school at Lambaréné. He was a successful businessman at Mouila between 1943 and 1952. He was elected to the Territorial Assembly from the N'Gounié Province in March 1952 and was re-elected to the Legislative Assembly in March 1957 where he belonged to the Bloc Démocratique Gabonais. He was appointed Minister of Agriculture & Livestock in the first government council in March 1957. He held ministerial posts until becoming Vice-President of the Government in February 1961 and also served in the National Assembly. President Mba replaced him as Vice-President in November 1966 with Albert-Bernard Bongo. [642, 682]

BIBLIOGRAPHY

Introduction

There is no comprehensive introduction to Gabon or to its history. Those interested in the country must turn to specialized studies and to general works on all Equatorial Africa or all former French Black Africa. Among specialized works, Jacqueline Bouquerel [11] provides a good introduction to the economy, geography, and demography but is weak on history. An excellent geography text by two Gabonese teachers, Frédéric Meyo-Bibang and Jean-Martin Nzamba [478], is particularly strong for economic geography. The most comprehensive works on the peoples of Gabon, including their history, are those by André Raponda Walker [251] and Hubert Deschamps [189]. Marcel Soret [247] treats the peoples of the south and southeast who also inhabit the Congo Republic. Studies by K. David Patterson [232] and Henry Bucher [170-173] ably treat the history of the northern coastal regions through 1875. Phyllis Martin [214] deals with the portions of the southern coast under the sway of Loango through 1870. François Gaulme [197] analyzes the evolution of Nkomi society through the nineteenth century. Other works on individual peoples, including the impact of colonial rule, are those on the Fang by Georges Balandier [261] and James Fernandez [283, 286] and on the Bakota by Louis Perrois [235]. The only work which treats the entirety of Gabonese history is Meyo-Bibang's [221] outline for the secondary schools. Though sketchy, it is useful for the periods up to 1918. But its omissions create erroneous impressions about the country's political evolution during later periods. Helpful for understanding political developments from the Second World War through the end of the Mba regime are works by John Ballard [335, 336], Brian Weinstein [381], and Charles and Alice Darlington [347]. An authoritative article by Gilbert Comte [344] treats the Mba period and the early years of the Bongo regime. There is nothing comparable for Bongo's second seven-year term as president (1973-1980). Useful for both the politics and economics of the period 1945-1959 are the chapters in the detailed survey by Virginia Thompson and Richard Adloff [108]. Articles by David Gardinier [446, 448, 449] introduce educational developments since independence as well as the history of western education. Christian missionary activities in the nineteenth century have been recently studied by Penelope Campbell [505, 506] and David Gardinier [517, 518]. The best older work on Catholic evangelization in this period is that of Alexandre Le Roy [528]. André Raponda Walker and Roger Sillans [556] treat the traditional religions and beliefs of Gabon's peoples.

Students of contemporary affairs should start with the Gabon sections of several annual surveys: *Africa Contemporary Record* [637], *Africa South of the Sahara* [640], *Année Africaine* [647], *Année Politique Africaine* [648], *Annuaire du Tiers-Monde* [649], and the annual reference issue of *Europe-France-Outre-Mer* [684] (e. g. June 1978, Nov. 1979). News digests and press summaries are contained in the *Africa Research Bulletin* [639] and *Africa Report* [638]. Economic and political news are found in the *Quarterly Economic Review of Gabon* [680], the *Bulletin de l'Afrique Noire* [661], *Marchés Tropicaux et Méditerranéens* [707], and *Europe-France-Outre-Mer* [684]. *Africa Confidential* [636] has unsigned but usually reliable reports from time to time.

Continuing bibliographical sources for books and articles include *Afrique Contemporaine* [644], *Africana Journal* [643], *Current Bibliography of African Affairs* [670], and *International African Bibliography* [703]. For articles of interest to historians, see the Africa section of *Recently Published Articles* [720]. Unfortunately, the annual bibliography of works in French prepared by CARDAN [665] between 1969 and 1977 has no apparent successor.

Abbreviations in the Bibliography

AC	Armand Colin
AENA	*Annales de l'Ecole Nationale d'Administration*
AHA	American Historical Association
AJ	*Africana Journal*
ASA	African Studies Association
BDPA	Bureau pour le Développement de Production Agricole
Bibl.	Bibliography

BIEC	*Bulletin de l'Institut d'Etudes Centrafricaines*
BIFAN	*Bulletin de l'Institut Français d'Afrique Noire*
BIRSC	*Bulletin de l'Institut de Recherche Scientifique Centrafricaine*
B-L	Berger-Levrault
BMBCEAEC, ES / *BMBEAC, ES*	*Bulletin Mensuel de la Banque Centrale des Etats de l'Afrique Equatoriale et du Cameroun, Etudes Statistiques* / *Bulletin Mensuel de la Banque des Etats de l'Afrique Centrale, Etudes Statistiques.*
BSPPG	*Bulletin de la Société Préhistorique et Protohistorique Gabonaise*
BSRC	*Bulletin de la Société de Recherches Congolaises*
Bv.	Brazzaville
CEA	*Cahiers d'Etudes Africaines*
CJAS	*Canadian Journal of African Studies*
CNRS	Centre National de Recherche Scientifique
CNRST	Centre National de Recherche Scientifique et Technologique
CO-M	*Cahiers d'Outre-Mer*
CORSTOM, SSH	*Cahiers de l'Office de la Recherche Scientifique et Technique d'Outre-Mer*, série *Sciences Humaines*
CRMSASO-M / *CRTSASO-M*	*Comptes Rendus Mensuels des Séances de l'Académie des Sciences d'Outre-Mer* / *Comptes Rendus Trimestriels des Séances de l'Académie des Sciences d'Outre-Mer*
DF	La Documentation Française
Diss.	Dissertation
ed.	editor, edited
Ed.	Editions
FCS	*French Colonial Studies*
G-A	*Genève-Afrique*
HA	*History in Africa*
IJAHS	*International Journal of African Historical Studies*
Impr.	Imprimerie
IN	Imprimerie Nationale
IO	Imprimerie Officielle
IPN	Institut Pédagogique National

JA / JAS	Journal des Africanistes / Journal de la Société des Africanistes
JAH	Journal of African History
L.	London
Lv.	Libreville
MTM	Marchés Tropicaux et Méditerranéens
n. d.	no date
NED	Notes et Etudes Documentaires
no.	number
n. s.	new series, nouvelle série
N. Y.	New York
ORSTOM	Office de la Recherche Scientifique et Technique d'Outre-Mer
P.	Paris
PA	Présence Africaine
P&D-A	R. Pichon & R. Durand-Auzias
PB	Paul Bory
PDG	Parti Démocratique Gabonais
PFCHS	Proceedings of the French Colonial Historical Society
PUF	Presses Universitaires de France
RFEPA	Revue Française d'Etudes Politiques Africaines
RFHO-M / RHCF	Revue Française d'Histoire d'Outre-Mer / Revue d'Histoire des Colonies Françaises
RG	Réalites Gabonaises
RJP	Revue Juridique et Politique
RTM	Revue du Tiers-Monde
SME	Société des Missions Evangéliques
Tr.	Translation
U.	University
UP	University Press
v.	volume

Scope of the Bibliography

The bibliography includes the 740 books, articles, reports, and theses most useful for understanding Gabon and its history. It omits outdated works as well as most political and economic ephemera. A few of the latter are included on important matters where no larger studies are available. Some citations have been briefly annotated in brackets where their titles do not indicate their contents sufficiently. Nearly all publications on Gabon are in French and English and most of the remainder are in German.

Following the format of the series of Historical Dictionaries, the writings are grouped into fourteen subject categories. In addition, each item has been numbered individually so that the most important sources for the entries in the Dictionary portion of the volume can be readily identified. These references are given in brackets after each entry. The fourteen subject categories are:

I. GENERAL WORKS

1 Abelin, Pierre. Rapport sur la politique française de coopération. P.: DF, 1975. 78 pp.

2 Ammi-Oz, Moshe. "Les impératifs de la politique militaire française en Afrique Noire à l'époque de la décolonisation," RFEPA (Feb. 1977), pp. 65-89.

3 Ansprenger, Franz. Politik im Schwarzen Afrika. Cologne: Westdeutscher Verlag, 1961. 516 pp.

4 Ayouné, Jean-Rémy. "Occidentalisme et Africanisme," Renaissances (Brazzaville) (Oct. 1944).

5 ______. "Points de vue d'intellectuels d'Afrique centrale," Renaissances (Brazzaville) (Oct. 1944).

6 ______. "Valeurs et christianisme," La Semaine de l'Afrique Equatoriale Française (Brazzaville) (Jan. 29, 1955), p. 4; (Feb. 5, 1955), p. 4; (Feb. 19, 1955), p. 4.

7 Baer, Barbara. "The British Views of the Importance of French Africa to the Allied War Effort, 1940-1944," PFCHS, v. 2 (1977), pp. 16-23.

8 Betts, Raymond F. Tricouleur: The French Overseas Empire. L.: Cremona, 1978. 174 pp.

9 Binet, Jacques. "La République Gabonaise," NED (no. 3703, June 27, 1970). 36 pp.

10 Borella, François. L'évolution politique et juridique de l'Union Française depuis 1946. P.: P&D-A, 1958. 499 pp.

11 Bouquerel, Jacqueline. Le Gabon. P.: PUF, 2nd ed., 1976. 128 pp.

12 Bourges, Yvon. La politique française d'aide au développement. P.: DF, 1971. 30 pp.

13 Bourrinet, Jacques. La coopération économique eurafricaine. P.: PUF, 1976. 189 pp.

14 Brownlie, Ian. African Boundaries. A Legal & Diplomatic Encyclopedia. L.: C. Hurst, 1979. 1355 pp. [texts].

15 Bruel, Georges. L'Afrique Equatoriale Française. P.: Larose, 1935. 558 pp.

16 Brunschwig, Henri. "French Exploration and Conquest in Tropical Africa from 1865 to 1898," in P. Duignan and L. H. Gann, eds., The History and Politics of Colonialism, 1870-1914. L.: Cambridge UP, 1969, pp. 132-164.

17 ______. Mythes et réalités de l'impérialisme colonial français, 1871-1914. P.: AC, 1960. 204 pp. Tr. French Colonialism, 1871-1914; Myths & Realities. L.: Pall Mall Press, 1966. 228 pp.

18 Buell, Raymond Leslie. The Native Problem in Africa. N.Y.: Macmillan, 1928. 2 v., 1049 pp.

19 Charbonneau, Jean & René. Marchés et marchands de l'Afrique noire. P.: Ed. du Vieux Colombier, 1961. 150 pp.

20 Charbonnier, François, ed. Gabon, Terre d'Avenir. P.: Encyclopédie d'Outre-Mer, 1957. 151 pp.

21 Chemery, J. Histoire de la mise en valeur minière des territoires d'Afrique Centrale. P.: Bureau d'Etudes Géologiques et Minières Coloniales, 1960. 175 pp.

22 Cohen, William B. Black Encounter: French Images of Africa, 1500-1885. Bloomington: Indiana UP, 1979.

23 Cominardi, Giuliano, and Ducci, Paolo. Gabon: République Gabonaise. Rome: Istituto Italo-Africano, 1975. 112 pp.

24 "La coopération entre la France, l'Afrique Noire d'Expression française et Madagascar," NED (no. 3330, Oct. 25, 1966). 47 pp.

25 Coquery-Vidrovitch, Catherine. "Colonisation ou impérialisme: la politique africaine de la France entre les deux guerres," Mouvement Social (Apr.-June 1979), pp. 51-76.

26 ______. "French Colonization in Africa to 1920: Administrative and Economic Development," in P. Duignan and L. H. Gann, eds., The History & Politics of Colonialism, 1870-1914. L.: Cambridge UP, 1969, pp. 165-198.

27 ______. "L'Afrique coloniale française et la crise de 1930: crise structurelle et genèse du sous-développement. Rapport d'ensemble," RFHO-M, v. 53 (no. 3-4, 1977), pp. 386-424.

28 _______. "La mise en dépendance de l'Afrique Noire: Essai de périodisation, 1800-1970," CEA, v. 16 (no. 1-2, 1976), pp. 7-58.

29 _______. "Les idées économiques de Brazza et les premières tentatives de compagnie de colonisation au Congo Français, 1885-1898," CEA, v. 5 (no. 1, 1965), pp. 57-82.

30 _______. "L'impérialisme français en Afrique Noire: Idéologie impériale et politique d'équipement, 1924-1975," Relations Internationales (Autumn 1976), pp. 261-282.

31 _______. "Mutation de l'impérialisme colonial français dans les années 30," African Economic History (Fall 1977), pp. 103-152.

32 _______, and Moniot, Henri. L'Afrique Noire de 1800 à Nos Jours. P.: PUF, 1974. 462 pp.

33 Corbett, Edward M. The French Presence in Black Africa. W.: Black Orpheus Press, 1972. 209 pp.

34 Cornevin, Marianne. Histoire de l'Afrique contemporaine de la deuxième guerre mondiale à nos jours. P.: Payot, 1972. 426 pp.

35 _______, and Cornevin, Robert. Histoire de l'Afrique des origines à la deuxième guerre mondiale. P.: Payot, 4th ed., 1974. 411 pp.

36 Cornevin, Robert. L'Afrique noire de 1919 à nos jours. P.: PUF, 1973. 251 pp.

37 _______. Histoire de l'Afrique. P.: Payot, 1962, 1966, 1975. 3 v. 453, 638, and 700 pp.

38 _______. Histoire des Peuples de l'Afrique Noire. P.: B-L, 1960. 715 pp.

39 Curtin, Philip, et al. African History. Boston: Little, Brown, 1978. 612 pp.

40 Daget, Serge. "L'abolition de la traite des noirs en France de 1814 à 1831," CEA, v. 11 (no. 1, 1971), pp. 14-58.

41 D'Arjanse, Jean. Les Conquérants au Gabon. P.: Jules Tallandier, 1933. 92 pp.

42 Decraene, Philippe. "Gabon 1968," CRMSASO-M, v. 28 (June 1968), pp. 297-312.

43 Delavignette, Robert L. "French Colonial Policy in Black

Africa, 1945 to 1960," in P. Duignan and L. H. Gann, ed., The History and Politics of Colonialism, 1914-1960. L.: Cambridge UP, 1970, pp. 251-285.

44 Denis, Martin J. M., ed. Histoire militaire de l'Afrique Equatoriale Francaise. P.: IO, 1931. 516 pp. [Gabon, pp. 84-124].

45 Denis, Jacques; Vennetier, Pierre; and Wilmet, Jules. L'Afrique Centrale et Orientale. P.: PUF, 1971. 294 pp.

46 Deschamps, Hubert, ed. Histoire générale de l'Afrique noire, de Madagascar et des archipels. V. I. Des origines à 1800; V. II. De 1800 à nos jours. P.: PUF, 1970-1971. 576 & 720 pp.

47 ______. "France in Black Africa & Madagascar Between 1920 & 1945," in P. Duignan and L. H. Gann, eds., The History & Politics of Colonialism, 1914-1960. L.: Cambridge UP, 1970, pp. 226-250.

48 ______. Histoire de la traite des Noirs de l'antiquité à nos jours. P.: Fayard, 1972. 338 pp.

49 ______. Les méthodes et doctrines de colonisation de la France. P.: AC, 1953. 222 pp.

50 ______, et al. Afrique au XXe siècle, 1900-1965. P.: Sirey, 1966. 908 pp.

51 Duhamel, Olivier. "L'AUPELF et la coopération universitaire ou de la francophonie au dialogue des cultures," RFEPA (Feb. 1976); pp. 30-59.

52 Durand-Réville, Luc. "Albert Schweitzer ou la Coopération avant l'heure," CRTSASO-M, v. 35 (no. 2, 1975), pp. 307-318.

53 French Equatorial Africa. High Commissioner's Office. Annuaire statistique de l'Afrique Equatoriale Française. V. I, 1936-1950; V. II. 1950. Bv.: IO, 1951. 289 pp.

54 ______. Service for Coordination of Economic Affairs and the Plan. L'Afrique Equatoriale Française économique et sociale, 1947-1958. Avec l'aide du FIDES. P.: Ed. Alain, 1959. 112 pp.

55 Le Gabon Après Léon M'Ba. Special no. Europe-France-Outre-Mer (Nov. 1967). 60 pp.

56 Gabon, Données statistiques sur les activités économiques, culturelles et sociales. P.: Ministry of Cooperation, 1976. 241 pp.

57 Gabon, République du. P.: Office de la Coopération, DF, 1970.

58 Gardinier, David E. "French Equatorial Africa," Current History, v. 34 (Feb. 1958); pp. 105-110.

59 Gifford, Prosser, and Louis, Wm. Roger, eds. France and Britain in Africa: Imperial Rivalry & Colonial Rule. New Haven: Yale UP, 1971. 989 pp.

60 Goulven, J. L'Afrique Equatoriale Française (Ancien Congo Français): Son Organisation Administrative, Judiciaire, Financière. P.: Larose, 1911. 250 pp.

61 Great Britain Naval Intelligence Division. French Equatorial Africa and the Cameroons. L.: His Majesty's Stationery Office, 1942. 542 pp.

62 Grébert, F. Au Gabon (Afrique Equatoriale Française). P.: SME, 3rd ed., 1948. 216 pp.

63 Hallett, Robin. Africa to 1875: A Modern History. Ann Arbor: U. of Michigan Press, 1970. 503 pp.

64 _______. Africa Since 1875. Ann Arbor: U. of Michigan Press, 1974. 807 pp.

65 Hayter, Teresa. French Aid. L.: Overseas Development Institute, 1966. 230 pp.

66 Hegba, Meinrad. Emancipation d'Eglises sous Tutelle: Essai sur l'Ere Post-Missionnaire. P.: PA, 1976. 174 pp.

67 Jalloh, Abduh. Political Integration in French-Speaking Africa. Berkeley: Institute of International Studies, U. of California, 1973. 208 pp.

68 Jeanneney, Marcel. La politique de coopération avec les pays en voie de développement. P.: DF, 1963.

69 Kabongo-Kongo, Kola. Traité des rapports franco-africains. Kinshasa: Office national de la recherche et du développement, 1972. 295 pp.

70 Leduc, Michel. Les Institutions monétaires africaines des pays francophones. P.: Pedone, 1965. 397 pp.

71 Leymarie, Philippe. "L'Agence de coopération culturelle et technique ou la francophonie institutionnelle," RFEPA, (Feb. 1976); pp. 13-29.

72 Ligot, Maurice. Les accords de coopération entre la France et les Etats africains et malgache d'expression française. P.: DF, 1964. 187 pp.

73 Londres, Albert. Terre d'Ebène. P.: Albin Michel, 1929. 268 pp.

74 Lusignan, Guy de. French-Speaking Africa Since Independence. N. Y.: Praeger, 1969. 416 pp. Tr. L'Afrique Noire depuis L'Indépendance. L'Evolution des Etats francophones. P.: Fayard, 1970. 410 pp.

74a Marshall, D. Bruce. The French Colonial Myth and Constitution-Making in the Fourth Republic. New Haven: Yale UP, 1973. 363 pp.

75 Martin, Gaston. L'Ere des Negriers (1714-1774): Nantes au XVIIIe siècle d'après des documents inédits. P.: Alcam, 1931. 452 pp.

76 ________. Histoire de l'esclavage dans les colonies françaises. P.: PUF, 1948. 318 pp.

77 Ménier, Marie Antoinette. "Conceptions politiques et administratives de Brazza, 1885-1898," CEA, v. 5 (no. 1, 1965), pp. 83-95.

78 Merle, Marcel, ed. Les Eglises Chrétiennes et la Décolonisation. P.: AC, 1969. 519 pp.

79 Morris-Jones, Wyndraeth, and Fischer, Georges, eds. Decolonisation & After: The British & French Experience. L.: Frank Cass, 1980.

80 Mortimer, Edward. France and the Africans; 1944-1960: A Political History. L.: Faber, 1969. 390 pp.

81 Mytelka, Lynn Krieger. "A Genealogy of Francophone West & Equatorial African Regional Organisations," JMAS, v. 12 (no. 2, 1974), pp. 257-320.

82 Neuhoff, Hans Otto. Gabun. Bonn: Schroeder, 1967. 176 pp.

83 ________. Geschichte, Struktur und Probleme des Aufsfuhrwirtschaft eines Entwicklungs Landes. Berlin & N. Y.: Springer Verlag, 1967. 273 pp.

84 Ngango, Georges. Les Investissements d'origine extérieure en Afrique Noire francophone: leur statut et incidence sur le développement. P.: PA, 1973. 451 pp.

85 Oschswald, Pierre. Randonnée au Gabon. P.: SME, 1956. 48 pp.

86 Pedler, Frederick. Main Currents of West African History, 1940-1978. L.: Barnes & Noble, 1979. 301 pp. [interstate organizations].

87 Poquin, Jean-Jacques. Les relations économiques extérieures des pays d'Afrique Noire de l'Union Française, 1925-1955. P.: AC, 1957. 297 pp.

88 Pounah, Paul Vincent. Concept gabonais. Monaco: Ed. PB, 1968. 88 pp.

89 ______. Dialectique gabonaise, pensées d'hier, opinion aujourd'hui. Monaco: Ed. PB, 2nd ed., 1975. 144 pp.

90 Priestly, Herbert Ingram. France Overseas: A Study of Modern Imperialism. N.Y.: Appleton-Century, 1938. 463 pp.

91 "La République Gabonaise," NED (no. 2795, July 1961). 56 pp.

92 Robarts, Richard. French Development Assistance: A Study in Policy & Administration. Beverly Hills: Sage, 1974. 82 pp.

93 Roberts, Stephen H. History of French Colonial Policy (1870-1925). L.: King, 1929. 2 v. 741 pp.

94 Saintoyant, Jules. L'affaire du Congo, 1905. P.: Ed. de l'Epic, 1960. 162 pp.

95 Senegas, Louis. Cher Gabon. P.: S.O.S., 1976. 191 pp.

96 Servel, André. L'Organisation administrative et financière de l'Afrique Equatoriale Française. P.: Larose, 1912. 298 pp.

97 "Le Service de la Coopération culturelle, scientifique et technique avec les Etats Francophones Africains et Malgache: Bilan et Perspectives," NED (no. 3787, May 4, 1971). 34 pp.

98 Sicé, André. L'Afrique Equatoriale Française et le Cameroun au service de la France, 26-27-28 août 1940. P.: PUF, 1946. 200 pp.

99 Sorum, Paul Clay. Intellectuals and Decolonization in France. Durham: U. of N. Carolina Press, 1977. 305 pp.

100 Sousatte, René-Paul. L'Afrique Equatoriale Française--Berceau de l'Union Française. P.: Brodard & Taupin, 2nd ed., 1963. 143 pp.

101 Spiegler, James S. Aspects of Nationalist Thought Among French-Speaking West Africans, 1921-1939. D. Phil. Diss., Oxford U., 1968. [Film, Center for Research Libraries, Chicago.]

102 Stein, Robert Louis. The French Slave Trade in the Eighteenth

Century: An Old Regime Business. Madison: U. of Wisconsin Press, 1979. 256 pp.

103 Suret-Canale, Jean. Afrique noire, Ere Coloniale (1900-1945). P.: Ed. Sociales, 1964. 637 pp. Tr. French Colonialism in Tropical Africa, 1900-1945. N.Y.: Pica, 1971. 521 pp.

104 ______. Afrique Noire occidentale et centrale. P.: Ed. Sociales, 3rd ed., 1968. 321 pp.

105 ______. Afrique Noire occidentale et centrale. De la colonisation aux indépendances (1945-1960). P.: Ed. Sociales, 1972. 430 pp.

106 ______. "Difficultés du néo-colonialisme français en Afrique tropicale," CJAS, v. 8 (no. 2, 1974), pp. 211-234.

107 Susset, Raymond. La vérité sur le Cameroun et l'Afrique Equatoriale Française. P.: Ed. de la Nouvelle Revue Critique, 1934. 218 pp.

108 Thompson, Virginia, and Adloff, Richard. The Emerging States of French Equatorial Africa. Stanford: Stanford UP, 1960. 595 pp.

109 ______, and ______. "French Economic Policy in Tropical Africa," in P. Duignan and L. H. Gann., eds., The Economics of Colonialism. L.: Cambridge UP, 1975, pp. 95-126.

110 Tixier, Gilbert. "Les conventions fiscales passées par la France avec les pays en voie de développement," RJP, v. 29 (Apr.-June 1975): pp. 252-262.

111 Trenezem, Edouard. L'Afrique Equatoriale Française. P.: Ed. Maritimes et Coloniales, 3rd ed., 1955. 208 pp.

112 Vaudiaux, Jacques. L'Evolution politique et juridique de la coopération franco-africaine et malgache. P.: Pedone, 1971. 47 pp.

113 Vennetier, Pierre. L'Afrique Equatoriale. P., PUF, 1972. 128 pp.

114 Vignes, Daniel. L'Association des Etats Africains et Malgache à la C.E.E. P.: AC, 1970. 224 pp.

115 Wall, Irwin. "Communism, Decolonisation, and the Fourth Republic," FCS (Spring 1977), pp. 82-99.

116 Weinstein, Brian. Eboué. N.Y.: Oxford UP, 1971. 350 pp.

117 West, Richard. Brazza of the Congo: European Exploration

& Exploitation in French Equatorial Africa. L.: Cape, 1972. 304 pp.

118 White, Dorothy S. Black Africa & De Gaulle: From the French Empire to Independence. U. Park: Penn State U. Press, 1979. 314 pp.

119 ______. "De Gaulle & the Decolonization of Black Africa," PFCHS, v. 1 (1976): 52-63.

120 Wodie, F. Les institutions internationales régionales en Afrique occidentale et centrale. P.: P&D-A, 1970. 274 pp.

121 Yacono, Xavier. Les Etapes de la décolonisation française. P.: PUF, 1971. 127 pp.

122 Zartman, I. William. "Europe and Africa: Decolonization or Dependency," Foreign Affairs. v. 54 (Jan. 1976), pp. 325-343.

123 ______. The Politics of Trade Negotiations Between Africa and the European Community. Princeton: Princeton UP, 1971. 243 pp.

124 Zieglé, Henri. Afrique Equatoriale Française. P.: B-L, 1952. 190 pp.

II. EARLY HISTORICAL AND EXPLORATION ACCOUNTS (BEFORE 1914)

125 Ancel, Jacques. "Etude historique: La formation de la colonie du Congo français (1843-1882)," Renseignements Coloniaux et Documents, Afrique Française. (no. 4, 1902), pp. 79-94; (no. 5, 1902), pp. 99-120; (no. 6, 1902), pp. 132-134.

126 Barbot, John [Jean]. A Description of the Coasts of North and South-Guinea and of Ethiopia Inferior, Vulgarly Angola. L. 1732.

127 Bosman, William [Willem]. A New and Accurate Description of the Coast of Guinea: Divided into the Gold, Slave, and Ivory Coasts. L.: Frank Cass, 1967. 577 pp. [Tr. of Dutch ed. of 1704].

128 Bouët-Willaumez, Louis-Edouard. Commerce et Traite des Noirs aux Côtes Occidentales d'Afrique. P.: IN, 1848. 227 pp. Reprint, Geneva: Slatkin Reprints, 1978.

129 ______. Description Nautique des Côtes de l'Afrique Occidentale, comprises entre la Sénégal et l'Equateur. P.: Paul Dupont, 2nd. ed., 1849. 98 pp.

129a Bowdich, Thomas Edward. Mission from Cape Coast Castle to Ashantee. L.: J. Murray, 1819. 3rd. ed. L.: Frank Cass, 1966. 512 pp.

130 Burton, Richard Francis. Two Trips to Gorilla Land & the Cataracts of the Congo. L.: Marston, Low & Searle, 1876. 355 pp. Reprint, N. Y.: Johnson Reprints, 1967.

131 Compiègne, Louis Victor Dupont. L'Afrique Equatoriale Française; Gabonais, Pahouins, Gallois. P.: Plon, 2nd ed., 1876. 359 pp. Reprint, P.: Plon, 1976.

132 ______. L'Afrique Equatoriale Française: Okanda, Bangouens, Osyéba. P.: Plon, 3rd. ed., 1885. 360 pp.

133 Dapper, Olfert. Description de l'Afrique. Amsterdam: Wolfgang Waesberge, 1686. 534 pp. [Tr. of Dutch ed. 1668].

134 Du Chaillu, Paul B. A Journey to Ashango-land and Further Penetration into Equatorial Africa. N. Y.: Harper, 1874. 501 pp.

135 ______. Exploration and Adventures in Equatorial Africa. N. Y.: Harper, 1861. 531 pp. Reprint, N. Y.: Negro UP, 1969. Tr. Voyages et aventures dans l'Afrique Equatoriale (1856-1859). P.: Michel Levy, 1863. 546 pp.

136 ______. My Apindji Kingdom. N. Y.: Harper, 1871. 254 pp.

137 ______. Stories of the Gorilla Country. N. Y.: Harper, 1899. 292 pp.

138 ______. The Country of the Dwarfs. N. Y.: Harper, 1872. 314 pp. Reprint, N. Y.: Negro UP, 1969.

139 ______. Wild Life Under the Equator. N. Y.: Harper, 1868. 231 pp.

140 Kingsley, Mary H. Travels in West Africa--Congo Français, Corisco & Cameroons. N. Y.: Macmillan, 1897. 743 pp. Reprint, L.: Frank Cass, 1965.

141 Le Cour, A. Rapport sur la colonisation du Gabon et de l'Afrique centrale. Nantes: Impr. William Busseuil, 1848. 16 pp.

142 Marche, Alfred. Trois Voyages dans l'Afrique Occidentale. Sénégal-Gambie, Casamance, Gabon-Ogooué. P.: Hachette, 1882. 376 pp.

143 Morel, Edward Dene. The British Case in the French Congo. L.: Heinemann, 1903. 215 pp.

144 Nassau, Robert Hamill. My Ogowe: Being a Narrative of Daily Incidents During Sixteen Years in Equatorial West Africa. N. Y.: Neale, 1914. 708 pp.

145 Ney, Napoleon, ed. Conférences et lettres de Pierre Savorgnan de Brazza sur ses trois explorations dans l'Ouest Africain. P.: Maurice Dreyfous, 1887.

146 Payeur-Didelot, N. Trente Mois au Continent Mystérieux: Gabon-Congo et la Côte Occidentale de l'Afrique. P.: B-L, 1889. 403 pp.

147 Proyart, Liévain Bonaventure. Histoire de Loango, Kakongo et autres Royaumes d'Afrique. P.: Berton and Craport, 1776. 393 pp. Tr. History of Loango, Kakongo, and Other Kingdoms in Africa in John Pinkerton, ed. V. 16, A General Collection of the Best and Most Interesting Voyages and Travels, L., 1808-1814.

148 Rouget, Fernand. L'Expansion coloniale au Congo Français. P.: Larose, 1906. 942 pp.

149 Wilson, John Leighton. Western Africa: Its History, Condition & Prospects. N. Y.: Harper, 1856. 527 pp. Reprint, Negro UP, 1970.

III. HISTORICAL STUDIES

150 Alexandre, Pierre. "Proto-histoire du groupe beti-bulu-fang: essai de synthèse provisoire," CEA, v. 5 (no. 4, 1965), pp. 503-560.

151 Ambouroué Avaro, Joseph. Le Bas-Ogooué au XIXe Siècle (Gabon). Histoire intérieure. Doctoral Thesis, U. of P., 1969. 518 pp.

152 Annet, Armand. Aux heures troublées de l'Afrique française, 1939-1947. P., 1952.

153 Aubry, Fernand. Don Fernando. P.: Robert Laffont, 1972. 428 pp. [1919-1929].

154 Avelot, R. "Notice historique sur les Bakalé," Anthropologie, v. 24 (1913), pp. 197-240.

155 Balesi, Charles J. "A 19th-century Anglo-French Dispute: The Issue of African Free Laborers," PFCHS, v. 2 (1977), pp. 75-86.

156 Beauchêne, Guy de. "La préhistoire du Gabon," Objets et Mondes, v. 3 (no. 1, 1963), pp. 3-16.

157 Berger, Augustin. "Le premier et désastreux voyage du Père Bessieux vers le Gabon (1843-1844)," CRTSASO-M, v. 36 (no. 2, 1976): pp. 257-268.

158 Birmingham, David. "Central Africa from Cameroun to the Zambezi," in R. Gray, ed. Cambridge History of Africa. V. 4. From c. 1600 to c. 1790. L.: Cambridge UP, 1975, pp. 325-383.

159 _______. "Central Africa from Cameroun to the Zambezi," in R. Oliver, ed. Cambridge History of Africa. V. 3, From c. 1050 to c. 1600. L.: Cambridge UP, 1977, pp. 519-566.

160 _______. "The Forest and Savanna of Central Africa," in J. Flint, ed., Cambridge History of Africa. V. 5, C. 1790 - C. 1870. L.: Cambridge UP, 1976, pp. 222-269.

161 Blankoff, Boris. "L'état des recherches préhistoriques au Gabon," Etudes et Documents Tchadiens, Mémoire (No. 1, 1969).

162 _______. "Quelques découvertes préhistoriques récentes au Gabon," Proceedings of the Pan-African Congress for Prehistory, V. 5 (1965), pp. 191-206.

163 Bouche, Denise. Les Villages de Liberté en Afrique Noire Française, 1887-1910. P.: Mouton, 1968. 280 pp.

164 Brunschwig, Henri, ed. Brazza explorateur: L'Ogooué, 1875-1879. P.: Mouton, 1966. 215 pp.

164a _______. "Expéditions punitives au Gabon (1875-1877)," CEA, v. 2 (no. 3, 1962), pp. 347-361.

165 _______. "Les factures de Brazza, 1875-1878," CEA, v. 4 (no. 1, 1963), pp. 14-21.

166 _______. "La troque et la traite," CEA, v. 2 (no. 3, 1962), pp. 339-346.

167 Bucher, Henry H. "Canonization by Repetition: Paul du Chaillu in Historiography," RFHO-M. Forthcoming.

168 _______. "Liberty and Labor: The Origins of Libreville Reconsidered," BIFAN. Forthcoming.

169 _______. "John Leighton Wilson and the Mpongwe: The 'Spirit of 1776' in Mid-Nineteenth-Century Africa," Journal of Presbyterian History, v. 54 (Fall 1976), pp. 291-316.

170 _______. The Mpongwe of the Gabon Estuary: A History to 1860. Ph. D. Diss., U. of Wisconsin, Madison, 1977. 455 pp.

171 ______. "Mpongwe Origins: Historiographical Perspectives," HA, v. 2 (1975), pp. 59-90.

172 ______. "The Settlement of the Mpongwe Clans in the Gabon Estuary: An Historical Synthesis," RFHO-M, v. 64 (no. 1, 1977), pp. 149-175.

173 ______. "The Village of Glass and Western Intrusion: An Mpongwe Response to the American & French Presence in the Gabon Estuary," IJAHS, v. 6 (no. 3, 1973), pp. 363-400.

174 Capperon, L. "Bouet-Willaumez en Afrique Occidentale et au Gabon (1836-1850)," Revue Maritime, n. s. (Sept. 1953), pp. 1085-1103.

175 Catala, René. "La question de l'échange de la Gambie britannique contre les comptoirs français du Golfe de Guinée de 1866 à 1876," RHCF, v. 35 (1948), pp. 114-137.

176 Chamberlin, Christopher. "Bulk Exports, Trade Tiers, Regulation and Development: An Economic Approach to the Study of West Africa's Legitimate Trade," Journal of Economic History. v. 39 (June 1979), pp. 419-438.

177 ______. "The Migration of the Fang into Central Gabon During the Nineteenth Century: A New Interpretation," IJAHS, v. 11 (no. 3, 1978), pp. 429-456.

178 ______. Competition and Conflict: The Development of the Bulk Export Trade in Central Gabon During the 19th Century. Ph. D. Diss., U. of California at Los Angeles, 1977.

179 Clark, J. Desmond. "The Legacy of Prehistory: An Essay on the Background to the Individuality of African Cultures," in J. D. Fage, ed., Cambridge History of Africa. V. 2, C. 500 B. C. to A. D. 1050. L.: Cambridge UP, 1978, pp. 11-86.

180 Cookey, S. J. S. "The Concession Policy in French Congo and the British Reaction, 1897-1906," JAH, v. 7 (no. 2, 1966), pp. 263-278.

181 Coquery-Vidrovitch, Catherine, ed. Brazza et la prise de possession du Congo. La Mission de l'Ouest Africain, 1883-1885. P.: Mouton, 1969. 502 pp.

182 ______. Le Congo au Temps des Grandes Compagnies Concessionnaires, 1898-1930. P.: Mouton, 1972. 598 pp.

183 ______. "De Brazza à Gentil: la politique française en Haute-Sangha à la fin du XIXe siècle," RFHO-M, v. 52 (1965), pp. 22-40.

184 ________. "L'échec d'une tentative économique: L'impôt de capitation au service des compagnies concessionnaires du 'Congo français' (1900-1909)," CEA, v. 8 (no. 1, 1968), pp. 96-109.

185 ________. "L'intervention d'une société privée à propos du contesté franco-espagnol dans la Rio Muni. La Société d'exploration coloniale, 1899-1924," CEA, v. 3 (no. 1, 1962), pp. 22-68.

186 Couture, Claude-Paul. Le Commandant Emile Dubos, héros de Sheï Poo (1852-1935). Rouen: Author, 1963.

187 Dermigny, Louis, and Serre, Gérard. "Au Gabon, le district du 'bout du monde,'" CO-M, v. 7 (July-Sept. 1954), pp. 213-224.

188 Deschamps, Hubert. Quinze Ans de Gabon: Les débuts de l'établissement français, 1839-1853. P.: Société française d'histoire d'outre-mer, 1965. 98 pp.

189 ________. Traditions orales et archives au Gabon. P.: B-L, 1962. 172 pp.

190 Dupré, G. "Le commerce entre sociétés lignagères: les nzabi dans la traite à la fin du XIXe siècle (Gabon-Congo)," CEA, v. 12 (no. 4, 1972), pp. 616-658.

191 Eboué, Félix. La Nouvelle Politique Indigène (pour l'Afrique Equatoriale Française). P.: Office Français d'Ed., 1944, & Bv.: Afrique Française Libre, 1941. 61 pp.

192 Farine, B. "Le Néolithique de Moanda," BSPPG (no. 5, 1966), pp. 79-94.

193 ________. Sites préhistoriques Gabonais. Lv., Ministry of Information, 1964. 64 pp.

194 Fernandez, James W. "The Sound of Bells in a Christian Country: The Quest for the Historical Schweitzer," Massachusetts Review, v. 5 (Spring 1964), pp. 537-562.

195 Fyfe, Christopher. "Freed Slave Colonies in West Africa," in J. Flint, ed., Cambridge History of Africa. V. 5, C. 1790-C. 1870. L.: Cambridge UP, 1976, 170-199.

196 Garfield, Robert. A History of São Tomé Island, 1470-1665. Ph.D. Diss., Northwestern U., Evanston, 1971. 337 pp.

197 Gaulme, François. L'Ancien Pays du Cama: Société et Organisation du XVIe au XIXe Siècle. Doctoral Thesis, U. of P., 1975. 349 pp.

198 _______. "Un problème d'histoire du Gabon. Le sacre du Père Bichet par les Nkomi en 1897," RFHO-M, v. 61 (no. 3, 1974), pp. 395-416.

199 Gautier, Jean M. Etude historique sur les Mpongoués et tribus Avoisinantes. Montpellier: Impr. Lafitte-Lauriol for the Institut d'Etudes Centrafricaines, 1950. 69 pp.

200 Gollnhofer, Otto. Bokodu. Ethno-histoire ghetsogho: Essai sur l'histoire générale de la tribu après la tradition orale. Doctoral Thesis, U. of P, 1967. Mimeographed, 1971.

201 _______; Noel, Bernard; and Sillans, Roger. "L'historicité des paroles attribuées au premier évêque du Gabon à propos du maintien du comptoir entre 1871 et 1873," RFHO-M, v. 59 (no. 4, 1972), pp. 611-644.

202 Government-General of French Equatorial Africa. Souvenirs sur le Gabon. Bv.: IO, 1950. 21 pp.

203 Guillot, B. "Note sur les anciennes mines de fer du Pays Nzabi dans la région de Mayako," CORSTOM, SSH v. 6 (no. 2, 1969), pp. 93-99.

204 Hadjigeorgiou, C., and Pommeret, Yvan. "Présence du Lumpembien dans la région de l'Estuaire," BSPPG (no. 3, 1965), pp. 111-131.

205 Ikele, P. "La guerre de Wongo dans l'Ogooué-Lolo," RG (no. 34, 1969), pp. 17-23.

206 Kouambila, J. La révolte des Awandji, Gabon, 1928. Memoir for the Master's, U. of P., 1975.

207 Labat, René. Le Gabon devant de gaullisme. Bordeaux: Delmas, 1941. 79 pp.

208 Lagarde, Georgette. La migration pahouine au Gabon. Doctoral Thesis, U. of P., 1966.

209 Lasserre, Guy. "Bordeaux et les origines de Libreville," Actes du VIIIe Congrès d'Etudes Régionales. Bordeaux et sa Région dans le Passé et dans le Présent. Bordeaux: Bière for the Fédération Historique du Sud-Ouest, 1956, pp. 159-168.

210 Leterrier, R. P. "A propos du sacre du Père Bichet," RFHO-M, v. 62 (no. 4, 1975), p. 674.

211 Le Testu, Georges. "La soumission des Bawandji," BSRC (no. 14, 1931), pp. 11-28.

212 Mangongo-Nzambi, A. "La délimitation des frontières du

Gabon (1885-1911)," CEA, v. 9 (no. 1, 1969), pp. 5-53.

213 _______. La pénétration française et l'organisation administrative du Nord-Gabon. Doctoral Thesis, U. of P., 1968. 377 pp.

214 Martin, Phyllis M. The External Trade of the Loango Coast, 1576-1870: The Effects of Changing Commercial Relations on the Vili Kingdom of Loango. Oxford: Clarendon, 1972. 193 pp.

215 M'Bokolo, Elikia. "French Colonial Policy in Equatorial Africa in the 1940s and 1950s," in P. Gifford and Wm. R. Louis, eds., Transfer of Power in Africa. New Haven: Yale UP. Forthcoming.

216 _______. La France et les Français en Afrique Equatoriale. Le Comptoir du Gabon, 1839-1874. Doctoral Thesis, U. of P., 1975. 385 pp.

217 _______. "La résistance des Mpongwe du Gabon à la création du comptoir français (1843-1845)," Afrika Zamani (Dec. 1978), pp. 5-32.

218 _______. "Le Roi Denis," in Charles-André Julien, ed., Les Africains, v. 6. P.: Ed. Jeune Afrique, 1977, pp. 69-95.

219 _______. Le Roi Denis: la première tentative de modernisation du Gabon. P.: Afrique Biblioclub & Dakar: Nouvelles Ed. Africaines, 1976. 94 pp.

220 Metegue N'nah, Nicolas. Le Gabon de 1854 à 1886: 'Présence' Française et Peuples Autochtones. Doctoral Thesis, U. of P., 1974.

221 Meyo-Bibang, Frédéric. Aperçu historique du Gabon. Lv.: IPN, 1973. 171 pp.

222 Minlamèze, E. "La grande famine de trois ans au Woleu-N'tem (1925-1928)," RG (no. 25, 1965), pp. 47-49.

223 N'Doume-Assembe. Emane-Tole et la résistance à la conquête française dans le Moyen-Ogooué. Memoir for the Master's, U. of P., 1973.

224 Neuhoff, Hans-Otto. "German-Gabonese Relations from the Mid-19th Century to the Present Day," Afrika, (Aug. 1964), pp. 122-127.

225 _______. "Les rapports germano-gabonais depuis la seconde moitié du XIXe siècle jusqu'au présent," Africa (Rome) v. 20 (June 1965), pp. 200-202.

226 Nkoghve-Mve, Moïse. "Le docteur Albert Schweitzer et la colonisation," RG (Jan.-Mar. 1977), pp. 21-26.

227 Oliver, Roland, and Fagan, Brian. "The Emergence of Bantu Africa," in J. D. Fage, ed. Cambridge History of Africa. V. 2. 500 B.C. to 1050 A.D. L.: Cambridge UP, 1978, pp. 342-409.

228 Oudima Epigat, G. Franceville (Gabon) des origines à la deuxieme guerre mondiale. Memoir for the Master's, U. of P., 1974.

229 Pambo-Louega, C. F. La crise de 1929 au Gabon. Memoir for the Master's, U. of P., 1974.

230 Patterson, K. David. "Early Knowledge of the Ogowe River and the American Exploration of 1854," IJAHS, v. 5 (no. 1, 1972), pp. 75-90.

231 _______. "Paul B. Du Chaillu & the Exploration of Gabon, 1855-1865," IJAHS, v. 7 (no. 4, 1974), pp. 648-667.

232 _______. The Northern Gabon Coast to 1875. Oxford: Clarendon, 1975. 167 pp.

233 _______. "The Vanishing Mpongwe: European Contact and Demographic Change in the Gabon River," JAH, v. 16 (no. 2, 1975), pp. 217-238.

234 Perrois, Louis. "Tradition orale et histoire: intérêt et limites d'une enquête de terrain sur les migrations Kota (Gabon)," CORSTOM, SSH, v. 13 (no. 2, 1976), pp. 143-146.

235 _______. "Chronique du pays kota (Gabon)," CORSTOM-SSH v. 8 (no. 2, 1970), pp. 15-110.

236 Pommeret, Yvan. Civilisations préhistoriques au Gabon. Lv.: Ministry of National Education, 1966. 2v. 65 & 45 pp.

237 Pounah, Paul Vincent. Carrefour de la discussion. Coulonges sur l'Antize: Impr. Reynaud, 1971. 101 pp. [Galoa origins].

238 _______. Notre passé. P.: Société d'impressions techniques, 1970. 105 pp. [Galoa].

239 _______. La recherche du Gabon traditionnel: hier Edongo, aujourd'hui Galwa. P.: Impr. Loriou, 1975. 277 pp.

240 Rabut, Elisabeth. "Le Mythe Parisien de la Mise en Valeur des Colonies Africaines à l'aube du XXe Siècle: La Commission des Concessions Coloniales, 1898-1912," JAH, v. 20 1979), pp. 271-288.

241 Ratanga-Atoz, Ange. "Commerce, économie et société dans le Gabon du XIXe siècle--début XXe siècle," AENA v. 3 (1979), pp. 83-96.

242 ______. "Fang et Miènè dans le Gabon du XIXe siècle," RG (Jan.-Mar. 1977), pp. 9-20.

243 ______. Les Résistances Gabonaises à l'Imperialisme de 1870 a 1914. Doctoral Thesis, U. of P., 1973. Microfiche ed. P.: CNRS; N.Y.: Clearwater Publishers.

244 Reynard, Robert. "Notes sur l'activité économique des côtes du Gabon au début du XVIIe siècle," BIEC, n.s., (no. 13-14, 1957), pp. 49-54.

245 ______. "Recherches sur la présence des Portugais au Gabon XVe-XIXe siècles," BIEC, n.s. (no. 9, 1955), pp. 15-66 & (no. 11, 1956), pp. 21-27.

246 Schnapper, Bernard. La politique et le commerce français dans la Golfe de Guinée. P.: Mouton, 1961. 286 pp.

247 Soret, Marcel. Histoire du Congo. Capitale Brazzaville. P.: B-L, 1978. 237 pp. [peoples of Gabon also].

248 Vansina, Jan. "Equatorial Africa before the 19th Century" and "A Trade Revolution in Equatorial Africa," in P. Curtin, et al., African History. Boston: Little, Brown, 1978, pp. 249-276, 419-443.

249 ______. "Finding Food in the History of Pre-Colonial Equatorial Africa: A Plea," African Economic History (Spring 1979), pp. 9-20.

250 Vaucaire, Michel. Paul du Chaillu: Gorilla Hunter. N.Y.: Harper, 1930. 322 pp. Tr. from French.

251 Walker, André Raponda. Notes d'histoire du Gabon. Montpellier: Impr. Charité for the Institut d'Etudes Centrafricaines, 1960. 158 pp.

252 ______. "Toponymie de l'Estuaire du Gabon et de ses environs," BIRSC (no. 2, 1963), pp. 87-116.

253 ______, and Reynard, Robert. "Anglais, Espagnols et Nord-Américains au Gabon au XIXe siècle," BIEC, n.s. (no. 12, 1956); pp. 253-279.

IV. ANTHROPOLOGY, ETHNOLOGY, AND SOCIOLOGY

254 Aboughe Obame, Jean. Acculturation et sous-développement au Gabon. Doctoral Thesis, U. of P., 1975.

255 Agondjo-Okawe, Pierre-Louis. Structures Parentales et Développement au Gabon: Les Nkomis. Doctoral Thesis, U. of P., 1967.

256 Akwa, Dikwa Guillaume Betoté. Bible de la sagesse Bantu: Choix d'aphorisme, devinettes et mots d'esprit du Cameroun et du Gabon. P.: Centre artistique et culturel camerounais, 1955. 147 pp.

257 Alexandre, Pierre, and Binet, Jacques. Le Groupe dit Pahouin: Fang-Boulou-Beti. P.: PUF, 1958. 152 pp.

258 Alikanga, M. Structures communautaires traditionnels et perspectives coopératives dans la société altogovéenne (Gabon). Doctoral Diss., St. Thomas Aquinas U. of Pontifical Studies, Rome, 1976. 625 pp.

259 Avaro, A. "La notion d'Anyambie (Dieu) dans les civilisations claniques du Gabon avant les blancs," PA (no. 4, 1969), pp. 96-102.

260 Balandier, Georges. Afrique Ambigue. P.: Plon, 1957. 294 pp. Tr. Ambiguous Africa. N.Y.: Pantheon, 1966. 276 pp.

261 ______. Sociologie actuelle de l'Afrique Noire. P.: PUF, 2nd. ed., 1963. 532 pp. Tr. Sociology of Black Africa. L.: Deutsch, 1970. 540 pp.

262 ______, and Pauvert, Jean-Claude. Les villages gabonais. Bv.: Institut d'Etudes Centrafricaines, 1952. 90 pp.

263 Bascou-Brescane, R. Etude des conditions de vie à Libreville (1961-1962). Lv.: INSEE-Coopération, 1969. 142 pp.

264 Biffot, Laurent. Articles et communications sociologiques (1962-1972). Lv.: CNRST, 1977. 219 pp.

265 ______. Comportements et attitudes de la jeunesse scolaire gabonaise. Doctoral Thesis, U. of P., 1971. 146 pp.

266 ______. Contribution à la connaissance et compréhension des populations rurales du Nord-Est du Gabon. Lv.: Collection "Sciences Humaines Gabonaises," July 1977. 239 pp.

267 ______. Facteurs d'intégration et de désintégration du

travailleur gabonais à son entreprise. P.: ORSTOM, 1960-1961. 153 pp.

268 ______. "Genèse des classes sociales au Gabon," AENA, (no. 1, 1978), pp. 31-48, & (no. 2, 1978), pp. 17-32.

269 ______. Genèse des classes sociales au Gabon. Lv.: CNRST, 1977. 51 pp.

270 ______. "La jeunesse gabonaise face au monde rurale et au monde urbain," L'Enfant en Milieu Tropical, v. 20 (1966), pp. 21-34.

271 Binet, Jacques. Afrique en question de la tribu à la nation. Tours: Mame, 1965. 252 pp.

272 Bodinga-Bwa-Bodinga, S. Traditions orales de la race Eviya. P.: T.M.T., 1969. 56 pp.

273 Bôt Ba Njock, H. M. "Prééminences sociales et systèmes politico-religieux dans la société traditionnelle bulu et fang," JSA, v. 30 (no. 2, 1960), pp. 151-172.

274 Bouet, Claude. "Pour une introduction à l'étude des migrations modernes en milieu sous-peuplé: situation actuelle du salariat et de l'emploi au Gabon," CORSTOM, SSM, v. 10 (no. 2-3, 1973), pp. 295-306.

275 ______. "Problèmes actuels de main d'oeuvre au Gabon: conditions d'une immigration controlée," CO-M, v. 31 (Oct.-Dec. 1978), pp. 375-394.

276 Bourdes-Ogouliguende. L'évolution du statut de la femme gabonaise. Doctoral Thesis, U. of Paris, 1972.

277 Boussoukou-Boumba. "L'organisation de la chefferie indigène à Ntima et à Divenie (Congo) (1923-1941)," PA (no. 3, 1978), pp. 111-134.

278 Breitengross, Jens P. "Sozio-ökonomische Aspekte der Bevölkerungsentwicklung in Zentralafrika," Afrika Spectrum, v. 10 (no. 2, 1975), pp. 119-140.

279 Briault, Maurice. Dans la fôret du Gabon. P.: Grasset, 1930. 195 pp.

280 Cabrol, Claude, and Lehuard, Raoul. La civilisation des peuples batéké. Lv.: Multipress, & Monaco: Ed. PB, 1976. 96 pp.

281 Eckendorff, Jean. "Note sur les tribus des subdivisions de Makokou et de Mékambo (Gabon)," BIEC, n.s., v. 1 (no. 1, 1945), pp. 87-95.

282 Edzang, S. "Gabon's Population Policy," African Population Newsletter (Dec. 1976), pp. 4-6.

283 Fernandez, James W. "Affirmation of Things Past: Alar Ayong & Bwiti as Movements of Protest," in R. Rotberg and Ali Mazrui, eds., Protest and Power in Black Africa. N. Y.: Oxford UP, 1970, pp. 427-457.

284 _______. "Christian Acculturation and Fang Witchcraft," CEA, v. 2 (no. 2, 1961), pp. 244-270.

285 _______. "Fang Representations Under Acculturation," in P. Curtin, ed., Africa and the West: Intellectual Responses to European Culture. Madison: U. of Wisconsin Press, 1972, pp. 3-48.

286 _______. Redistributive Acculturation and Ritual Reintegration in Fang Culture. Ph. D. Diss., Northwestern U., Evanston, 1963. 346 pp.

287 Gollnhofer, Otto, and Sillans, Roger. "Phénoménologie de la possession chez les Mitsogho: Aspects psychosociaux," Psychopathologie Africaine, v. 10 (no. 2, 1974), pp. 187-210.

288 _______, and _______. "Phénoménologie de la possession chez les Mitsogho (Gabon). Rites et techniques." Anthropos, v. 74 (no. 5-6, 1979), pp. 737-752.

289 Guillot, B. "Le Village de Passia: Essai sur le Système Agraire Nzabi," CORSTOM, SSH, v. 7 (no. 1, 1970), pp. 47-94.

290 _______. "Le Pays Bandzabi au Nord de Mayoko et les déplacements récents de population provoqués par l'axe COMILOG (Cie. Minière de l'Ogooué)," CORSTOM, SSH, v. 4 (no. 3-4, 1967), pp. 37-56.

291 Hagenbucher, Sacripanti, Frank. Les fondements spirituels du pouvoir au Royaume de Loango, République du Congo. P.: ORSTOM, 1973. 214 pp.

292 Hartweg, R. La vie secrète des pygmées. P.: Ed. du Temps, 1961. 118 pp.

293 Hauser, André. "Les Babingas," Zaïre, v. 7 (Feb. 1953), pp. 146-179.

294 _______. "Notes sur les Omyènè du bas Gabon," BIFAN, v. 16 (1954), pp. 402-415.

295 Hervo-Akendengue, A. "Social Security in Gabon," in African Social Security. Geneva, Mar. 1967, pp. 3-56.

296 Jean, Suzanne. Organisation sociale et familiale et problèmes fonciers des populations banjabi et bapunu de la N'Gounié-Nyanga. P.: BDPA, 1960.

297 Leblanc, Loïc. "L'évolution du Code du travail gabonais," AENA (no, 2, 1978), pp. 45-66.

298 Le Testu, Georges. Notes sur les coutumes bapounou de la circonscription de la Nyanga. Caen: J. Haulard la Brière, 1920. 212 pp.

299 Maclatchy, A. R. "L'organisation sociale des populations de la région de Mimongo (Gabon)," BIEC, n. s., v. 1 (no. 1, 1945), pp. 53-86.

300 Mba, Léon. "Essai de droit coutumier pahouin," BSRC, (no. 25, 1938), pp. 5-51.

301 Mbah, Jules. Coutumes gabonaises et civilisation française. Memoir, Ecole Nationale de la France d'Outre-Mer, Paris, 1958-1959. [Fang].

302 Mbot, Jean Emile. Binga dzi dzi akong: "Nous mangions la lance" (comportements de guerre chez les Fang du Gabon). Memoir for the Master's, U. of P., 1971.

303 Miletto. "Notes sur les ethnies de la région du Haut-Ogooué," BIEC, n. s., (no. 2, 1951), pp. 19-48.

304 Milligan, Robert H. The Fetish Folk of West Africa. N. Y., 1912. 328 pp. Reprint, N. Y.: AMS Press, 1970. [Mpongwe, Fang].

305 Nassau, Robert Hamill. Fetichism in West Africa: Forty Years' Observations of Native Customs and Superstitions. N. Y.: Scribners, 1904. 389 pp. Reprint, N. Y.: Negro UP, 1969.

306 Ndombet, Marie-Augustine. "La femme et la pratique du droit coutumier au Gabon: baptême, mariage, decès," in Société Africaine de Culture, La civilisation de la Femme dans la tradition africaine. P.: PA, 1975, pp. 328-336.

307 Nnanga Kon. Ebolowa, Cameroon: American Presbyterian Mission Press, 1948. [in Fang].

308 Nzaou-Mabika, Jeanne. "Initiative et pouvoir créateur de la femme. L'exemple du Gabon," in Société Africaine de Culture, La civilisation de la Femme dans la tradition africaine. P.: PA, 1975, pp. 286-295.

309 Ogoula-M'Beye, Pastor. Galwa ou Edonga d'antan. P.: Impr. Loriou, 1978. 214 pp.

310 Ondoua, Engute, ed. Dulu Bon be Agin Kara [The Journey of the Children of Africa]. Ebolowa, Cameroon: American Presbyterian Mission Press, 194?. [In Fang].

311 Panyella, Augusto. Esquema de etnología de los Fang Ntumu de la Guinea Española. Madrid: Consejo superior de investigaciones cientificas, 1959. 79 pp.

312 Papy, Louis. "Les populations batéké," CO-M, v. 2 (Apr.-June 1949), pp. 112-134.

313 Perrois, Louis. "La circoncisión Bakota (Gabon)," CORSTOM, SSH, v. 5 (no. 1, 1968), pp. 1-109.

314 Rey, Pierre Philippe. "Articulation des modes de dépendances et des modes de réproduction dans deux sociétés lignagères (Punu et Kunyi du Congo-Brazzaville)," CEA, v. 9 (no. 3, 1969), pp. 415-440.

315 Sautter, Gilles. "Les paysans noirs au Gabon sepentrional. Essai sur le peuplement et l'habitat du Woleu-N'tem," CO-M, v. 4 (Apr.-June 1951), pp. 119-159.

316 Shank, Floyd Aaron. Nzabi Kinship: A cognitive Approach. Ph. D. Diss., Indiana U., 1974. 512 pp.

317 Sillans, Roger. Motombi. Mythes et Enigmes initiatiques des Mitsoghos du Gabon Central. Doctoral Thesis, U. of P., 1967.

318 Siroto, Leon. Masks and Social Organization Among the Bakwele People of Western Equatorial Africa. Ph. D. Diss., Columbia U., N. Y., 1969. 325 pp.

319 Soret, Marcel. "Carte ethno-démographique de l'Afrique Equatoriale Française. Note préliminaire," BIECF n. s., v. 11 (1956), pp. 26-52.

320 Trenezem, Edouard. "Notes ethnographiques sur les tribus Fan du Moyen-Ogooué (Gabon)," JSA, v. 6 (no. 1, 1936), pp. 65-93.

321 Trilles, Henri. L'Ame du Pygmée d'Afrique: Au Coeur de la Fôret Equatoriale. P.: Le Cerf, 1945. 262 pp.

322 ________. Les Pygmées de la Fôret Equatoriale. P.: Blonde & Gay, 1932. 530 pp.

323 Van Den Audenaerde, F. E. Thys. Les Tilapia du Sud Cameroun et du Gabon. Tervuren: Musée Royal d'Afrique Centrale, 1968. 98 pp.

324 Walker, André Raponda. "Remarques sur les noms propres gabonais," BIEC, n. s. (no. 11, 1956), pp. 81-90.

325 _______. "Les Tribus du Gabon," BSRC (no. 4, 1924), pp. 55-101.

V. POLITICS SINCE 1945, ADMINISTRATION AND LAW

326 Agondjo-Okawe, Pierre-Louis. "Les droits fonciers coutumiers au Gabon," RJP, v. 24 (Oct. 1970), pp. 1135-1152.

327 _______. "Les Droits Fonciers Coutumiers au Gabon (Société Nkomi, Groupe Myènè)," Rural Africana (Fall 1973), pp. 15-30.

328 Ajami, S. M. Les Institutions Constitutionnelles de la République Gabonaise. Lv.; Faculté de Droit et Sciences Economiques, Mar. 1976. 118 pp.

329 _______. "Les institutions constitutionnelles du présidentialisme gabonais," RJP, v. 29 (Oct.-Nov. 1975), pp. 436-466.

330 _______. "Le rôle prédominant du parti unique institutionnaliste au Gabon," RJP, v. 30 (Jan.-Mar. 1976), pp. 114-129.

331 Ambouroué, M.-A. "La femme en droit coutumier gabonais," RJP, v. 28 (Oct.-Dec. 1974), pp. 673-680.

332 Anchouey, Michel. La vie politique du Gabon de 1960 à 1965. Memoir, U. of Poitiers, 1965.

333 Aubame, Jean-Hilaire. "La conférence de Brazzaville," in E. Guernier, ed. L'Afrique Equatoriale Française, P.: Ed. Coloniales et Maritimes, 1950, pp. 183-186.

334 _______. Renaissance gabonaise. Programme de regroupement des villages. Bv.: IO, 1947. 12 pp.

335 Ballard, John A. The Development of Political Parties in French Equatorial Africa. Ph.D. Diss., Fletcher School, Tufts U., Medford, Mass., 1964.

336 _______. "Four Equatorial States," in Gwendolyn Carter, ed., National Unity and Regionalism in African States. Ithaca: Cornell UP, 1966, pp. 231-336.

337 Bongo, Albert-Bernard. Dialogue et participation: avec Bongo aujourd'hui et demain. Monaco: Ed. PB, 1973. 117 pp.

338 _______. Gouverner le Gabon. Monaco: Ed. PB, 1968. 139 pp.

339 ______. Pensée et action sociales. Monaco: Ed. PB, 1974. 127 pp.

340 ______. Rénovation: pensées politiques. Lv.: PDG, 1973. 63 pp.

341 Bongo, El Hadj Omar. Le dialogue des nations. L'Afrique dans le nouvel ordre politique et économique mondiale. P.: Ed. ABC, 1977. 130 pp.

342 Boumah, Augustin. "Un Nouveau Code de Procédure Civile Gabonais," Penant, v. 89 (Oct.-Dec. 1979), pp. 373-378.

343 Cathala, Michel. La politique étrangère de la République gabonaise. Doctoral Thesis, U. of Toulouse, 1975. 169 pp.

344 Comte, Gilbert. "La république gabonaise: treize années d'histoire," RFEPA, (June 1973), pp. 39-57.

345 Conférence africaine française. Bv.: IO, 1944, & Algiers, IO, 1944. 122 pp.

346 Coulon, Christian. "Gabon," in Année africaine, 1964. P.: Pedone, 1966, pp. 213-230.

347 Darlington, Charles F. and Alice B. African Betrayal. N.Y.: David McKay, 1968. 359 pp.

348 Decraene, Philippe. "Esquisse d'une nouvelle politique étrangère gabonaise," RFEPA, (June 1972), pp. 58-66.

349 Duhamel, Olivier. "Le parti démocratique gabonais: étude des fonctions d'un parti unique africain," RFEPA (May 1976), pp. 24-60.

350 Essone-Ndong, Laurent-Thierry. "Les syndicats au Gabon," AENA, v. 3 (1979), pp. 45-54.

351 Filippi, Jean-Michel. L'Evolution politique du Gabon depuis 1958. Memoir, U. of Nice, 1967. 66 pp.

352 "Gabon, Guinée équatoriale: le conteste insulaire," RFEPA (Jan. 1973), pp. 25-27.

353 Gabon. Ministry of Information. Hommage à Léon Mba. Lv., 1971. 100 pp.

354 ______. L'Oeuvre du Président Léon Mba, 1900-1965. Lv., 1965. 70 pp.

355 Hippolyte, Mirlande. Les Etats du groupe de Brazzaville aux Nations Unies. P.: AC, 1970. 333 pp.

356 Hughes, Anthony. "Interview with Omar Bongo, President of the Republic of Gabon," Africa Report, v. 22 (May-June 1977), pp. 2-5.

357 Interafrique Presse. Le "putsch du Gabon" à travers la presse parisienne & quelques notes sur le processus d'un coup d'Etat. P., 1964. 16 pp.

358 Issembé, Georges. Constantes Variables et Tendances de la Politique Extérieure des jeunes Etats Africains: Les Exemples du Congo et du Gabon. Memoir, U. of P., 1978. 128 pp.

359 Klintberg, Robert. Equatorial Guinea-Macias Country. Geneva: International U. Exchange Fund, 1978. 89 pp.

360 Latappy, Denis. Le système politique gabonais. Memoir, U. of Bordeaux, 1973. 197 pp.

361/2 Livre blanc sur l'affaire Jean-Bernard Eyi: Enlèvement, séquestration et violences corporelles. Lv.: Gabonese Republic, 1971. 21 pp.

363 Matongo, Julien. Les assemblées législatives dans les Etats de l'ancienne Afrique Equatoriale Française. Doctoral Thesis, U. of P., 1968. 436 pp.

364 Mauric, Alain. Gabon de la Loi-Cadre au Référendum. Memoir, Ecole Nationale de la France d'Outre-Mer, Paris, May 1959. 121 pp.

365 Mba, Léon. Le Président Léon Mba vous parle. P.: Ed. Diloutremer, 1960. 102 pp.

366 Mébiame, Léon. "La commune et la collectivité rurale au Gabon," RJP, v. 22 (July-Sept. 1968), pp. 909-918.

367 Mercier, Jean-Louis. "La condition juridique des personnels de la Fonction publique au Gabon," AENA, v. 3 (1979), pp. 97-110.

368 Nguema, Isaac. "Aspects traditionnels da la nationalité gabonaise," RJP, v. 25 (no. 4, 1971), pp. 503-511.

369 ______. Le nom dans la tradition et la législation gabonaise (Essai de droit coutumier). Doctoral Thesis, U. of P., 1969.

370 ______. "La terre dans le droit traditionnel Ntumu," RJP, v. 24 (Oct. 1970), pp. 1119-1134.

371 N'Toutoume, Jean-François. La crise politique gabonaise en 1964. Memoir, U. of P., 1966. 199 pp.

372 _______. L'Evolution de la vie politique gabonaise de 1958 à 1968. Doctoral Thesis, U. of Rennes, 1969. 342 pp.

373 Nze-Ekekang, Timothée. La "Rénovation." Analyse du Contenu des Idées Politiques du Président A. B. Bongo. Memoir, U. of P., 1973. 125 pp.

374 Parti Démocratique Gabonais. Le Deuxième Congrès Extra-ordinaire du P. D. G. Special No., Dialogue (no. 62, August 17, 1979). 104 pp.

375 Peter, Jean E. "Gabon 1975: Le new deal," RJP, v. 29 (July-Sept. 1975), pp. 328-335.

376 Remondo, Max. "L'administration gabonaise," Bulletin de l'Institut d'Administration Publique, (July-Sept. 1973), pp. 443-464.

377 _______. L'Administration Gabonaise. P.: B-L, 1974. 54 pp.

378 Republic of Congo. Ministry of Information. Félix Tchicaya. Premier Parlementaire Congolais (1903-1961). In Memoriam. Bv.: IO, 1961. 23 pp.

379 Spero, Joan Edelman. Dominance-Dependence Relationship: The Case of France and Gabon. Ph. D. Diss., Columbia U., N. Y., 1973.

380 Wadlow, Rene. "Après un coup d'état à rebours," La Tribune de Genève (Mar. 1-2, 1964).

381 Weinstein, Brian. Gabon: Nation-Building on the Ogooué. Cambridge, Mass.: M.I.T. Press, 1966. 287 pp.

382 _______. "Léon Mba: The Ideology of Dependence," Genève-Afrique, v. 6 (no. 1, 1967), pp. 49-63.

VI. ECONOMICS

383 Anguilé, André-Gustave, and David, Jacques. L'Afrique sans Frontières. Monaco: Ed. PB, 1965. 311 pp.

384 Bertin, A. Les Bois du Gabon. P.: Larose, 1929. 306 pp.

385 Binet, Jacques. "Activité économique et prestige chez les Fangs du Gabon," RTM, v. 33 (Jan.-Mar. 1968), pp. 25-42.

386 Bouanga, Jean-Christophe. L'Absorption du Capital au Gabon. Memoir, U. of P., 1977. 180 pp.

387 Bouquerel, Jacqueline. "Le pétrole au Gabon," CO-M, v. 20 (Apr.-June 1967), pp. 186-199.

388 ______. "Port-Gentil, centre économique du Gabon," CO-M, v. 20 (July-Sept. 1967), pp. 247-274.

389 Cabrol, Claude. "Perspectives de réalisation du chemin de fer Transgabonais," Afrique Contemporaine, (Mar.-Apr. 1973), pp. 2-6.

390 ______. "Les transports au Gabon. Le Transgabonais, historique des réalisations dans le temps, situation actuelle," AENA (no. 2, 1978), pp. 77-92.

391 Carouet, Bernard. "Activités immobilières et travaux d'urbanisme au Gabon," BMBCEAEC, ES (May 1972), pp. 309-320.

392 Chauput, Jean-Louis. "Les voies navigables au Gabon," BMBEAC, ES (June-July 1974), pp. 368-378.

393 Courbot, Roger. Le Mouvement Commercial du Gabon de 1928 à 1939. Memoir, Ecole Nationale de la France d'Outre-Mer, Paris, 1944-45.

394 Daverat, Geneviève. "Un producteur africain de pétrole, le Gabon," CO-M, v. 30 (Jan.-Mar. 1977), pp. 31-56.

395 Distelhorst, Lynn Harris. Impact of American Aid and Trade on Resource Development of Gabon. M.A. Thesis, George Washington U., 1969. 260 pp.

396 Dix ans d'économie gabonaise, août 1963. Lv.: Chamber of Commerce, 1964. 43 pp.

397 Doupamby-Matoka. Les Investissements Etrangers et la Politique Gabonaise du Développement. Memoir, U. of P., 1970. 81 pp.

398 Dreux-Brezé, Joachim de. Le Problème de Regroupement en Afrique Equatoriale. Du Régime Colonial à l'Union Douanière et Economique de l'Afrique Centrale. P.: P&D-A, 1968. 214 pp.

399 Durand-Réville, Luc. L'assistance de la France aux Pays insuffisamment développés. P.: Ed. Génin, 1962. 128 pp.

400 L'Economie gabonaise. Special no., Bulletin de l'Afrique Noire. P.: Ediafric, 1976. 163 pp.

401 Ekagha-Assey, Jean. L'économie moderne et les relations inter-ethniques dans la région de Lambaréné (Gabon). Doctoral Thesis, U. of P., 1974.

401a Frediani, Lorenzo. The Banking System of Gabon and the Central Bank of Equatorial Africa & Cameroon. Tr. Système Bancaire du Gabon. Milan: Casse di Risparmio della Provincie Lombarde, 1974. 343 pp.

402 Le Gabon, Afrique de Demain. Session d'Etude 15 août -8 septembre 1971. Rapport des Participants. Brussels: Centre Interuniversitaire de Formation Politique Indépendant de Tout Parti, 1971. 297 pp.

403 "Gabon, 1960-1980." MTM (no. 1646, 1977), pp. 1246-1467.

404 Gabon, 1960-1970. Dix ans d'Expansion Economique. Monaco: Société nouvelle de l'Impr. nationale de Monaco, 1970.

405 "Gabon: La nouvelle politique économique," Eurafrica, v. 21 (Jan.-Mar. 1976), pp. 61-67.

406 Gaudio, Attilio, ed. "L'Industrialisation des Etats de l'Union Douanière et Economique de l'Afrique Centrale (UDEAC)," NED (no. 3830, Oct. 25, 1971). 43 pp.

407 Hance, William, and Van Dongen, Irene S., "Gabon and Its Main Gateways: Libreville and Port-Gentil," Tidjschrift voor Economischen en Sociale Geografie, v. 52 (no. 11, 1961), pp. 286-295.

408 International Monetary Fund. Surveys of African Economies. V. 1. Cameroon, CAR, Chad, Congo (Brazzaville) & Gabon. Tr. Etudes générales sur les économies africaines. V. 1. Cameroun, République Centrafricaine, Tchad, Congo (Brazzaville) & Gabon. W.: Internationaal Monetary Fund, 1968. 365 & 393 pp.

409 Jalloh, Adbul Aziz. "Foreign Private Investments & Regional Political Integration in UDEAC," Cahiers Economiques et Sociaux, v. 17 (June 1979), pp. 174-197.

410 Lasserre, Guy. "Okoumé et chantiers forestiers au Gabon," CO-M, v. 8 (Apr.-June 1955), pp. 118-160.

411 Leret, S. "Le manganèse au Gabon," CO-M, v. 19 (Oct.-Dec. 1966), pp. 354-363.

412 Lotito, Gaston. "Le développement économique de Gabon," CO-M, v. 23 (Oct.-Dec. 1970), pp. 425-439.

413 Lukusa, Théophile. "Intégration économique et données nationales: la création de l'Union des Etats d'Afrique Centrale," Etudes Congolaises, v. 11 (Apr.-June 1968), pp. 68-119.

414 Mba, Casimir Oye. Les problèmes juridiques posés par

l'exploitation de sous-sol au Gabon. Doctoral Thesis, U. of P., 1969. 348 pp.

415 Meli, Marcel. "L'industrie forestière dans l'économie du Gabon," BMBEAC, ES (Feb. 1976), pp. 69-87.

416 Minko, Henri. "Le régime domanial de la République gabonaise," RJP, v. 24 (Oct. 1970), pp. 775-782.

417 _______. "Le régime foncier et la République gabonaise: l'immatriculation," RJP, v. 24 (Oct. 1970), 695-698.

418 Ndongko, Wilfred A. "Trade and Development Aspects of the Central African Customs and Economic Union (UDEAC)," Cultures et Développement, v. 8 (no. 2, 1975), pp. 339-356.

419 Nyingone, Pauline. "Les sociétés d'économie mixte et le développement économique du Gabon," RJP, v. 32 (Jan.-Mar. 1978), pp. 85-96.

420 Ovono-N'Goua, Fabien. La politique fiscale comme instrument de développement économique dans les pays sous-développés: le cas du Gabon: appréciation. Memoir, U. of P., 1976. 167 pp.

421/2 Peting, Isaac. Fiscalité et développement: le cas du Gabon. U. of Paris, 1977. 86 pp.

423 Ping, Jean. Quelques facteurs externes de freinage de la croissance et du blocage du développement au Gabon. Memoir, U. of P., 1970. 70 pp.

424 Prats, R. Le Gabon: La mise en valeur et ses problèmes. Doctoral Thesis, U. of Montpellier, 1955. 272 pp.

425 Rapontchombo, Gaston, and M'Bouy Boutzit, E. A. Libreville, capitale de la République gabonaise. Lv.: Société gabonaise d'éd., 1973. 131 pp.

426 Republic of Gabon. Plan de Développement Economique et Sociale, 1966-1970. Lv.: IO, 1966. 3 v. 555 pp.

427 Rey, Pierre Philippe. Colonialisme, néo-colonialisme, et transition au capitalisme. Exemple de la "Comilog" au Congo-Brazzaville. P.: Maspero, 1971. 526 pp. [Loango].

428 Roumegous, M. "Port-Gentil: Quelques aspects sociaux du développement industriel," CO-M, v. 19 (Oct.-Dec. 1966), pp. 321-353.

429 "Le rush sur le Gabon," RTM, v. 18 (Jan.-Mar. 1977), pp. 155-157.

430 Sabolo, Y. "Some Comments on Foreign Private Investments and the Economic and Social Development of Gabon," African Development (no. 4, 1975), pp. 499-534.

431 ______. Quelques Réflexions sur les investissements privés étrangers et le développement économique et social du Gabon. Geneva: B. I. Travas, 1975. 58 pp.

432 Saint-Aubin, G., de. La forêt du Gabon. Nogent-sur-Marne: Ed. du Centre technique forestier tropical, 1963. 208 pp.

433 Schaetzen, Y., de. "L'économie gabonaise," RFEPA, (June 1973), pp. 67-94.

434 Stern, M. L'Okoumé au Gabon, 1930-1960. Memoir for the Master's, U. of P., 1977.

435 "Le Troisième Plan du Gabon, 1976-1980," MTM, v. 32 (Nov. 5, 1976), pp. 3061-3064.

436 Vennetier, Pierre. "Les ports du Gabon et du Congo-Brazza," CO-M, v. 22 (Oct.-Dec. 1969), pp. 337-355.

437 Villien-Rossi, Marie-Louise. La Compagnie de l'Ogooué. Son Influence Géographique au Gabon et au Congo. P.: Honoré Champion, 1978. 700 pp.

438 Voss, Harald. Kooperation in Afrika: Das Beispiel Aquatorials-Afrikas. Hamburg: Verlag-Weltarchiv, 1965. 87 pp.

439 Waller, Peter P. "Petrodollars und Entwicklungsstrategie--der Fall Gabun," Afrika Spectrum, v. 11 (no. 1, 1976), pp. 187-196.

440 Walter, R. Le Développement de Libreville. Doctoral Thesis, U. of Aix-Marseilles, 1976.

VII. EDUCATION

441 Ango, E. Moure, and Becquelin, J. Les Besoins Futurs en Ressources à la Lumière des Perspectives du Développement de l'Education au Gabon. P.: Unesco, June 1978. 28 pp.

442 Banga, Luther. Proverbe et éducation chez les Bulu-Fan-Beti: Une Etude socio-éducative des proverbes. Doctoral Thesis, U. of P., 1972. 479 pp.

443 Botti, Marc, and Venizet, Paul. Enseignement au Gabon. P.: SEDES, 1965. 351 pp.

444 Erny, Pierre. L'Enfant et son milieu en Afrique Noire. Essais sur l'éducation noire. P.: Payot, 1972. 311 pp.

445 French Equatorial Africa. Government-General. Histoire et organisation générale de l'enseignement en Afrique Equatoriale Française. Bv.: IO, 1931. 97 pp.

446 Gardinier, David E. "Education in French Equatorial Africa, 1842-1945," PFCHS, v. 3 (1978), pp. 121-137.

447 _______. "Education in the States of Equatorial Africa: A Bibliographical Essay," Africana Journal, v. 3 (no. 3, 1972), pp. 7-20.

448 _______. "Gabon," in Asa Knowles, ed. International Encyclopedia of Higher Education. San Francisco: Jossey-Bass, 1977, pp. 1789-1795.

449 _______. "Schooling in the States of Equatorial Africa," CJAS, v. 8 (no. 3, 1974), pp. 517-538.

450 Labrousse, André. La France et l'aide à l'Education dans 14 Etats africaines et malgache. P.: International Institute of Educational Planning, 1971. 166 pp.

451 Ministry of National Education. "Reforme et rénovation de l'enseignement au Gabon," Recherche, Pédagogie, et Culture (May-Aug. 1976), pp. 16-24.

452 Smith, Jasper K. A Planning Model for Educational and Economic Development: Educational Requirements of Economic Development. M.A. Thesis, Howard U., Wash., 1966.

453 Swiderski, Stanislas. "Les agents éducatifs traditionnels chez les Apindji," Revue de Psychologie des Peuples, v. 21 (no. 2, 1966), pp. 194-220.

454 Swiderski, Stanislaw. "Education traditionnelle chez les Apindji," Lud-Polsko (no. 52, 1968), pp. 27-63. [In Polish; French summary].

455 Weiland, Heribert. Erziehung und Nationale Entwicklung in Gabun. Munich: Weltforum Verlag, 1975. 245 pp.

VIII. PHYSICAL SCIENCES AND GEOGRAPHY

456 Antoine, Philippe, & Cantrelle, Pierre. "Enregistrement des decès et étude de mortalité urbaine. Etat civil de Libreville, Gabon," CORSTOM, SSH, v. 13 (no. 3, 1976), pp. 267-281.

457 Aubreville, A. Etude sur les Fôrets d'Afrique Equatoriale Française et du Cameroun. Nogent-sur-Marne: Section technique agricole tropicale, May 1948. 131 pp.

458 ________, ed. Flore du Gabon. P.: Musée National D'Histoire Naturelle, 23 v., 1961-1973.

459 Bensaid, Anita. "Niveau nutritionnal des pays gabonais: une analyse factorielle en componantes principales," Bulletin de l'Institut National de la Statistique et des Etats Economiques (Paris) (May-Sept. 1970), pp. 11-44.

460 Bensaid, Georges. Economie et Nutrition: Essai à partir d'une enquête alimentaire sur deux régions du Gabon. 1963. P.: INSEE Coopération, 1970, 2 v. 288 and 554 pp. [Woleu N'Tem & N'Gounié Provinces].

461 Caperan. "Notes sur l'état sanitaire des populations M'Fangs du Woleu-N'Tem, BSRC, v. 12 (1930), pp. 103-125.

462 Esteve, H. "Enquête démographique comparative en pays Fang, District d'Oyem." Médicine Tropicale, v. 17 (1957), pp. 85-105.

463 Ford, Henry A. Observations on the Fevers of the West Coast of Africa. N.Y.: Edward Jenkins, 1856.

464 François, Michel. "Gabon," in John C. Caldwell, ed., Population Growth and Socio-Economic Change in West Africa. N.Y.: Columbia UP, 1975, pp. 630-656.

465 Gabon. National Statistical Service. Recensement général de la population, 1969-1970. Méthodologie. République Gabonaise. Lv.: IO, 1971. 59 pp.

466 Gabon. Enquête démographique au Gabon, 1960-1961. P.: Ministry of Cooperation, 1963. 32 pp.

467 Gabon. Recensement et enquête démographiques, 1960-1961. Ensemble du Gabon. Résultats définitifs. P.: Ministry of Cooperation, 1965. 148 pp.

468 Ghenassia, Jean-Claude, ed. Libreville, capitale de la république gabonaise. Lv.: Société gabonaise d'éd., 1973. 130 pp.

469 Hamono, B., and Chauliac, G. "La situation démographique des districts du Franceville, Leconi, et Moanda dans le département du Haut-Ogooué (Gabon)." Médicine Tropicale, v. 31, (no. 21, 1971), pp. 215-224.

470 Hodder, P. W. "Equatorial Africa," in D. R. Harris, ed. Africa in Transition. L.: Methuen, 1967, pp. 259-291.

471 Jeannel, Camille. La Sterilité en République Gabonaise. Geneva: Offenberg Press, 1962.

472 Koechlin, Jean. Les savanes du Sud-Gabon. Bv.: ORSTOM, 1957.

473 Lasserre, Guy. Libreville: la ville et sa région, Gabon, Afrique Equatoriale Française: étude de géographie humaine. P.: AC, 1958. 347 pp. Microfiche, P.: CNRS, and N. Y.: Clearwater.

474 _______. "Les mécanismes de la croissance et les structures démographiques de Libreville (1953-1970)," in La Croissance Urbaine en Afrique Noire et Madagascar. P.: CNRS, 1972, pp. 719-738.

475 _______. "Le paysage urbain des Libreville noires," CO-M, v. 9 (Oct.-Dec. 1956), pp. 363-388.

476 Leroy-Deval, J. R. Biologie et sylviculture de l'okoumé; Aucoumea klaineana Pierre. Nogent-sur-Marne: Centre technique forestier tropical, 1976. 2 v. 355 and 76 pp.

477 Le Testu, Georges. "Notes sur les cultures indigènes dans l'intérieur du Gabon," Revue de botanique appliquée et d'agriculture tropicale, (Aug.-Sept. 1940), pp. 540-556.

478 Meyo-Bibang, Frédéric, and Nzamba, Jean-Martin. Notre Pays. Le Gabon. Géographie. P.: Edicef, 1975. 80 pp.

479 Naudet, Roger. "The Oklo Nuclear Reactors: 1800 Million Years Ago," Interdisciplinary Scientific Review (Mar. 1976), pp. 72-84.

480 Neuhoff, Hans Otto. Contribution à la connaissance géographique du Gabon. Bonn: Ed. Schroeder, 1967. 177 pp.

481 Perrusset, André-Christian. "Aménagements routiers en zone équatoriale forestière et accidentée: l'Exemple des Monts de Cristal (Gabon)," CO-M, v. 30 (Oct.-Dec. 1977); 404-411.

482 _______. Le Gabon: Géographie physique équatoriale. L.: U. Nationale du Gabon, 1977. 170 pp.

483 Résultats de l'enquête agricole au Gabon. P.: INSEE Coopération, 1969. 139 pp.

484 Sautter, Gilles. De l'Atlantique au Fleuve Congo. Une Géographie de Sous-Peuplement. P.: Mouton, 1966. 2 v. 1102 pp.

485 Walker, André Raponda, and Sillans, Roger. Les plantes utiles au Gabon. P.: Paul Lechevalier, 1961. 614 pp.

486 Waltisperger, D. "La mortalité au Gabon," Démographie en Afrique d'expression française. Bulletin de Liaison, Special no. 9 (Nov. 1976), pp. 5-80.

IX. RELIGION AND MISSIONS

487 Annuaire de l'Archdiocèse de Libreville et du Diocèse de Mouila. Lv., 1964. 54 pp.

488 Annuaire de l'Eglise Catholique en Afrique Francophone (Missions Catholiques), 1978-1979. V. 2. P.: ONPC-R. F., 1978. 688 pp.

489 Annuaire de l'Eglise Evangélique du Gabon. Lv.: Apr. 1973. 15 pp.

490 Babel, Henry. Schweitzer tel qu'il fut. P.: Payot, 2nd ed., 1970. 198 pp.

491 Bessuges, J. Lambaréné à l'ombre de Schweitzer. Limoges: Dessagne, 1968. 152 pp.

492 Binet, Jacques. "Drogue et mystique: les bwiti des Fangs," Diogènes, v. 86 (Apr.-June 1974), pp. 34-57. Tr. "Drugs and Mysticism: The Bwiti Cult of the Fang," Diogenes, v. 86 (Summer 1974), pp. 31-54.

493 ________; Gollnhofer, Otto; and Sillans, Roger. "Textes religieux du Bwiti-Fan et de ses confréries prophétiques dans leurs cadres rituels," CEA, v. 46 (1972), pp. 197-257.

494 Birinda, M. [Birinda de Boudieguy]. La Bible secrète des Noirs selon le Bouity. P.: Omnium Littéraire, 1952. 141 pp.

495 Blanc, René; Blocher, Jacques; and Kruger, Etienne. Histoire des Missions Protestantes Françaises. Flavion, Belgium: Ed. Le Phare, 1970. 448 pp.

496 Brasseur, Paule. "A la recherche d'un absolu missionnaire: Mgr. Truffet, vicaire apostolique des Deux Guinées," CEA, v. 15 (no. 2, 1975), pp. 259-286.

497 ________. "Missions catholiques et administration française sur la côte d'Afrique de 1815 à 1870," RFHO-M, v. 62 (no. 3, 1975), pp. 415-446.

498 Briault, Maurice. Le Vénérable Père François Marie Pierre Libermann: La Reprise des Missions d'Afrique au Dix-neuvième Siècle. P., 1946.

499 _______. Sur les pistes de l'Afrique Equatoriale Française. P.: Ed. Alsatia, 1945. 285 pp.

500 Brown, Arthur Judson. One Hundred Years. N. Y.: Revell, 1936. [Presbyterian missions].

501 Bureau, René. "'Connais-tu la mort?' Les trois nuits rituelles du Bwiti fang," Annales de l'U. d'Abidjan, Série D, v. 6 (1973), pp. 231-303.

502 _______. "Le Harrisme et Le Bwiti: Deux Réactions Africaines à l'Impact Chrétien," Recherches de Sciences Religieuses, v. 63 (Jan.-Mar. 1975), pp. 83-100.

503 _______. La Religion d'Eboga. 1. Essai sur le Bwiti-Fang. 2. Lexique du Bwiti-Fang. Lv.: Service de Réproduction des Thèses, 1972. 562 & 241 pp.

504 Cadier, Charles. Lumière sur l'Ogooué. Formation de la Jeune Eglise de Samkita. The Author, 196?. 149 pp.

505 Campbell, Penelope. "American Protestant Evangelism and African Responses: The American Presbyterians in Gabon & Equatorial Guines, 1850-1925," Paper, AHA, Dallas, Dec. 1977. 22 pp.

506 _______. "Presbyterian West African Missions: Women as Converts and Agents of Social Change," Journal of Presbyterian History, v. 56 (Summer 1978), pp. 121-133.

507 "Centenaire de la naissance d'Albert Schweitzer," Communautés et Continents, v. 67 (Jan.-Mar. 1975), pp. 3-36.

508 Clark, Henry. The Philosophy of Albert Schweitzer. L.: Methuen, 1964. 241 pp.

509 Clémenceau, Macaire. "Saint Gabriel au Gabon: Ecole Montfort (1900-1948)," Chronique de Saint-Gabriel (Oct. 1949), pp. 45-73.

510 Delcourt, J. Au Congo Français. Monseigneur Carrie, 1842-1904. P.: The Author, n. d. 2 v. 459 pp. [Loango].

511 Duhamelet, Geneviève. Les Soeurs Bleues de Castres. P.: Grasset, 1934. 241 pp.

512 Durand-Réville, Luc. "Albert Schweitzer: le grand docteur blanc," Revue des Deux Mondes (Nov. 15, 1965), pp. 230-241.

513 Eglise Evangélique du Gabon, 1842-1961. Alençon: Impr. Corbière et Jugain, 1962. 52 pp.

514 Eglise Evangélique de Gabon. Constitutions, après les modifications adoptées par le Synode extraordinaire de Janvier 1970 à Libreville. Oyem, Ed. CLE, 1970. 39 pp.

515 Fanguinoveny, Thérèse. A History of American Protestant Missions in Gabon, 1842-1893. Memoir for the Master's, Faculty of Protestant Theology, P., 1978. 56 pp.

516 Faure, Félix. Christ in the Great Forest. N. Y.: Friendship Press, 1936. 181 pp. Tr. Le Christ dans la grande Fôret. P.: SME, 2nd ed., 1953. [1st ed., 1934].

517 Gardinier, David E. "American Protestant Evangelism and African Responses: The ABCFM in Gabon, 1842-1870," Paper, AHA, Dallas, Dec. 1977. 75 pp.

518 ______. "The Beginnings of French Catholic Evangelization in Gabon and African Responses, 1844-1883," FCS, (no. 2, 1978), pp. 49-74.

519 Goettman, Alphonse. L'Evangile de la Miséricorde. Hommage au Dr. Schweitzer. P.: Ed. du Cerf, 1964. 448 pp.

520 Gollnhofer, Otto, and Sillans, Roger. "Recherche sur le mysticisme des Mitsogho--peuple de montagnards du Gabon Central (Afrique Equatoriale)," in Réincarnation et Vie mystique en Afrique Noire. P.: PUF, 1965, pp. 143-173.

521 Gross, Helmut. Albert Schweitzer, Grösse und Grenzen. Munich: Ernst Reinhardt Verlag, 1974. 841 pp.

522 Hamilton, Benjamin A. The Environment, Establishment and Development of Protestant Missions in French Equatorial Africa. Ph. D. Diss., Grace Theological Seminary, Goshen, Indiana, 1959. 352 pp.

523 Haygood, William Converse. "With Schweitzer at Lambaréné: Noel Gillespie's Letters from Africa," Wisconsin Magazine of History (Spring 1971), pp. 167-203.

524 Keller, Jean. "The Churches of Equatorial Africa," Practical Anthropology, v. 10 (Jan.-Feb. 1963), pp. 16-21.

525 Koren, Henry J. The Spiritans: A History of the Congregation of the Holy Ghost. Pittsburgh: Duquesne U. Press, 1958. 641 pp.

526 Lavignotte, Henri. L'Evur, croyance des Fan du Gabon. P.: SME, 3rd ed., 1952. 118 pp.

527 Leperdriel, A. "Colonisation et évangélisation au Gabon," Missions Catholiques, (Jan. 1960), pp. 62-72.

528 Le Roy, Alexandre, "Missions d'Afrique: le Congo Français, le Gabon," in J. B. Piolet, ed., Les Missions Catholiques Françaises au XIXe Siècle. V. 5. P.: AC, 1902, pp. 219-254.

529 Mallo, Eugène. "Les difficultés de l'Eglise Evangélique du Gabon," Flambeau (May 1971), pp. 128-130.

530 Marie-Germaine, Sister. Le Christ au Gabon. Louvain: Museum Lessianum, 1931. 170 pp.

531 Marschall, George, and Poling, David. Schweitzer: A Biography. N.Y.: Doubleday, 1971. 342 pp.

532 Mboumba-Bouassa, Florent. Genèse de l'Eglise du Gabon: Etude Historique et Canonique. LL.D. Diss., U. of Strasbourg, 1972. 335 pp.

533 Minder, Raynold, ed. Rayonnement d'Albert Schweitzer. Le Livre du Centenaire. P.: Ed. Alsatia, 1975. 301 pp.

534 Ndong, Amvame. "L'Eglise Evangélique du Gabon au lendemain de son Autonomie," in C. Bonzon, et al., L'Appel. P.: SME, 1962, pp. 61-72.

535 "Persécutions religieuses en Guinée Equatoriale," Parole et Société, v. 87 (no. 3, 1979), pp. 184-189.

536 Preston, Jane S. Gaboon Stories. N.Y.: American Tract Society, 1872.

537 Pujadas, Tomás Luis. La Iglesia en la Guinea Ecuatorial: Fernando Po. Madrid: I. de Paz, 1968. 528 pp.

538 Roques, L. Le Pionnier du Gabon. Jean-Rémi Bessieux. P.: Ed. Alsatia, 1971. 176 pp.

539 Schweitzer, Albert. On the Edge of the Primeval Forest. London, 1926. 180 pp. Reprinted 1955. Tr. A l'orée de la forêt vierge. P.: Payot, 1929. 231 pp.

540 _______. From My African Notebook. L.: Allen & Unwin, 1938. 132 pp.

541 _______. Histoire de la forêt vierge. P.: Payot, 1950. 174 pp.

542 _______. More from the Primeval Forest. L.: A. &. C. Black, 1931. 173 pp.

543 Swiderski, Stanislas. "Le Bwiti, société d'initiation chez les Apindji au Gabon," Anthropos, v. 60 (no. 1-6, 1963), pp. 541-576.

544 _______. "Le rite de la renaissance spirituelle chez les Bouiti, Gabon," Anthropos, v. 73 (no. 5-6, 1978), pp. 845-886.

545 _______. "Synretyzm religijny w Gabonie," Przeglad Sojologie (no. 26, 1975), pp. 133-174.

546 Swiderski, Stanislaw. "Aperçu sur la trinité et la pensée triadique chez les Fang au Gabon," CJAS, v. 9 (no. 2, 1975), pp. 235-258.

547 _______. "La conception psycho-religieuse de l'homme dans la religion syncrétique Bouiti au Gabon," Africana Marburgensia, v. 9 (no. 2, 1976), pp. 32-66.

548 _______. "La fonction psychologique et socio-religieuse des drogues sacrées au Gabon," Journal of Religion in Africa, v. 8 (no. 2, 1976), pp. 123-132.

549 _______. "Notions théologiques dans la religion syncrétique Bouiti au Gabon," Eglise et Théologie, v. 6 (Oct. 1975), pp. 391-394.

550 _______. "Remarques sur la philosophie religieuse des sectes syncrétiques au Gabon," CJAS, v. 8 (no. 1, 1974), pp. 43-54.

551 Teuwissen, Raymond W. Robert Hamill Nassau, 1835-1921: Presbyterian Pioneer Missionary to Equatorial West Africa. M. Th. Thesis, Louisville Theological Seminary. 1973.

552 Vernaud, G. Etablissement d'une mission du plein Evangile au Gabon. Pesseux-NE: Ed. Evangéliques, 1957.

553 _______. Reveil au Gabon. Les Andelys, Eure: Viens et Vois, n. d. 69 pp.

554 Wadlow, René V. L. "An African Church and Social Change (Eglise Evangélique du Gabon)," Practical Anthropology, v. 16 (Nov.-Dec. 1969), pp. 257-264.

555 Walker, André Raponda. "Frère Dominique Fara: Religieux Gabonais," Revue du Clergé Africain, v. 9 (Nov. 1954), pp. 600-609.

556 _______, and Sillans, Roger. Rites et croyances des peuples du Gabon. P.: PA, 1962. 377 pp.

557 Woytt-Secretan, M. Albert Schweitzer construit l'hôpital de Lambaréné. Strasbourg; Dernières Nouvelles de Strasbourg, 1975. 111pp. [Tr. of Albert Schweitzer baut Lambaréné].

X. LITERATURE AND POETRY

558 Abessolo, J.-B. Les aventures de Biomo. Lv.: IPN, 1975. 36 pp.

559 ______. Contes de gazelle. Les aventures de Biomo. L'Arbre du voyageur. P.: L'Ecole, 1975. 63 pp.

560 Adam, J.-J. Folklore du Haut-Ogooué, proverbes, devinettes, fables mbédé. Issy-les-Moulineaux: Impr. Saint-Paul, 1971. 360 pp.

561 Alexandre, Pierre. "Introduction to a Fang Oral Art Genre: Gabon & Cameroon Meet," Bulletin of the School of African & Oriental Studies, U. of London, v. 37 (no. 1, 1974); pp. 1-7.

562 Bidzo, Hauban. Poèmes choisis. Lv.: IPN, Apr. 1975. 19 pp.

563 Contes. Special no., L'Educateur Gabonais (Dec. 1970). 94 pp. [93 stories]

564 Cornevin, Robert. Littératures d'Afrique noire de langue française. P.: PUF, 1976. 273 pp.

565 Damas-Aleka, Georges. L'Homme Noir. Monaco: Ed. PB, 1970.

566 Koumba Koumba, Rufin. Poèmes choisis. L.: IPN, Apr. 1975. 11 pp.

567 Leyimangoye, Jean-Paul. Olende ou le chant du monde. Légende populaire traduite et adaptée par l'auteur. Lv.: Ministry of National Education, 1976. 67 pp.

568 Mbot, Jean-Emile. "La Tortue et le léopard chez les Fang du Gabon (Hypothèse de travail sur les contes traduits)," CEA, v. 14 (no. 4, 1974), pp. 651-670.

569 Meye, François. Les récits de la forêt. Monaco: Ed. PB, 1970. 93 pp.

570 Ministry of National Education. Anthologie de la littérature gabonaise. Montréal: Ed. Littéraires, 1976. 357 pp.

571 Ndong Ndoutoume, Tsira. Essais. Lv.: Ministry of National Education, 1975. 33 pp.

572 ______. Le Mvett. P.: PA, 1970. 157 pp.

573 Ndouna-Depenaud. Rêves à l'aube. Lv.: IPN, May 1975. 13 pp.

574 _______. Passages. Lv.: IPN, May 1975. 24 pp.

575 Nkoghe-Mve, Moïse. Fables et poèmes choisis. Lv.: IPN, May 1975. 19 pp.

576 Pounah, Paul Vincent. Chant du Mandola alias Pégase. Fontenay-le-Comte: Impr. Loriou, 1978. 132 pp.

577 Towo-Atangana, G. "Le mvet, genre majeur de la littérature orale des populations Pahouines (Bulu, Beti-Fang-Ntumu)." Abbia (July-Aug. 1965), pp. 163-179.

578 Trilles, Henri. Contes et légendes pygmées. Bruges: Librairie de l'Oeuvre St. Charles, 1935. 186 pp.

579 Walker, André Raponda. Contes gabonais. P.: PA, 1968. 384 pp.

580 Walker-Deemin, Henri, ed. Ecrivains, artistes et artisans gabonais. Monaco: Ed. PB for the IPN, 1966. 93 pp.

581 Zotoumbat, Robert. Histoire d'un enfant trouvé. Ed. CLE, 1971. 59 pp.

XI. LINGUISTICS

581a Adam, J. J. "Dialectes du Gabon--la famille des langues téké," BIEC, n. s. (no. 7-8, 1954), pp. 33-107.

582 _______. Grammaire composée Mbédé, Adumu, Duma. Montpellier: Impr. Charité, 1954. 173 pp.

583 Alexandre, Pierre. "Aperçu sommaire sur le Pidgin Afo du Cameroun," CEA, v. 3 (no. 4, 1963), pp. 577-582.

584 Bates, George L. A Grammar of the Fang Language as Spoken on the Como and Benito Rivers. Libreville-Baraka: 1899. 113 pp.

585 Bonneau, J. Grammaire Pounou et Lexique Pounou-Français. Montpellier: Impr. Charité, 1956. 177 pp.

586 _______. "Grammaire pounou," JSA, v. 10 (1940), pp. 131-162; v. 17 (1947), pp. 23-50; v. 22 (1952), pp. 43-94.

587 Dalby, David. Language Map of Africa and the Adjacent Islands. L.: International African Institute, 1977. 63 pp.

588 Galley, Samuel. Dictionnaire français-fang, fang-français. Neuchâtel: Ed. Henri Messeiller, 1964. 588 pp.

589 Guthrie, Malcolm. The Bantu Languages of Western Equatorial

Africa. L.: Oxford UP for the International African Institute, 1953. 94 pp.

590 _______. Comparative Bantu: An Introduction to the Comparative Linguistics & Pre-History of the Bantu Languages. L.: Gregg, 1967-1970. 4 v.

591 _______. "Notes on Nzabi (Gabon)," Journal of African Languages. v. 7 (no. 2, 1968), pp. 101-129.

592 _______. "The Western Bantu Languages," in Thomas A. Sebok, ed., Linguistics in Sub-Saharan Africa. P.: Mouton, pp. 357-366.

593 International Institute of African Languages and Cultures. Practical Orthography of African Languages. L.: Oxford UP for the IIALC, 1930. 24 pp.

594 Jouin, Michel. La terminologie de parenté Mpongwe. Lv.: ORSTOM, 1973. 187 pp.

595 Mbot, Jean-Emile. Ebughi bifia "Démonter les expressions" (Enonciation et situations sociales chez les Fang du Gabon). P.: Institut d'Ethnologie du Musée de l'Homme, 1975. 150 pp.

596 Perrou, R. P. Lexique français-ikota. Makoukou: Mission catholique, 1964. 2 v.

597 Preston, Ira M., and Best, Jacob, eds. A Grammar of the Bakele Language with Vocabularies. N.Y.: Prall, 1854. 117 pp.

598 Trenezem, Edouard. "Vocabulaire Inzabi," JSA, v. 2 (1932), pp. 75-84.

599 Tucker, A. N. "Orthographic Systems & Conventions in Sub-Saharan Africa," in Thomas A. Sebok, ed., Linguistics in Sub-Saharan Africa. P.: Mouton, 1971, pp. 618-653.

600 Walker, André Raponda. Dictionnaire Français-Mpongwe suivi d'Eléménts de Grammaire. Bv.: Ed. St. Paul, 1961.

601 _______. Dictionnaire Mpongwe-Français suivi d'Eléments de Grammaire. Metz: La Libre Lorraine, 1934. 640 pp.

602 _______. Essai de grammaire tsogo. Bv.: Impr. du Gouvernement, 1937. 37 pp.

603 Wilson, John Leighton. A Grammar of the Mpongwe Language with Vocabularies. N.Y.: Snowden and Prall, 1847. 94 pp.

XII. ART AND MUSIC

604 Cornet, Joseph. "Introduction à la musique africaine," Etudes Scientifiques (Dec. 1977), pp. 2-37.

605 Fernandez, James W. Fang Architectonics. Philadelphia: Institute for Study of Human Issues, 1977. 41 pp.

606 ________. "Principles of Opposition and Vitality in Fang Aesthetics," Journal of Aesthetics and Art Criticism, v. 25 (1966), pp. 53-64.

607 ________, & Fernandez, R. L. "Fang Reliquary Art: Its Quantities and Qualities," CEA, v. 15 (no. 4, 1975), pp. 723-746.

608 Gollnhofer, Otto; Sallée, Pierre; and Sillans, Roger. Art & Artisanat Tsogho. Lv.: Musée des Arts et Traditions du Gabon & ORSTOM, 1975. 126 pp.

609 Grébert, F. "L'art musical chez les Fang du Gabon," Archives suisses d'anthropologie générale, v. 5 (1928) pp. 75-86.

610 Grimaud, Yvette. Notes sur la musique des Bochiman comparée à celle des Pygmees Babinga. P.: Musée de l'Homme, 1957. 20 pp. [text in French & English].

611 Hall, H. U. "Two Masks from French Equatorial Africa," The Museum Journal [U. of Pennsylvania] (Dec. 1927), pp. 381-409.

612 Lehuard, Raoul. "Le musée de Libreville," Arts d'Afrique Noire. v. 11 (1974), pp. 5-8.

613 Maquet, Jacques. "Sculpture traditionnelle et classes sociales," Bulletin des Séances de l'Académie Royale des Sciences d'Outre-Mer, (no. 3, 1976), pp. 452-467. [Fang].

614 Mbot, J.-E. Un siècle d'histoire du Gabon raconté par l'iconographie. Lv.: Musée de la Culture et des Arts, 1977. n. p.

615 Nguema, Zwé. Un mvet. Chant épique fang. P.: AC, 1972. 473 pp. [plus three 45 rpm records].

616 Perrois, Louis. "L'art Kota-Mahongwe. Les figures funéraires du Bassin de l'Ivindo (Gabon-Congo)," Arts d'Afrique Noire, v. 20 (1976), pp. 15-37.

617 ________. "Aspects de la sculpture traditionnelle du Gabon," Anthropos, v. 63-64 (1968-1969), pp. 869-888.

618 ________. Problèmes d'analyse de l'art traditionnel au Gabon. P.: Institut d'Ethnologie, U. of P., n. d. 75 pp.

619 ________. "Le statuaire des Fang du Gabon," Arts d'Afrique Noire, v. 7 (1973), pp. 22-42.

620 ________. Le Statuaire Fan. Gabon. P.: ORSTOM, 1972. 421 pp.

621 ________ et al. Gabon. Cultures et Techniques. Catalogue du Musée des Arts et Traditions. Lv.: ORSTOM, 1969. 84 pp.

622 Roy, Claude. Le M'Boueti des Mahongoué. P.: Galerie Jacques Kerache, 1967. 79 pp.

623 Sallée, Pierre. Etude d'une harpe à 8 cordes des populations gabonaises dans contexte socio-culturel. Doctoral Thesis, U. of P., 1969.

624 Segy, Ladislav. "Bakota Funerary Art Figures," Zaire, v. 6 (May 1952), pp. 451-460.

625 Siroto, Leon. "The Faces of Bwiti," African Arts (Spring 1968), pp. 22-27.

626 Swiderski, Stanislaw. "Tradition et nouveauté des concepts religieux dans l'art sacré contemporain au Gabon," Anthropos, v. 74 (no. 5-6, 1979), pp. 803-816.

627 ________. "La harpe sacrée dans les cultes syncrétiques au Gabon," Anthropos, v. 65 (no. 5-6, 1970), pp. 833-857.

628 Vulysteke, M. Musique du Gabon. P.: Office de Coopération Radiophonique, 1968. 12 pp. [plus record no. 41, OCR].

XIII. TOURISM

629 D'Herville, François. Le Gabon. P.: Solar, 1976. 63 pp.

630 Fendeler, Gérard. Guide de Libreville et du Gabon. Dakar: Société africaine d'ed., 1975. 96 pp.

631 Gabun gestern und heute. Hildesheim: Roemer-Pelizaeus Museum, 1973. 72 pp. [German and French texts].

632 Houlet, Gilbert, ed. Afrique Centrale. Les Républiques d'Expression Française. P.: Hachette, 1962. 533 pp.

633 Ngabissio, N. N. Découvrir le Gabon touristique. P.: Novafric, 1976. 166 pp.

634 Rémy, Mylène. Le Gabon Aujourd'hui. P.: Ed. Jeune Afrique, 1977. 263 pp.

XIV. REFERENCE AND BIBLIOGRAPHY

635 Académie des Sciences d'Outre-Mer. Travaux et Mémoires, n. s. Hommes et Destins. Dictionnaire Biographique d'Outre-Mer. P.: V. 1, 1975; V. 2 in 2 parts, 1977.

636 Africa Confidential. L. Semi-monthly.

637 Africa Contemporary Record. L.: African Research/Rex Collins, 1968+.

638 Africa Report. N. Y.: African American Institute. Bi-monthly, 1957+.

639 Africa Research Bulletin. Series A. Political, Social, Cultural. Series B. Economic, Financial, Technical. Exeter, England, monthly, Jan. 1964+.

640 Africa South of the Sahara. L.: Europa Publications, 1971+.

641 Africa Year Book & Who's Who. L.: Africa Journal Ltd., 1976+.

642 African Biographies. Bonn: Research Institute of the Friedrich-Ebert Stiftung, 1967+. [Loose-leaf].

643 Africana Journal. N. Y.: Africana Publishers, quarterly, 1970+.

644 Afrique Contemporaine. P.: DF, Bi-monthly, 1959+.

645 L'Afrique Noire de A à Z. P.: Ediafric, 1975.

646 Alalade, F. O. "French-Speaking Africa-France Relations: A Critical Bibliographic Survey with Particular References to the Ivory Coast," CBAA, v. 9 (no. 1, 1976-1977), pp. 84-93.

647 Année africaine. P.: Pedone, 1963+.

648 Année Politique Africaine. Dakar: Société Africaine d'Ed., 1966+.

649 Annuaire du Tiers-Monde. P.: B-L, 1976+.

650 Annuaire Parlementaire des Etats d'Afrique Noire. Députés et Conseillers Economiques. P.: Ediafric, 1962.

651 Asamani, J. O., Comp. Indexus Africanus. Stanford: Hoover Institution Press, 1975. 659 pp.

652 Balandier, Georges, and Maquet, Jacques, eds. Dictionnaire des Civilisations Africaines. P.: Hazan, 1968. 448 pp. Tr. Dictionary of Black African Civilization. N. Y.: Leon Amiel, 1974. 350 pp. [Fang and Mpongwe]

653 Ballard, John C. "Politics and Government in Former French West and French Equatorial Africa: A Critical Bibliography," JMAS, v. 3 (Dec. 1965), pp. 589-605.

654 Belinga, Thérèse Baratte-Eno, Comp. Bibliographie. Auteurs africains et malgache de langue française. P.: Office de Radiodiffusion et Télévision française, 4th ed., 1979.

655 Berman, Sanford, Spanish Guinea: An Annotated Bibliography. M. L. S. Thesis, Catholic U. of America, W, 1961. 2 v. 597 pp. [chronologies; Fang].

656 Boston U. Gabon: Selected Bibliography. Boston: Boston U. African Studies Press, 1965.

657 Brasseur, Paule, and Maurel, Jean-François. Les sources bibliographiques d'Afrique de l'Ouest et de l'Afrique Equatoriale d'expression française. Dakar: Bibliothèque de l'U. de Dakar, 1970. 88 pp.

658 Bruel, Georges. Bibliographie de l'Afrique Equatoriale Française. P.: Larose, 1914. 326 pp.

659 Bucher, Henry H. "Archival Resources in Gabon," HA, v. 1 (1974), pp. 159-160.

660 ________. "The Robert Hamill Nassau Collection in Gabon's National Archives: A Bibliographical Essay," JA, v. 47 (no. 1, 1977), pp. 186-195.

661 Bulletin de l'Afrique noire. P.: Ediafric weekly, 1957+.

662 Bulletin de la Société Préhistorique et Protohistorique Gabonaise. Lv., Irregular, 1965+.

663 Cailloux, S. Le Gabon: repertoire bibliographique des études de sciences humaines (1970-1974). Lv.: Ministry of Culture and the Arts, 1975. 43 pp.

664 Carson, Patricia. Materials for West African History in French Archives. L.: Althone Press, U. of London, 1963. 170 pp. [includes Gabon].

665 Centre d'Analyse et de Recherche Documentaires pour l'Afrique Noire (CARDAN). Bulletin d'information et de liaison:

Recherche, enseignement, documentation africaniste francophone. P., 1969-1977.

666 Chroniques d'Outre-Mer. P.: Ministry of Overseas France, 10 times a year, 1951-1958.

667 Chronologie politique africaine. P.: Fondation Nationale des Sciences Politiques, bimonthly, 1960-1970.

668 Couret, René, ed. Guide bibliographique sommaire d'histoire militaire et coloniale française. P.: IN, 1969. 522 pp.

669 Cros, Anne, comp. Ouvrages sur le Gabon. Lv.: Centre Saint-Exupéry, 1978. 81 pp.

670 Current Bibliography of African Affairs. W.: African Bibliographic Center, N.S., quarterly, 1968+.

671 Current Contents Africa. Oxford: Hans Zell, 1978+. [Formerly published at Frankfurt, 1975-1977]

672 Darkowska-Nidzgoroka, L. Olenka. Connaissance du Gabon: Guide Bibliographique. Lv.: U. Nationale du Gabon, 1978. 151 pp.

673 Dokumentations-Leitstelle Afrika. Special Bibliography no. 9. Economic & Social Policy in Central Africa (Gabon, Cameroon, Congo, Chad, CAR). Hamburg: Deutsche Institut für Afrika-Forschung, 1974.

674 Duffy, David, ed. A Survey of the United States Government's Investments in Africa. Waltham, Mass.: ASA, 1978. 112 pp. Also published as Issue, v. 8 (no. 2-3, 1978), pp. 1-112.

675 Draguet, Zoé. Le Gabon: Repertoire Bibliographique des Etudes de Sciences Humaines (1967-1970). Lv.: ORSTOM, Feb. 1971. 33 pp.

676 Duignan, Peter, ed. Guide to Research and Reference Works on Sub-Saharan Africa. Stanford: Hoover Institution Press, 1971. 1102 pp.

677 _______, and Gann, L. H., ed. A Bibliographical Guide to Colonialism in Sub-Saharan Africa. L.: Cambridge UP, 1977. 552 pp.

678 Easterbrook, David L. "Bibliography of Africana Bibliographies, 1965-1975," AJ, v. 7 (no. 2, 1976), pp. 101-148.

679 _______. "Bibliography of African Bibliographies, 1975-1976," AJ, v. 8 (no. 3, 1977), pp. 232-242.

680 Economist Intelligence Unit. Quarterly Economic Review of Gabon, Congo, Cameroon, CAR, Chad and Madagascar. L.: 1976+. [also Quarterly Economic Review of former French Equatorial Africa, Cameroon and Madagascar, 1968-1975, and Quarterly Economic Review of former French Tropical Africa, 1960-1967.]

681 Les élites africaines. Cameroun--Gabon. P.: Ediafric, 1971. 298 pp.

682 Les élites gabonaises: Who's Who in the Republic of Gabon. P.: Ediafric, 1977. 217 pp.

683 Etudes Africaines: Liste mondiale des périodiques spécialisés. P.: Mouton, 1969. 214 pp.

684 Europe-France-Outre-Mer. P., Monthly, 1923+.

685 Gabon. Annuaire International. Lv., Irregular, 1960+.

686 Gabon. Annuaire national officiel de la République gabonaise. Lv.: Agence Havas, 1973+.

687 Gabon. Bulletin Mensuel de la Chambre de Commerce, d'Agriculture, d'Industrie et des Mines du Gabon. Lv., 1960+.

688 Gabon. Journal Officiel. Lv., Semimonthly, Apr. 1959+.

689 Gabon. Ministry of Finances. Budget de l'Etat. 1959+. [also Budget local, 1949-1958.]

690 Gabon. Ministry of Information. Annuaire national. P.: 1966+.

691 Gabon. Ministry of National Education. Statistiques de l'Enseignement au Gabon. Annual.

692 Gabon. National Statistical Service. Bulletin mensuel de statistique. Apr. 1959+.

693 "Gabon," in George T. Kurian, ed. Encyclopedia of the Third World. V. 1. N.Y.: Facts on File, 1978, pp. 500-510.

694 "Gabon," in S. Taylor, ed. The New Africans. N.Y.: Putnam, 1967, pp. 128-145.

695 Gabon Matin. Lv., Daily newspaper, 1977+.

696 Gardinier, David E. "Decolonization in French, Belgian, & Portuguese Africa," in P. Gifford and Wm. R. Louis, eds., Transfer of Power in Africa. New Haven: Yale UP, 1980. Forthcoming. [Bib. and Historiography].

697 _______. "French Colonial Rule in Africa [1914-1962]: A Bibliographical Essay," in P. Gifford & Wm. Roger Louis, eds., France and Britain in Africa: Imperial Rivalry and Colonial Rule. New Haven: Yale UP, 1971, pp. 787-902.

698 _______. "Resources in Paris Missionary Archives and Libraries for the History of Gabon," HA, v. 7 (1980), pp. 159-160.

699 Gaulme, François. "Bibliographie critique pour servir à anthropologie historique du littoral gabonais (époque précoloniale XVIe-XIXe siècles," JA, v. 47 (no. 1, 1977), pp. 157-175.

700 Guernier, Eugène, ed. L'Afrique Equatoriale Française (V. 5 of L'Encyclopédie de l'Union Française). P.: Ed. Coloniales et Maritimes, 1950. 590 pp.

701 Henige, David P., comp. Colonial Governors from the 15th Century to the Present: A Comprehensive List. Madison: U. of Wisconsin Press, 1970. 401 pp.

702 Hoover Institution. United States and Canadian Publications on Africa. Stanford: Hoover Institution Press, 1961-1966.

703 International African Bibliography. L.: Mansell, quarterly, 1971+.

704 International Council for Archives (Unesco). Guide to the Sources of the History of Africa. Multi-volume. French volumes: Sources de l'Histoire de l'Afrique au Sud du Sahara dans les Archives et Bibliothèques françaises. V. 1 Archives. V. 2 Bibliothèques. Switzerland: Interdocumentation Co., A. G. Zug, 1971 & 1976.

705 Lafont, Francis. Petit Atlas du Gabon. P.: Ed. Alain, 1958. 46 pp.

706 Liniger-Goumaz, Max. "Gabon--Guinée Equatoriale: problème frontalier," G-A, v. 12 (no. 1, 1973), pp. 99-102.

707 Marchés tropicaux et méditerranéens. P., Weekly, Nov. 1945+.

708 Miller, Joseph. Equatorial Africa. W.: American Historical Association, 1976. 70 pp. [historiography].

709 Ministry of Cooperation. Service of Studies and International Questions. République Gabonaise. P.: Dec. 1978.

710 _______. Gabon. Données Statistiques sur les Activités Economiques, Culturelles, et Sociales. P.: Sept. 1976, 241 pp.

711 Nicholas, Blaise, and Costisella, Monique, comp. Bibliographie des auteurs gabonais. Lv.: IPN, Mar. 1975. 17 pp.

712 Panofsky, Hans E. A Bibliography of Africana. Westport, Conn.: Greenwood Press, 1975. 350 pp.

713 Pansini, G. Gabon. Réorganisation des archives nationales. P.: Unesco, 1973. 20 pp.

714 Patterson, K. David. "Disease and Medicine in African History: A Bibliographical Essay," HA, v. 1 (1974), pp. 141-148.

715 ________, comp. Infectious Diseases in Twentieth-Century Africa: A Bibliography of Their Distribution and Consequences. Waltham, Mass.: Crossroads Press, 1980.

716 Perrois, Françoise. Le Gabon: Repertoire Bibliographique des Etudes de Sciences Humaines, 1960-1967. Lv., ORSTOM, 1969. 58 pp.

717 Perrot, Claude. Le Gabon: Repertoire Bibliographique relatif aux Sciences Humaines. P.: BDPA, 1962. 44 pp.

718 Personnalités publiques de l'Afrique Centrale: Cameroun, RCA, Congo, Gabon, Tchad. P.: Ediafric, 1968. 373 pp.

719 Réalités Gabonaises: Revue Pédagogique et Culturelle du Gabon. Lv., Apr. 1959+.

720 Recently Published Articles. W.: AHA, Three times a year, 1976+. [Africa section]

721 Republic of Gabon. Annuaire, 1966. Brussels, 1966. [trade statistics].

722 Sanner, P. Bibliographie ethnographique de l'Afrique Equatoriale Française, 1914-1948. P.: IN, 1949. 107 pp.

723 Scheven, Yvette. Bibliographies for African Studies, 1970-1975. Waltham, Mass.: Crossroads Press, 1979.

724 Sims, Michael, and Kagan, Alfred, comp. American and Canadian Doctoral Dissertations and Master Theses on Africa, 1886-1974. Waltham, Mass.: ASA, 1976. 365 pp.

725 South, Aloha P., ed. Guide to Federal Archives and Manuscripts Relating to Africa. Waltham, Mass.: Crossroads Press, 1977. 556 pp.

726 ________. Guide to Non-Federal Archives and Manuscripts Relating to Africa. Waltham, Mass.: Crossroads Press. Forthcoming.

727 Standing Conference on Library Materials on Africa. United Kingdom Publications & Theses on Africa. Cambridge: Heffer, 1963+.

728 Statistical Office of the European Communities. République du Gabon. Annuaire, 1951-1966. Brussels, 1968. 134 pp.

729 U. of London. School of Oriental and African Studies. Library. Library Catalogue. Boston: G. K. Hall, 1963. 29 v. Supplement, 1968.

730 U. S. Library of Congress. African Section. Africa South of the Sahara: Index to Periodical Literature, 1900-1970. Boston: G. K. Hall, 1971. 4 v. Supplement, 1973.

731 _______. Sub-Saharan Africa. A Guide to Serials. W.: 1970. 409 pp.

732 _______. United States and Canadian Publications on Africa in 1960. W.: 1962. 98 pp.

733 U. S. Office of Geography. Gabon. Official Standard Names approved by the U. S. Board of Geographic Names. W.: GPO, 1962. 113 pp.

734 Welsch, Erwin K., ed. Research Resources France: Libraries & Archives in France. N. Y.: Council for European Studies, 1979. 146 pp.

735 Witherell, Julian W., ed. The U. S. and Africa: Guide to U. S. Official Documents & Government Sponsored Publications on Africa, 1785-1975. W., 1978. 949 pp.

736 _______, comp. French-Speaking Central Africa. A Guide to Official Publications in American Libraries. W., 1973. 314 pp.

737 _______, comp. Official Publications of French Equatorial Africa, French Cameroons & Togo, 1946-1958. W., 1964. 78 pp.

738 Zell, Hans M. Livres africains disponibles: index par auteurs, matières et titres. P.: Ed. France Expansion, 1978. 2 v. 332 & 895 pp.

739 _______, ed. The African Book Publishing Record: A Directory. Oxford: Hans Zell, 1977. 296 pp.

740 _______, and Silver, Helene, ed. A Reader's Guide to African Literature. N. Y.: Africana Publishers, 1971. 218 pp.

XV. MAP

741 Soret, Marcel. Afrique centrale. Esquisse ethnique générale. Bv.: Institut Géographique National, 1962.